The wounds of nations

MANCHESTER
1824

Manchester University Press

The wounds of nations

Horror cinema, historical trauma and national identity

Linnie Blake

Manchester University Press
Manchester and New York
distributed exclusively in the USA by Palgrave

Published by Manchester University Press
Oxford Road, Manchester M13 9NR, UK
and Room 400, 175 Fifth Avenue, New York, NY 10010, USA
www.manchesteruniversitypress.co.uk

Distributed exclusively in the USA by
Palgrave, 175 Fifth Avenue, New York,
NY 10010, USA

Distributed exclusively in Canada by
UBC Press, University of British Columbia, 2029 West Mall,
Vancouver, BC, Canada V6T 1Z2

British Library Cataloguing-in-Publication Data
A catalogue record for this book is available from the British Library

Library of Congress Cataloging-in-Publication Data applied for

ISBN 978 0 7190 7593 3 *hardback*

First published 2008

17 16 15 14 13 12 11 10 09 08   10 9 8 7 6 5 4 3 2 1

Edited and typeset
by Frances Hackeson Freelance Publishing Services, Brinscall, Lancs
Printed in Great Britain
by MPG Books Ltd, Bodmin, Cornwall

Contents

Introduction: traumatic events and international horror cinema

> In a catastrophic age ... trauma itself may provide the very link between cultures: not as a simple understanding of the pasts of others but rather, within the traumas of contemporary history, as our ability to listen through the departures we have all taken from ourselves.[1]

> Horror is everywhere the same.[2]

Since the late 1970s psychoanalytically informed and often Holocaust-focused academics have brought into being an interdisciplinary area within the Humanities known as Trauma Studies. Broadly speaking, this is a theoretical caucus that attempts to articulate and critique the diverse ways in which traumatic memories have been inscribed as wounds on the cultural, social, psychic and political life of those who have experienced them, and those cultural products that seek to represent such experiences to those who have not. Such articulation and critique is intimately concerned with the ways in which ideas of integrated and cohesive identity may be violently challenged by traumatic events such as genocide, war, social marginalisation or persecution, being part of a broader academic project to give voice to the historically silenced. Trauma Studies can thus be seen as a body of theoretical scholarship that addresses itself to cultural memory, to the modes in which traumatic historical events are representationally transmitted in time and space, to the politics of memorialising such events and experiences and to the cultural significance of vicarious modes of witnessing trauma. And as such, it is an entirely apposite discipline through which to read that most traumatic and traumatised of film genres – cinematic horror, a genre here shown to undertake precisely the kind of cultural work that Trauma Studies takes as its subject.

Profoundly concerned with the socio-cultural and psychological ramifications of trauma, both Trauma Studies and the trauma-raddled and wound-obsessed genre that is horror cinema can be seen to address themselves to 'the psychic and social sites where individual and group identities are constituted, destroyed and reconstructed';[3] both by the wounds inflicted by trauma and by those psychological, social and cultural attempts to bind those wounds in the interests of dominant ideologies of identity. For by virtue of its generic strategies, its representational practices and its recurrent thematic concerns, I will argue, horror cinema is ideally positioned to expose the psychological, social and cultural ramifications of the ideologically expedient will to 'bind up the nation's wounds' that is promulgated by all aspects of the culture industry in post-traumatic contexts in an attempt, in Abraham Lincoln's words, to 'achieve and cherish a just and lasting peace'[4] for the nation and its people.

Following Dominick LaCapra, this study understands traumatic events to be man-made historical phenomena such as genocide or war that may be theorised retrospectively in the conceptual vocabulary of disciplines such as sociology or psychology.[5] It does so in the awareness, however, that such retrospective philosophising does not heal the traumatised subject who, lacking a pre-existing frame of reference within which to locate the traumatic experience, is unable to assimilate it into normative conceptions of the world.[6] For this is where cultural artefacts such as genre films can be seen to enact what Freud would term *Trauerarbeit* or the work of mourning; exploring trauma by remembering it and repeating it in the form of diagetically mediated symbolisations of loss. For as I will argue, horror cinema can function precisely in this way; for by focusing on the sites where ideologically dominant models of individual and group identity are sequentially formed, dismantled by trauma and finally re-formed in a post-traumatic context, such narratives can be seen to demand not only a willingness on behalf of audiences to work through the anxiety engendered by trauma, but a willingness also to undertake a fundamental questioning of those ideologically dominant models of individual, collective and national identity that can be seen to be deployed across post-traumatic cultures, as a means of binding (hence isolating and concealing) the wounds of the past in a manner directly antithetical to their healing.

Since at least the early 1990s it has been a critical common-place for trauma theorists such as Hayden White to assert that the stylistic experimentation of literary modernism may represent the reality of events such as the Holocaust in a way that 'no other ver-sion of realism could do'[7] precisely because 'the kinds of anti-narra-tive non-stories produced by literary modernism offer the only prospect for adequate representation of the kind of "unnatural" events – including the Holocaust – that mark our era and distinguish it absolutely from all of the "history" that has come before it.'[8] Con-testable in its conception of the post-traumatic uniqueness of our age, White's predilection for high-cultural modernism thus occludes, quite deliberately, the ways in which popular culture since the 1960s has repeatedly returned to narratives that privilege both the abject and the uncanny as core signifiers of traumatic historical events, establishing in the process what Andreas Huyssen would term a popu-lar 'culture of memory'[9] that is unstable, aporetic and often very frightening indeed.

This study is, then, a response to the longstanding occlusion of popular cultural forms (specifically those such as horror cinema that are generically driven by the abject and the uncanny) from con-temporary theorisations of the cultural legacy of trauma. It focuses on film, a medium that is 'sufficiently plastic to render the shifting colors [sic] and shapes of human experience as it manifests inter-nally, and externally, in things that happen and are perceived by witnesses and participants'[10] and is concerned specifically with hor-ror cinema, as a genre that attracts consumers by virtue of being 'expressly repulsive'[11] while appearing 'to take pleasure from the fact that so many people find it disturbing, distasteful, or even down-right unacceptable.'[12] Thus offering 'a portrait of ourselves and of the kind of life we have chosen to lead,'[13] horror cinema exists at the conjunction of cultural analysis and cultural policy – being the popu-lar genre most prone to legislative regulation through censorship from above.[14] For if the twentieth and early twenty-first centuries have been characterised not only by a bewildering array of traumatic happenings, from genocidal and nuclear holocausts to ideologically driven neo-colonialist war to spectacular terrorist outrage, then as I will argue, they have also been characterised by an escalating public interest in horror films that bespeak a public will to understand the experience of traumatic events while self-reflexively exploring the function of mass cultural representations of such trauma.

Such a tendency has, of course, been visible in horror film criticism from as early as 1965, when Robin Wood's analysis of *Psycho* (1960) illustrated how horror cinema may enable us to understand the spatio-temporal and inter-cultural legacy of traumatic events such as the holocaust.[15] Thus, following Wood, I will explore how horror film criticism may enable us to shift the emphasis of trauma critique away from high-modernist cultural artefacts and onto the popular cultural forms as they are daily consumed by millions across the globe; either as victims, perpetrators or witnesses to historical trauma. In terms of my interest in historical trauma, national identity and horror cinema, moreover, my study is thus closely related to that of Adam Lowenstein, whose excellent *Shocking Representations: Historical Trauma, National Cinema and the Modern Horror Film* (2005) I regrettably discovered only in the final stages of writing this book. With conceptual recourse to Benjamin's *The Origin of German Tragic Drama* (1928) and 'Theses on the Philosophy of History' (1940), Lowenstein addresses my own matrix of concerns by conceiving of what he terms the 'allegorical moment' in horror cinema; being that which conforms 'to neither the naive verisimilitude of realism, nor to the self-conscious distanciation of modernism' but invites us 'to unite shocking cinematic representation with the need to shock the very concept of representation in regard to historical trauma.'[16] Hence, engaging with Lyotard's conceptualisation of the *differend* as a means of finding new idioms for that which is unspoken by the victim of trauma (silenced by the conflicting idioms of those who speak of that trauma otherwise) Lowenstein's study sets out to illustrate how horror cinema may be seen to circumvent Trauma Studies' self-defeating tendency to respectfully silence testimonies of trauma deemed so horrific as to be 'unspeakable.' Like myself, he does this through engagement with both cinematic genre studies and debates concerning national identity as they relate to formulations of national cinema. Thus, in keeping with my own project, Lowenstein argues for horror cinema's will to show that which can not otherwise be shown; to speak that which can not otherwise be spoken and in turn to set about 'blasting open the continuum of history.'[17] An impressively intelligent, informed and insightful study, Lowenstein's book not only illustrates horror film scholarship's most recent theoretical orientation, but in so doing makes a significant contribution to that scholarship. And it is to this new area of intellectual inquiry, that takes historical trauma and cinematic genre as its subject, that this book aims to contribute.

As I have already intimated, this study is concerned with the social, cultural and political function of horror cinema. It also addresses the ways in which the generic and sub-generic conventions of horror allow for a decoding of traumatic memories already encoded within the cultural, social, psychic and political life of the nation's inhabitants by shocking historical events. It does so, however, from a critical perspective that owes every bit as much to historical materialism as to the psychoanalytical preoccupations of both Trauma Studies and much horror film criticism. So, while this study engages with psychoanalytically informed debates concerning the formation and representation of individual gendered subjectivity inherited from the *Screen* generation (itself of great relevance to Trauma Studies' concern with individual responses to traumatic events and broader theorisations of the psychology of trauma) my approach is a broadly culturalist one. I am concerned, in other words, with the socio-cultural and economic vectors that locate narratives of national identity within a specific context of initial reception and specifically the ways in which mass culture as a global network of self-obfuscating exchange both narrativises and normalises such narratives. Such a process, I argue, is directly challenged by the nationally distinctive and ever mutating generic strategies of the horror film – a genre that, for all its own mass cultural status, insistently comments upon the manipulability of the human subject by normalising narratives of identity, of which nationalism is only one. Thus, with direct recourse to thinkers such as Adorno and Benjamin, Althusser and Jameson (though with consideration of variant perspectives drawn from feminism and postmodernism,

specifically those of Kristeva, Baudrillard and Lyotard) I will argue
that horror cinema's generic codes enable us, both as critics and audience members, to address not only the desires, quandaries and
anxieties of the psychological unconscious, but those of the political
unconscious that underpins them. The interface between the personal and the political remains, of course, of key interest here: specifically when normative conceptions of selfhood and socius are
themselves challenged by shocking events or experiences. To put it
most simply, the questions I set out to ask here are why, within a
specific national context, at a particular point in time, particular
people produce particular horror film texts for the enthusiastic consumption of both their fellow countrymen and those who live beyond the nation's borders? What socio-cultural and historic functions
might such films serve, moreover, with regard to the already
traumatised nature of modern life?[18] And what cultural work do
such films undertake in exposing dominant ideologies' will to deny
trauma's centrality to national identity formation by prematurely
binding (and hence concealing, denying) those wounds?

In its consideration of horror cinema, this work thus rests upon
broadly structuralist definitions of genre forged by critics such as
Rick Altman; genre being viewed as an loose and ever-mutating collection of arguments and readings that help to shape both aesthetic
ideologies and commercial strategies and that on examination can
tell us a great deal about the culture from which such arguments or
readings emerged. In this, as Altman has observed, 'it is instructive
to note just how closely the notion of genre parallels that of nation',
both being 'implicitly a permanent site of conflict among multiple
possible meanings and locations'[19] but both providing an extremely
useful means of exploring the relation of cultural artefacts to the
milieux in which they circulate. Thus, despite acknowledgement of
that strand of critical debate that has sought to problematise both
'genre' and 'national cinema' beyond deployment, I assert both the
use-value of genre studies to an understanding of the social processes of the cinema as a whole and specifically the horror film's
inherent ability to challenge models of national identity promulgated by a nation's economic and political masters through other
branches of mass culture, providing in the process a 'major new arena

… for the process of self-fashioning'[20] in a post-traumatic context. Thus, for all the cultural diversity of and sub-generic variation in the films I will consider, the works of 'national' cinema on which I focus are notable for a number of characteristics they share: the controversial nature of their production or consumption, the censorship to which they were subject, their critical marginalisation, neglect or misconstrual by other branches of the culture industry and the critical opportunities they afford for a comparative exploration of the formation and mass-cultural dissemination of models of national identity in times of crisis, following seismic social and political change and in the aftermath of cataclysmic events such as war.

This is not to claim, of course, that 'the nation' or 'national culture' are transparent to interpretation, both having been differentially defined historically in service of competing ideologies of identity and alterity. Most simply, this study conceives of the nation as existing 'within a complex of other nation-states' being 'a set of institutional forms of governance' that maintains 'an administrative monopoly over a territory with demarcated boundaries (borders), its rule being sanctioned by law and direct control of the means of internal and external violence.'[21] Thus despite differences between nations and the ongoing socio-cultural and political evolution of individual states in time, since the Enlightenment the abstract noun that is 'the nation' has evoked and entailed a number of associated elements, including the idea of community, a sense of linguistic homogeneity and geographical contiguity, a system of economic exchange and, most contestably, a common culture underpinned by a shared psychological make-up.[22] Thus, as Homi K. Bhabha has argued, such conceptions of nationhood can be seen to exist as 'a powerful historical idea in the West,' offering an ideologically expedient 'continuous narrative of national progress, the narcissism of self-generation, the primeval present of the *Volk*.'[23] Thus functioning in justification of modernity's will to 'progress, homogeneity, cultural organicism, the deep nation, [and] the long past', such definitions of the nation clearly 'rationalise the authoritarian, "normalising" tendencies within cultures in the name of the national interest or the ethnic prerogative'[24] while marginalising or silencing those that are excluded by or are resistant to such a programmatic.

Signifying what Benedict Anderson would term 'imagined community,' the distinctive cultural forms and practices of the nation that
have been historically manifested in icons, ceremonies and symbols
of national cohesion thus appear to validate modernity's will to hegemony. And nationalist ideology's logical and rigorous deployment
of such symbolic signifiers of nationhood can therefore be seen to
mediate our experience of the real, offering illusory resolution of the
conflicts of interest groups and contradictions of identity that in
actuality beset the nation state in its varied cultural products and
practices while binding up the wounds wrought to such an image of
nationhood by a means of ideologically expedient strategies and practices.[25]

In my exploration of the ways in which international horror
cinema articulates the trauma wrought to ideologically saturated
conceptions of nationhood by historical events and processes, and
in turn the denial of that trauma in the service of nationally specific
ends, I have thus remained sensitive to the 'greater social and actual
mobility, the fragmentation of classes, the growing importance of
consumption and the rise of 'identity politics' that have increasingly
influenced identity formation'[26] in recent years. In the light of post-
war globalisation that itself appears to repudiate ideas of identity as
embedded in a place or associated with a national culture moreover,
the nation's influence on and relevance to its cultural products and
the subjectivities that consume them is, I acknowledge, increasingly
open to debate. But I would also suggest that for all post-war
globalisation may appear to have made ideas of nationhood conceptually redundant, and for all Postcolonial Studies offers a ready challenge to occidental post-Enlightenment hegemonies, the nation
remains the social, cultural and economic construct that is the single
most significant determinant of cultural identity, being in Guibernau's
words 'the socio-historic context within which culture is embedded
and the means by which culture is produced, transmitted and received;'[27] often in opposition, of course, to the homogenising agenda
of nationalist discourse itself. In my definition of national horror
cinema, then, I find myself concurring both with Andrew Tudor's
belief that 'genres are not fixed, nor are they only bodies of textual
material [being] composed as much of the beliefs, commitments

and social practices of their audience as by texts'[28] and with G. Cubitt's sense of the nation as an 'imaginative field on to which different sets of concerns may be projected, and upon which connections may be forged between different aspects of social, political and cultural experience.'[29] Thus, while 'the national' may be a difficult concept to pin down, it does retain a 'common sense' resonance that in Tim Edensor's words 'provides a certain ontological and epistemological security, a geographical and historical mooring and a legal, political and institutional complex which incorporates (and excludes) individuals as national subjects.'[30] And horror film, as I will argue, is uniquely situated to engage with the insecurities that underpin such conceptions of the nation; to expose the terrors underlying everyday national life and the ideological agendas that dictate existing formulations of 'national cinemas' themselves. It is for this reason that, in contradistinction to Jay Lowenstein's focus on art house and New Wave cinema, I am predominantly concerned with commercially successful mainstream films, or low-budget offerings that over time have accrued a substantive following. In such films, I argue, one may witness a purposeful 'unbinding' of the wounds wrought to totalising or essentialising formulations of national identity by traumatic events, a process that simultaneously exposes and unpicks those reductive or hegemonising assertions of nationhood with which said wounds are dressed. Accordingly, what follows is a historically grounded, textually engaged and theoretically conversant study of the ways in which film makers from four distinctive nation-states have deployed the generic conventions of horror cinema to explore ideas of national identity; specifically as those conceptions have been informed and shaped by the traumatic historical happenings of the post-Second World War period. It is informed by cultural theory's long-standing interrogation of ideas of nationhood: of what composes the nation state as we conceptualise and experience it and accordingly how specific cultural products may be read as manifestations, articulations or repudiations of differentially defined models of national identity or idiolects of historic trauma.

In the first instance, then, this study is centred upon four distinct and yet historically and conceptually inter-related sites of

cultural trauma. The first of these is the Second World War, specifically the psycho-cultural legacy of Germany and Japan's military
defeat, the subsequent revelation of acts of Japanese brutality in the
Far East, the industrialised genocide perpetrated by the Nazis in
Europe and the attendant occupation and cultural colonisation of
both nations by victorious Allied forces; specifically those of the
United States. Subject to an enforced repudiation of wartime models of national identity at all levels of social organisation and cultural
production, the mainstream (non-horror) films of these nations, as
I will illustrate, tended to bind up any psychic injuries inflicted by
the war with a culturally pervasive avoidance of the issue of individual and national responsibility for acts of atrocity perpetrated in
the name of the nation and its people. As I will demonstrate however, this silence is shattered by German and Japanese body horror,
as the unquiet dead cinematically return in a variety of victim, perpetrator and witness positions to apportion blame, exact retribution, offer testimony and atone.

    This study begins, then, with an exploration of the politically
controversial yet critically occluded German film maker and critic
Jörg Buttgereit – the most self-consciously experimental of my chosen directors – whose pre- and post-reunification films *Nekromantik*
(1987) and *Nekromantik 2* (1991) find a place here because they
were subject to the most punitive censorship since the Nazi era;
encapsulating as they did the historical and moral culpability of the
German people for genocidal acts perpetrated in their name and in
ways far more visceral than the New German Cinema had dreamed
or mainstream German horror had adequately conceptualised. Similar concerns are echoed in my exploration of the work of the Japanese director Nakata Hideo, specifically his internationally successful
crossover work *Ringu* (1998). Set against the classics of post-war
Japanese horror *Onibaba* (1964), *Kwaidan* (1964) and *Kuruneko*
(1968) and read in the light of Gore Verbinski's Hollywood remake
The Ring (2002), Nakata's *Ringu* is seen to decode the traumatic
changes wrought to Japanese society and hence national self-image
by the militaristic build-up to the Second World War and its apocalyptic closure in the atomic bombing of Hiroshima and Nagasaki.
Thus, while Buttgereit's highly visceral and intermittently anti-realist

body horror is seen to allow for the revelation of the hitherto cultur-ally repressed trauma of the Nazi holocaust, Nakata's highly realist supernaturalism locates *Nihonjinron* or essentialised Japanese iden-tity in the historically silenced feminine abject that returns to wreak revenge on indigenous patriarchy and American cultural colonial-ism alike.

The United States's doomed foray into Vietnam provides me with a second site of national trauma as the generic conventions of horror cinema call into question culturally pervasive notions of na-tional destiny that differentially underpin both left-wing and right-wing formulations of what it means to call oneself an American. Against the background of the Cold War and the mainstream cin-ematic representations of nationhood it evinced, George A. Romero's allegory of Vietnam, *The Crazies* (1973), his critically marginalised tale of suburban vampirism, *Martin* (1976) and the parable of eco-nomic collapse and social implosion that is *Dawn of the Dead* (1978) will be read as evocations of the trauma wrought to the self-image of both liberal *and* conservative Americans by the defeated nation's anti-communist ideology of militaristic neo-colonialism. Evoking the covenant theology of America's seventeenth-century Puritan colo-nists, Romero thus illustrates how foundational dreams of coopera-tive social endeavour, as the guarantor of the perfectibility of the nation, meet their end both in the rice fields of South East Asia and in the bankrupt cities of the American 1970s. Romero's America thus emerges as a nation governed by a President whose very name would become a watchword for corruption of the body politic: a fact no binding-up of the nation's wounds by the revisionist Gerald Ford and others would heal. As I will subsequently argue, the socio-cultural and political legacy of this would manifest itself in the neo-conservative apocalypticism of the Reagan years, when a reactionary will to turn back time led not only to mainstream cinema's whole-sale valorisation of a mythicised pre-Vietnam past but to horror cinema's culturally significant elevation of the serial killer to totemic hero of America's last frontier: standing mid-way between the civilisation allegedly guaranteed by American Republicanism and the savagery inherent in all oppositional forms of social or political organisation. In the fictive Jason of the nine *Friday 13th* films (1980–93) and Freddie Krueger of the five *Nightmare on Elm Street*[s] (1984–89), but most specifically in Hannibal Lecter, the perverse anti-hero of *Manhunter* (1986), *The Silence of the Lambs* (1990), *Hannibal* (2001) and *Red Dragon* (2002), I believe we can see encoded a post-traumatic cultural struggle between the insistent individualism of America's neo-conservative ascendancy and its liberal imperative to social and economic co-operative conformity. Thus, as mainstream cinema of the Reagan years and beyond advocated a bellicose nationalism that entailed a reactionary nostalgia for a simulacral America in which Vietnam, Civil Rights and the counterculture had simply never happened, 1980s horror's fetishisation of the serial killer allowed for a working through of the traumas of the 1970s, the horrors of the neo-conservative present and those of the (eminently plausible) apocalypse to come.

The third site of cultural trauma explored by this study is the bombing of the United States by agents of Al Qaeda on 11 September 2001. Building on the work done on the traumatic legacy of the Vietnam and the rise of neo-conservatism in the US, I will here consider the responses of American horror cinema to the events of 9/11 and the Allied Forces' subsequent wars in Afghanistan and Iraq and, most importantly, the implications of the War on Terror for civil liberties and international conceptions of human rights. The traumatic dislocation of United States self-image wrought by the bombings and visually encapsulated in the fall of the twin towers has been echoed, I will argue, by the remarkable resurgence of a horror sub-genre that has allowed for an exploration of the terrors of urban-industrial capitalist militarism and its cultural products since the 1970s. That sub-genre I term 'hillbilly horror.' Through exploration of films such as *Wrong Turn* (2002), *Cabin Fever* (2002), *Wrong Turn* (2003) and *The Texas Chainsaw Massacre* (2003) we can therefore see the concerns of Vietnam-encoded classics *The Texas Chainsaw Massacre* (1974), *The Hills Have Eyes* (1977) and *Southern Comfort* (1981) being revisited in the modern age – specifically as the representation of the poor white rural South enables a potent critique of the nation-state, its modes of political organisation and representation and its pretensions to occupy the civilised pole of a static Orientalist binarism. In a post-9/11 climate of paranoia, economic self-interest and cultural essentialism, hillbilly horror can thus be seen to explore the traumatic cultural aftermath of terrorist atrocity illustrating how the bombing of the World Trade Center has been re-narrativised, re-visioned and re-remembered in the service of nationally-specific military-industrial ends. In so doing, of course, horror cinema can once more be seen to tear away the layers of ideological obfuscation promulgated by the state as means to its own nationally-specific ends.

Contemporaneous with the return of backwoods horror in the United States and furnishing this study's final manifestation of horror cinema's articulation and interrogation of cultural trauma is the post-imperial, post-industrial crisis in available models of British masculinity engendered by the seismic transformation of the British geo-political and socio-cultural landscape at the hands of Thatcherite Conservatism, and its consolidation by Tony Blair's brand of right-wing social democracy that under the guise of New Labour, replaced Britain's longstanding socialist traditions with the conceptually and ideologically hybrid Third Way. In the werewolves of *Dog Soldiers* (2001), the flesh-eating zombies of *Shaun of the Dead* (2004), the murderous infected of *28 Days Later* (2002) and the cannibalistic troglodytes of *The Descent* (2005) we can thus see a range of hybridised monsters emerging that allow for an exploration of the increasingly simulacral culture of the United Kingdom and of the crisis of masculine identity increasingly apparent since the late 1970s. In the perceptible militarisation of British films such as *The Bunker* (2001), *Reign of Fire* (2002) and *Deathwatch* (2002) moreover, we can see a range of British heroes doing battle with malevolent spirits, demons, dragons and themselves in their exploration of gendered national identity, now marked by increasing political apathy and a loss of faith in the democratic nature of the British parliamentary system. Trauma, I argue here, may be engendered every bit as effectively by a process as by an event and horror cinema is entirely capable of addressing the totality of that process and its ramifications for ideas of national identity.

From the outset, then, I will argue that the generically specific conventions of horror allow not only for the narrativised, symbolised or otherwise encoded articulation of hitherto repressed individual and national experiences of trauma but demand audience response through a form of genre-specific interpellation that is materially different from but affectively similar to the claims Hayden White makes for high modernism. Depending on the nature and the historical moment of the traumatic event and in ways specific to the national culture in which the film text is produced and consumed, such responses may be seen to vary from an ostensible acceptance of existential responsibility for atrocities perpetrated in the name of the nation to a sense of outraged and vengeful victimhood. But in each case, the representational strategies of post-1960s horror can be seen to actively discourage an easy acceptance of cohesive, homogenising narratives of identity, national or otherwise, promoting instead a form of encoded/decoded engagement with traumatic events that may allow for the cultural assimilation of traumatic experiences that is a vital prerequisite for healing. For as Cathy Caruth asserts in the epigraph to this Introduction, it is only through our awareness of the ways in which traumatic experience has disrupted and displaced our own identities that we may forge a trans-cultural commonality of experience that, in turn, may provide a much needed 'link between cultures.'[31] For as my epigraph from Bataille acknowledges in much the same spirit, 'Horror is everywhere the same.'[32]

Notes

1   Cathy Caruth, 'Trauma and Experience,' in Neil Levi and Michael Rothberg (eds), *The Holocaust: Theoretical Readings* (Edinburgh: Edinburgh University Press, 2003), p. 197.

2   Georges Batailles, 'History and Memory after Auschwitz,' in Cathy Caruth (ed.), *Trauma: Explorations in Memory* (Baltimore: Johns Hopkins University Press, 1996), p. 229.

3   Eric L. Santer, 'History Beyond the Pleasure Principle: Some Thoughts on the Representation of Trauma,' in Levi and Rothberg (eds), *The Holocaust*, p. 219.

4   'With malice toward none, with charity for all, with firmness in the right as God gives us to see the right, let us strive on to finish the work we are in, to bind up the nation's wounds, to care for him who shall have borne the battle and for his widow and his orphan, to do all which may achieve and cherish a just and lasting peace among ourselves and with all nations.' Abraham Lincoln, 'Second Inaugural

Address,' (4 March 1864). *University of Oklahoma, College of Law. Historical Documents*. http://www.law.ou.edu/ushistory/lincoln2.shtml. Accessed 2 November 2006.

5   Dominick LaCapra, 'Trauma, Absence, Loss,' *Critical Inquiry* (Summer 1998). Levi and Rothberg (eds), *The Holocaust*, pp. 199–206.

6   Cathy Caruth, *Unclaimed Experience: Trauma, Narrative and History* (Baltimore: Johns Hopkins University Press, 1996).

7   Hayden White, 'Historical Emplotment and the Problem of Truth,' in Saul Friedlander (ed.), *Probing the Limits of Representation: Nazism and the 'Final Solution'* (Cambridge, MA: Harvard University Press, 1992), p. 52.

8   Hayden White, 'The Modernist Event,' in V. Sobchack (ed.), *The Persistence of History: Cinema, Television and the Modern Event* (New York and London: Routledge, 1996), p. 32.

9   Andreas Huyssen, 'Trauma and Memory: A New Imaginary Temporality,' in Jill Bennett and Rosanne Kennedy (eds), *World Memory: Personal Trajectories in Global Time* (Basingstoke: Palgrave Macmillan, 2003), p. 16.

10 Janet Walker, *Documenting Incest and the Holocaust* (Berkeley, CA and London: University of California Press, 2005), p. xix.

11 Noel Carroll, *The Philosophy of Horror, or, Paradoxes of the Heart* (London and New York: Routledge, 1990), p. 158.

12 Ken Gelder, 'Introduction: The Field of Horror,' in Ken Gelder (ed.), *The Horror Reader* (London: Routledge, 2000), p. 5.

13 Rudolph Arnheim, 'A Note on Monsters,' in Rudolph Arnheim (ed.), *Toward a Psychology of Art* (Berkeley, CA: University of California Press, 1972), p. 257.

14 Mark Jancovich, 'Introduction,' in Jancovich (ed.), *Horror: The Film Reader* (London and New York: Routledge, 2002), pp. 1–19.

15 Robin Wood, *Hitchcock's Films.* (1965. New York: A.S. Barnes, 1969).

16 Adam Lowenstein, *Shocking Representations: Historical Trauma, National Cinema, and the Modern Horror Film* (New York: Columbia University Press, 2005), p. 4.

17 Lowenstein, *Shocking Representations*, p. 16.

18 See Yi-Fu Tuan, *Landscapes of Fear* (Oxford: Basil Blackwell, 1979).

19 Rick Altman, *Film/Genre* (London: Bfi Publishing, 1999), pp. 86–7.

20 John Thompson, *The Media and Modernity* (Cambridge: Polity Press, 1995), p. 43.

21 Antony Giddens, *The Nation State and Violence: A Contemporary Critique of Historical Materialism, Volume 2* (Cambridge: Polity Press, 1985), p. 119.

22   Joseph Stalin, 'The Nation,' in Bruce Franklin (ed.), *The Essential Stalin: Major Theoretical Writings 1905–1952* (London: Croom Helm, 1973), pp. 57–61.

23   Homi K. Bhabha, 'Narrating the Nation,' in Homi K. Bhabha (ed.), *The Nation and Narration* (London: Routledge, 1990), p. 1.

24   Bhabha, 'Narrating the Nation', p. 4.

25   As Althusser would put it: 'In ideology men … express not the relation between them and their conditions of existence, but the way they live the relation between them and their conditions of existence; this presupposes both a real relation and an "imaginary," "lived" relation. Ideology … is the expression of the relation between men and their "world," that is, the (overdetermined) unity of the real relation and the imaginary relation between them and their real conditions of existence.' Louis Althusser, *For Marx* (London: Allen Lane, 1969), pp. 233–4.

26   Stuart Hall, 'The Question of Cultural Identity,' in S. Hall, D. Held and A. McGrew (eds), *Modernity and Its Futures* (Cambridge: Polity Press, 1992), p. 172.

27   M. Guibernau, *Nationalisms: The Nation State and Nationalism in the Twentieth Century* (Cambridge: Polity Press, 1996), p. 79.

28   Andrew Tudor, 'Why Horror: The Peculiar Pleasures of a Popular Genre,' *Cultural Studies*, 11:3 (October 1997), 449.

29   G. Cubbitt, 'Introduction,' in G. Cubbitt (ed.), *Imagining Nations* (Manchester: Manchester University Press, 1998), p. 1.

30   Tim Edensor, *National Identity, Popular Culture and Everyday Life* (Oxford: Berg, 2002), p. 29.

31   Caruth, 'Trauma and Experience,' in Levi and Rothberg (eds), *The Holocaust*, p. 197.

32   Bataille, 'History and Memory after Auschwitz,' in Caruth (ed.), *Trauma*, p. 229.

PART I

**German and Japanese horror:
the traumatic legacy of the Second
World War**

Introduction

On 15 August 1945, shortly after the cataclysmic bombing of Hiroshima and Nagasaki, Emperor Hirohito took to the radio waves to acknowledge in highly circumspect courtly language that the 'war situation' had developed 'not necessarily to Japan's advantage.' In order to avoid what he termed 'the total extinction of human civilisation,' Hirohito proclaimed to a weeping public that Japan would have to 'endure the unendurable and suffer the un-sufferable' by accepting the nation's unconditional surrender to Allied, specifically American, forces.[1] In subsequent months, twenty-five of Japan's military leaders were tried for war crimes by the Military Tribunal of the Far East – seven were hanged while local military commissions condemned a further 920 war criminals to death and over 3,000 to prison.[2] But further trauma to Japanese self-image was to follow as, until 1952, Japan's entire cultural tradition was subject to radical and enforced transformation at the hands of the American Occupation. Introducing a new constitution, the Americans revised the education system 'with the aim of eliminating propaganda and the harmful nationalistic elements'[3] that had initially led to the nation's militarisation. Women were given the vote, the age of male suffrage was lowered to twenty, trade unions were allowed to develop while radical land reform led to a more equitable distribution of the nation's agricultural resources. Thus the Japanese people, traumatised both by the catastrophic militarisation of their nation (that had led to the death of some four million combatant and civilian Japanese) and by an enforced refashioning of Japanese culture and society (in the image of American capitalist democracy) now undertook a frantic quest for *Nihonjinron*: or what it now meant to call oneself Japanese.[4]

Some months earlier, of course, Japan's wartime ally Germany had itself conceded defeat, Germany also being subject to seismic alterations to its psycho-geographical and socio-cultural landscape as the nation was initially divided into zones differentially controlled by Allied forces and then partitioned into the Soviet-controlled communist East and the capitalist West, the economic recovery and socio-cultural rehabilitation of the latter being spearheaded once again by the United States, here under the auspices of the Marshall Plan. Thus Berlin, Germany's capital and the site of Hitler's ignominious suicide became home to the infamous Berlin Wall: the material and conceptual synecdoche for the Cold War between the superpowers that would dominate world politics for the next forty-five years. As the two halves of the nation struggled with its bifurcated identity, the wall thus became a site of trauma on which was inscribed the militarisation of Germany under Hitler, the horrors of the war years, the nation's military defeat, the catastrophic hardship that followed in the wake of the war, the social and cultural dislocations engendered by partition and, ultimately, the traumatic re-unification of the nation in the wake of 1989's collapse of the Soviet Union.

Japan too had its own material site of trauma, that being the city of Hiroshima, the original Ground Zero, whose bombing would become to the Japanese 'the supreme symbol of the Pacific War,' encapsulating 'all the suffering of the Japanese people, a symbol of absolute evil, often compared to Auschwitz.'[5] Thus, for unrepentant right-wing elements the A-bomb was the price Japan had paid for pursuing its territorial destiny in South Asia. For the Left it was a kind of 'divine punishment for Japanese militarism', providing the Japanese people with 'the sacred duty, to sit in judgment of others, specifically the United States, whenever they show signs of sinning against the "Hiroshima spirit"'.[6] Thus politically bifurcated, culturally dislocated and suffering from the ongoing psychological fallout of the war, modern Japan and modern Germany struggled into being. And although their political histories and cultural practices were very different, both countries would either encode the trauma of the war and subsequent struggles for a cohesive national identity in their popular culture or mark its occurrence in significant absences, slippages and silences that themselves stand as testimony to the existence of un-addressed and hence unassimilated horrific events in each nation's past.

In the immediate post-war period in Japan, then, a pervasive sense of outraged victimhood could be seen in the popularity of A-bomb films, such as *Hiroshima* (1953) and *Black River* (1969), the first insisting on Japan's victim status in its depiction of American tourists buying as souvenirs the bones of the Japanese dead, the latter advocating vengeance in the form of a radiation victim turned syphilitic prostitute whose chosen clients are American GIs. Clearly there were unresolved issues here. But if America's nuclear assaults on Hiroshima and Nagasaki had allowed Japan to stake a legitimate claim for victim status, and in so doing attempted to nullify the outrages perpetrated at the hands of nationalistic Japanese militarism, Germany had no such opportunity to evade responsibility for past misdeeds. For all its cities lay in ruins, for all its population starved in the streets, the revelation of the Nazis' systematic genocide of millions of Jews, communists, homosexuals, gypsies and disabled people nullified not only any claims to victim status, but called into question the German people's right to inclusion in the international community of nations. Hitler's *Endlosüng* (or Final Solution), it was revealed, had not only demanded the compliance of the now defunct Nazi military machine, but the selfsame industrial giants that continued to dominate the economic landscape were shown to have competitively tendered for a share in the profits of genocide. Millions of German individuals, of course, had also gone about their daily lives regardless of the slaughter occurring on their doorsteps. So, while Japan sought to bind up the traumatic wounds of pre-war militarism and military defeat by conceptual recourse to the bombing of Hiroshima, there was little that could conceal or attempt to heal Germany's psycho-social and politico-cultural injuries, for what it meant to call oneself a German had become inextricable from the industrialised and state-sponsored slaughter of millions. As Primo Levi put it, it was now impossible to establish how many people

> could *not not know* about the frightful atrocities being committed, how many knew something but were in a position to pretend that they did not know, and, further, how many had

the possibility of knowing everything but chose the more pru-
dent path of keeping their eyes and ears (and above all their
mouths) well shut.[7]

If the traumatised survivors of the Nazi genocide had become, in
Cathy Caruth's formulation, 'the symptom of a history that they
cannot entirely possess,'[8] repeatedly suffering from the events they
had survived while endlessly witnessing (from the site of trauma)
that trauma's rational impossibility, then those complicit in such
impossible events were themselves traumatised by deeds they dare
not own. For as Dominick LaCapra has argued, 'perpetrator trauma'
not only exists but must be worked through 'if perpetrators are to
distance themselves from an earlier implication in deadly ideologies
and practices.'[9]

The problem was, of course, the steadfast refusal of elements
of the Japanese and German nations to claim ownership, and hence
responsibility, for the horrors of the past. Thus, while Japan's post-
war devotion to peaceable business development would see it out-
strip all countries bar the United States in terms of international
economic might while domestically attaining 'greater equality of
income distribution than any other industrial economy'[10] in the
world, even the most cursory exploration of Japanese popular culture would seem to indicate a range of unresolved traumas relating
to wartime events and post-war cultural transformation that themselves function as a means of concealing, though not healing, the
wounds of the past. For a culture notionally driven by *Wa*, or awareness of the necessity of harmony between all elements of society,
Japanese popular culture continues to be strikingly saturated with
images of sexual violence whereby, as Ian Buruma has outlined at
length:

> photographs of nude women trussed up in ropes appear regu-
> larly in mass circulation newspapers; torture scenes are com-
> mon on television, even in children's programmes; glossy,
> poster-sized pictures of naked pre-pubescent girls are on dis-
> play in the main shopping-streets; [and] sado-masochistic
> pornography is perused quite openly by a large number of men
> on their way to work on the subway.[11]

Such barely-repressed violence, sitting so uneasily alongside the official values and cultural practices of Japanese society, would be echoed in the profound silence regarding the Holocaust that characterised German popular culture until the 1970s when the New German Cinema set about articulating *Die Unbewaltigte Vergangenheit*, or the prematurely silenced and highly traumatic past. Lacking external investment and hence the opportunity to attract an international audience, German cinema of the post-war years had confined itself to popular nativist genres – *Heimatfilmes*, for example, focusing on community and familial life in rural Germany, and adventure films based on popular German novels offering a slice of derring-do while historical films set in Imperial Austria allowed for a little escapism, even as romantic adventures and comedies set in picturesque locations provided undemanding amusement. What was not mentioned were the events of wartime: specifically the complicity of the German people in the genocide of millions. Not until the 1960s did things change as the Young German Cinema, later the New German Cinema, addressed the Hitler years – not 'from above' but as lived reality. With the 1970s emergence of films like Syberberg's highly theatrical *Hitler – A Film From Germany* (1977), Fassbinder's *The Marriage of Maria Braun* (1978), Kluge's *The Patriot* (1979) and Edgar Reitz's sixteen-hour television documentary *Heimat* (1984) an identifiably German cinema could be seen to emerge; one that operated in dialogue with the ways in which other nations had represented the German past. But for all these films sought to evoke the horrors of that past, often through witness testimony, the disgusting viscerality of the *Shoah*'s annihilation of millions was not a subject for graphic depiction. And this is where horror cinema can be seen to fulfil a significant socio-cultural and psycho-political function.

As argued in the Introduction to this study, critical engagement with a nation's horror cinema offers a significant means of not only grappling with the traumatic past and in so doing measuring the effects of social, political and cultural transformation of the nation on its citizens, but of exposing the layers of obfuscation, denial or revisionism with which those wounds are dressed in service of dominant ideologies of national identity. Accordingly Chapter 1 explores the ways in which the generic conventions of body horror, which by its very definition has the capacity to disgust and outrage audiences, allows for a powerful and potentially cathartic engagement with otherwise unrepresentable aspects of the German past. And that Buttgereit's films should have been subject to *the* most radical acts of state censorship in Germany since the Second World War bespeaks not only of the ongoing trauma of Germany's prematurely bound and hence unhealed historical wounds but of the cultural significance of this little-known cult film director. He finds a place in this study of predominantly mainstream horror cinema not only because the distinction, in Germany of this period, is considerably more permeable than is usually the case, but because of Buttgereit's own determination to peel back the bindings of the nation's wounds. Thus revelling in the dark irrationality of the Romantic tradition that had informed German Expressionism before him, Buttgereit sets out to address the trauma of the past by an insistent looking upon the dead and what may or may not be done with them, remembering the past and the possibility of remembering otherwise. It is a mode of film making that in all its viscerality forces the audience to look at that which they would rather avoid, offering a counter-memory to Nazi cinema's elision of its own bloody deeds and a representation of human desire that rejects the power dynamics of heterosexual pornography and slasher-horror alike.

Chapter 2 is similarly concerned with a range of post-war anxieties, here specifically Japanese. It argues that these were engendered initially by the militarisation of the nation, subsequently by its wartime defeat, by its social, political and cultural Americanisation and by Japanese reactions to that process. Focusing on the *onryou*, a narrative of supernatural female vengeance, the generic conventions of which stretch back to the oral tradition of popular storytelling, it explores how this horrific sub-genre allows for a decoding of traumatic memories that continue to fester in post-war Japanese culture, despite the bindings of American-style democracy. In the awareness of the cultural hybridity of the highly Americanised Japan, and of the Japanese people's self-appointed mission to monitor American contraventions of the 'Hiroshima spirit' therefore, the consideration of wartime trauma is extended to Gore Verbinski's recent Hollywood adaptation of Nakata Hideo's *Ringu*, examining how the *onryou's* generic conventions allow for an ongoing exploration of the perils of militarism in the neo-imperialistic American present; how the massive trauma of the Japanese engendered by Hiroshima may provide, as its survivors hoped, a lesson to the world about the evils of military ambition, the horrors of war and premature post-traumatic reaffirmations of ideologically dominant conceptions of national identity.

Notes

1   R.J.C. Butow, *Japan's Decision to Surrender* (Stanford: University of California Press, 1954), p. 248.

2   Paul Johnson, *A History of the Modern World from 1917 to the 1990s* (London: Weidenfeld & Nicolson, 1991), p. 428.

3   Joy Hendry, *Understanding Japanese Society* (Nissan Institute/Routledge Japanese Studies Series, London: Routledge, 1996), p. 17.

4   Johnson, *History of the Modern World*, p. 426.

5   Ian Buruma, *The Wages of Guilt: Memories of War in Germany and Japan* (London: Vintage, 1994), p. 92.

6   Buruma, *Wages of Guilt*, p. 98.

7   Primo Levi, 'The Drowned and the Saved,' in Levi and Rothberg (eds), *The Holocaust*, p. 31.

8   Caruth, 'Trauma and Experience,' in Levi and Rothberg (eds), *The Holocaust*, p. 194.

9   Dominick LaCapra, 'Trauma, Absence, Loss,' in Levi and Rothberg (eds), *The Holocaust*, p. 200.

10 Johnson, *History of the Modern World*, p. 734.

11 Ian Buruma, *A Japanese Mirror: Heroes and Villains of Japanese Culture* (London: Penguin, 1985), p. 220.

1

The horror of the Nazi past in the reunification present: Jörg Buttgereit's *Nekromantiks*

We are separated from yesterday not by a yawning abyss, but by the same situation. (Camus)

Everyone bears the guilt for everything, but if everyone knew that, we would have paradise on earth. (Dostoyevsky)

These two epigraphs, from the opening and closing titles of *Yesterday Girl* (1966), Alexander Kluge's pioneering work of Young German Cinema, provide an entirely apposite introduction to the concerns of this book; for here I will explore two recent works of experimental, historically grounded and hence political German films that effectively encapsulate my conceptual and critical agenda. They are Jörg Buttgereit's *Nekromantik* and *Nekromantik 2*. For although Buttergereit's much-banned necro-porn horrors have been frequently dismissed as little more than 'disappointingly witless' and 'morbidly titillating' attempts to 'disgust the most jaded conceivable audience,'[1] these films are not only more thematically complex and technically sophisticated than is popularly supposed, but they also share a set of artistic and ideological concerns more usually associated with the canonic auteurs of the Young German Cinema and the New German Cinema of the turbulent years of the 1960s and 1970s: specifically Volker Schlöndorff and Hans Jürgen Syberberg in the first generation and Werner Herzog and Rainer Werner Fassbinder in the second. So, even though the glory days of horror film production in Germany had been brought to a close by the Nazis, and horror directors of the 1960s had worked on budgets so low that the quality of their work was severely compromised and with the horror film entirely disappearing from the German mainstream by the 1970s, Buttgereit (alongside fellow horror directors such as Andreas Schnaas, Olaf Ittenbach and Christoph Schlingensief) brought about a resurgence of the genre's fortunes in the traumatic years that surrounded the 1989 fall of the Berlin Wall. Thus, in his distinctively alienated musings on the existential isolation of the desiring German subject, in his libidinally ambiguous re-animation of the deeply repressed historical past and in his highly self-reflexive plays on cinema's capacity for the dissemination and reproduction of regressive ideologies of race and gender (themselves designed to bind up the damage wrought to German self-image by the events of 1939–45) Buttgereit would deliver not, as has been argued, the 'limp, inane' message that 'it's okay to f**k [*sic*] the dead as long as you don't kill them'[2] but a considered and often playful exploration of one of the key subjects of recent German cinema and a core concern of this book – *die Unbewaltigte Vergangenheit* – the past that has not been adequately dealt with.

Born in 1963, the year following the *Oberhausen Manifesto*'s demands for a 'new German feature film' predicated upon 'new freedoms,' liberated from 'the influence of commercial partners' and 'the control of special interest groups,'[3] Buttgereit received his first Super-8 camera as a First Holy Communion present. He made his first film in 1977, as West Germany veered to the political right and various left-wing, feminist, anti-establishment and terrorist groups such as the Red Army Faction came to the cultural and political fore. In the face of ideological divisions at the heart of West German society, and the evolution of Kluge's Young German Cinema into the distinctively historically engaged New German Cinema, it is notable that while Buttgereit's early film career ranged across genres (from parodic monster and super-hero shorts to mock-rockumentaries set in the West Berlin punk scene),[4] it is nonetheless possible to trace a culturally engaged thematic continuity across these early works that shares a great deal with the art house films of the German avant garde and which underscores Buttgereit's often playful horror films with a deadly historical and political seriousness.

In 1981, Buttgereit covertly shot the six-minute short *Mein Papi*, a slice of *cinema verité* displaying for ridicule Buttgereit's elderly, overweight and vest-clad father. The film was screened in clubs, mostly as a back-projection to live performances by the experimental noise band *Einsturzende Neubaten*, with Buttgereit being paid for his art in vodka. The real payment however, as the director remarked in interview with David Kerekes, was the satisfaction of having 'whole audiences laughing at [his] father behind his back.'[5] The New German Cinema's location, in Thomas Elsaesser's words, of 'history in the home and Fascism in the family unit'[6] was here transmuted into a punkish mockery of the father as legitimate familial embodiment of totalitarian authority and law. It was a mockery echoed the following year, in *Bloody Excesses in the Leader's Bunker* (1982), a six-minute Super-8 short set in the final days of the Reich, with Hitler played by a performer better known for his obscene parodies of the much-loved folk musician Heino. While the Heino impersonator went down very well with contemporary audiences, it is nonetheless notable that Buttgereit's onetime inclusion of genuine concentration camp footage in the film proved too strong even for the punk denizens of the Berlin music scene to stomach. It nonetheless underscored Buttgereit's own decidedly inventive take on his nation's past, and the connection of that past to the politically divided and culturally confused present. It was a concern that would, most certainly, feed into the *Nekromantik* films and, in so doing, transform them into serious works of political film making. In 1985 came *Hot Love*, a self-consciously absurd tale of sexual infidelity, rape, suicide and the slaughter of the transgressive mother by a murderously mutant newborn. Already apparent was Buttgereit's sense that the present moment had been born of parental sin and that such transgressions must somehow be recognised and avenged in order for a future to be realised. Finally, with the Buttgereit-directed crucifixion sequence in Michael Brynntup's *Jesus: The Film* (1985–86) in which Christ (in vampire teeth) is simultaneously nailed to the cross and staked through the heart, the director's thematic machinery and collection of collaborators was complete. Like Syberberg before him, Buttgereit evidently recognised that strand of Romantic irrationalism that had lain at the heart of German culture long before

the originary unification of the nation in the 1870s – an irrationalism that had manifested itself in Goethe's rendering of the Faust
legend, Hoffman's tales of the *unheimlich* in prose and later still the
horror tales of Weimar cinema, such as Weine's *The Cabinet of Dr
Caligari* (1919) and Murnau's *Nosferatu* (1922). Like Syberberg before him, Buttgereit also recognised 'the emotional deadness of German society'[7] engendered by the Nazi appropriation of that Romantic
tradition and focused in his films on Germany's subsequent repression both of the memory of the Nazi past and the irrationalism that
underscored it, leaving Germany 'spiritually disinherited and dispossessed … a country without a homeland, without *"Heimat"'.*[8]
For if Syberberg had had the quintessentially irrational Germanic
unconscious rise from the grave in the guise of the Führer in *Hitler
– A Film From Germany* then in the *Nekromantik* films Buttgereit
would undertake a considerably more visceral, but no less politically
serious, act of resurrection.

Operating in a variety of roles and working with a small team,
including Manfred Jelinski as producer, Franz Rodenkirchen as co-
writer and co-director and actors such as Daktari Lorenz, Mark
Reeder and Monika M. amongst others; working to insanely unpre-
dictable shooting schedules and on ridiculously low budgets,
Buttgereit had clearly picked up the torch of the *Oberhausen
Manifesto*'s signatories in his attempt to make something new out of
the legacy of the past and the incertitudes of the present. The subject material he adopted (specifically his graphic depictions of sexual
encounters with the dead and of the killing and mutilation of people
and animals) alongside his decidedly idiosyncratic re-animation of
the German Romantic tradition (through his disruption of linear
temporality, insertion of dream sequences and absurdist parodies of
classic films) would moreover result in a scandal undreamed of by
Kluge himself, and swingeing censorship unheard of in Germany
since the days of the Third Reich.

The political climate into which *Nekromantik* was released in
West Germany was an extremely conservative one. And as in Britain
(see Chapter 6) this impacted directly on contemporary horror cinema. All horror films shown, both on video and in picture houses
were heavily cut, with numerous classics of the genre, such as *The*

Evil Dead (1982) and *The Texas Chainsaw Massacre* (1974) being banned outright on video. Refusing to submit *Nekromantik* to the agency responsible for implementing the code of *Freiwillige Selbst Kontrolle*, or 'voluntary self-control' under which directors were supposed to work, Buttgereit released the film directly to cinemas for screening to those over the age of eighteen. And nothing much in the way of reprisals ensued, either from the radical left which was known for its attacks on cinemas screening films they considered sexist or pornographic or from the authorities. Only in 1992, following the scandal surrounding *Nekromantik 2* was sale of the film by mail order briefly outlawed. The film, it seemed, was essentially too 'arty' for a mainstream horror audience and it passed without a great deal of notice at home, at least until its enthusiastic reception in the United States and elsewhere made it something of a *cause célèbre*. *Nekromantik 2*, however, released following the fall of the Berlin Wall and the re-unification of Germany, faced a considerably harder time of it, being placed on the list of 'seized videos' whereby it could neither be owned, watched or shown legally in Germany and orders were given, without hearing or trial, for its negatives, production-related and publicity materials to be destroyed. This was a move unprecedented in Germany since the war and it was echoed internationally, where until very recently the *Nekromantik* films have remained widely banned and largely unavailable.

So, what *is* so dreadful about the *Nekromantik* films that has driven governments to ban them and critics so consistently to neglect them?[9] Certainly, their heroes and heroines are decidedly unappealing, Rob and Betty of *Nekromantik* being bound together by their shared passion for the dead – Rob working as a 'street cleaner' with the Nazi-encoded *Joe's Sauberungsaktion*, the company logo of which is a skull and crossbones within a pentacle. It is an occupation that allows for the acquisition first of body parts and then of a complete corpse for this oddest of couples' mutual erotic delight. But this is no ordinary body. It is not the product of an automobile accident, as seems to be the case with many of Rob's acquisitions, but was once a young man who was accidentally shot while picking apples. The perpetrator of the crime, moreover, was a beer-guzzling, oompah-listening fat man, remarkably visually similar to Buttgereit's own father of *Mein Papi*, and extremely reminiscent of the kinds of characters depicted in the *Heimatfilms* of the 1950s – West Germany's most popular post-war genre.[10] Positioning the murderer in a back-yard deckchair as he shoots small birds that fly across the sky, Buttgereit simultaneously evokes and derides not only the *Heimatfilms* themselves – being essentially conservative and enor-mously popular depictions of morally unimpeachable familial and community lives being lived with no heed to the horrors of recent years, amidst the splendours of the German landscape – but also the culture that so enthusiastically consumed them. As Buttgereit makes clear then, neither Rob nor Betty have transformed the young apple-picker into a corpse. This has been accomplished by an ostensibly morally upstanding member of society who subsequently disappears from view, unpunished for his crimes. Buttgereit's mission, it seems, is to embrace that corpse and in so doing to look upon the culturally specific wounds inflicted on the national psyche by National Social-ism and its legacy. In doing this he would raise the question origi-nally posed by Alexander Mitscherlich, Director of the Sigmund Freud Institute in Frankfurt, as to why the collapse of the Third Reich had not provoked the reaction of conscience-stricken remorse that one might logically expect; why, in Thomas Elsaesser's words, '[i]nstead of confronting this past, Germans preferred to bury it.'[11] Like the New German Cinema before him, the purpose of Buttgereit's *Nekromantik* films is thus to dig into the place of burial (to rip away the grave clothing) and engage passionately with the rotting fruits of the past. It is an act which we the audience are forced also to em-brace visually through a highly self-conscious deployment of the technological mechanisms of cinematic production and the generic representational strategies of horror.

Fittingly for a Berliner who had grown up in an island city bisected by the Wall and its attendant ideologies, Buttgereit frequently adopts the metaphor of the border or boundary as a means of ar-ticulating the sense of existential isolation and cultural confusion experienced by his characters. Great emphasis is placed, for example, on the ways in which the most innocuous-looking of apartments, shot from the sanitised safety of the street, can nonetheless house the most grotesque and historically redolent realities. Focusing on the interiors of such apartments, Buttgereit not only participates in the New German Cinema's quasi-documentary focus on the real-life spaces inhabited by ordinary people, but points to essentially *unheimlich* nature of the German home. The apartment inhabited by Rob and initially Betty is one such space. Their bed, for example, is swathed in chicken wire, becoming a highly culturally resonant space of physical, emotional and historical entrapment whereby erotic shenanigans with the bony corpse inescapably evoke the cadaverous figures staring out from behind the concentration camp wire in films such as Alain Resnais' *Night and Fog* (1955), famously quoted as a commentary on the German present by director Margarethe von Trotta in the closing sequence of *The German Sisters* (1981). A bed is never just a bed in Buttgereit, just as a corpse is never simply a corpse, for here sexual desire, the world of dreams, the horrors of the past and death itself are self-consciously entwined in a cinematic spectacle that does indeed shock, but which shocks in a way that is intimately involved with the German past and encoded by German representational practices.

Subtly encoded Nazi semiology is apparent, for example, across both films: both Rob of *Nekromantik* and Monika of *Nekromantik 2* possessing a highly distinctive and highly nationally-specific ornament – a miniature version of *The Glass Man*. Originally created by Franz Tschackert of the German Hygiene Museum in Dresden in 1930, this was a life-size model of a male figure whose transparent skin allowed the observer to see the skeleton within and some of the internal organs. One of Hitler's favourite contemporary artefacts (there are pictures of him posing proudly alongside it) the model was assiduously promoted as an embodiment of Aryan racial perfection; its organs echoing the master race's purity of line and perfection of form, its transparency signalling the eugenic purity of the breed.[12] In possessing such an artefact, in playing with it and re-assembling its body parts with a certain loving care, necrophiliacs like Rob and Monika do seem to be engaging with a particular model of historically-grounded memorialising subjectivity that is overtly linked to the discourses of racial supremacism which underscored National Socialism and unleashed the Holocaust upon the world. But as Buttgereit again intimates through his *mise-en-scène*, such discourses were not the invention of the Nazis who simply appropriated them. After all, Rob's flat also contains a large collection of specimen jars holding an eyeball, a foetus, a hand and various unidentifiable organs. These too are highly reminiscent of the discourses of racial supremacy promulgated by Nazi science and explicitly dealt with in films such as Schlöndorff's *Tin Drum* (1979), when the squealing of the boy Oskar shatters the specimen jars of the doctor who seeks to cure him of his refusal to grow up into Fascism. But such imagery also existed before the rise of the Nazis, specifically in the Expressionist inflected 'mad-scientist' movies of the early years of the twentieth century, films such as *Homunculus* (1916), in which a decidedly Faustian scientist pre-empts Hitler's 'final solution' by setting out to overcome the bounds of human knowledge in the creation of his own Superman, a thematic echoed in both *The Golem* (1920) and *The Cabinet of Dr Caligari*. Thus Buttgereit seems to argue that beneath the rational consciousness of the street and beneath the present's repressions of the past there is an essential irrationality. As for Syberberg, this lies at the heart of German consciousness and can be seen in the nightmare world of the ghost train, the crazy logic of dreams and in the representational strategies of experimental cinema itself. Accordingly, both *Nekromantik* films contain lengthy or repeated dream sequences; Rob's rural visions of a white-clad, long-limbed woman striding across a rural landscape, carrying a severed head in a box before removing it to play a game of catch being echoed by Mark's drunken nightmare of burial up to his neck and having his own head first placed beneath a box and then stamped upon by a spike-heeled shoe. And there is also Monika's love song to death, sung with the accompaniment of an 'Eterna' piano as a giant blood-spattered skull revolves in the background. Surreal visions of death, desire and love coalesce here in a strange dream-logic that self-consciously questions not only the transparency of the cinematic medium but also the certitudes of rational discourse itself. What emerges is a historicised model of German subjectivity that is itself predicated on historical trauma and which accordingly reveals itself in classic post-traumatic mode in the form of 'repeated, intrusive hallucinations, thoughts and behaviours' and a simultaneous 'arousal to (and avoidance of) stimuli recalling the event.'[13]

Within a specifically German cultural context, it is therefore
notable that Rob and Betty's erotic desire for the corpse, their sexual
delight in it (and hence their very subjectivity as necrophiles) is seen
to be predicated upon an act of remembering. And that such subjectivity is also tightly bound to the act of looking further implicates
us, as spectators, in the necessary re-consideration of the horrors of
the past. Early on in *Nekromantik*, for example, a television psychiatrist talks at length on the ways in which phobic individuals can
become desensitised to the object of their fear. Such therapy is based
on the psychiatrist's observation that teenagers who repeatedly watch
video nasties can be seen to become inured to the horrors of what
they see. Desensitisation, the psychiatrist argues, is a product of visually experiencing the horrific, or mass-cultural renderings of the
horrific, again and again. But as Buttgereit realised early in his film-
making career, there are some things that German eyes find difficult
to look upon, whatever their political allegiances. The inclusion of
concentration camp footage in *Bloody Excesses in the Leader's Bunker*, for example, was simply too much for audiences to stomach,
regardless of their punk credentials. Might it be the case Buttgereit
appears to propose, that desensitisation to violence is just as likely to
happen when we refuse to look, when we turn our head away from
reality and look elsewhere – at the world of nature, the rural community, at the falsified present? Nazi cinema, of course, with its
promotion of a *volkish* ideology of national community and blood
and soil (which entailed the concomitant purgation of all liberal,
democratic, progressive or cosmopolitan elements) had effectively
instituted a cult of the beautiful as a means of aestheticising the
horrific actuality of industrialised genocide. Both the documentary
tradition instituted by Leni Riefenstahl's *Triumph of the Will* (1935)
and the concertedly anti-Semitic and anti-communist *Hetzfilms* such
as *Jud Süß* (1940) had counterposed the essentially wholesome,
healthy and beautiful world of National Socialism to the hideously
bestialised sexual threat that was the Jew or the communist. And
repeated viewing of such materials obviously naturalised the binarism,
printed it upon the national unconscious, desensitised the audience
to the aestheticisation of the political upon which the Final Solution rested. In his insistent looking upon the dead and what may or

may not be done with them Buttgereit thus appears to be proposing a radical de-aestheticisation of that past, a tearing-away of all obfuscatory bindings to engage in a form of truthful looking. Such a mode of looking would not only cut through the desensitising affect of revisionist history to lay the wounds of the past bare, but point to the pronouncedly ideological nature of the strategies of control that are implicit in all acts of cinematic viewing.

In both *Nekromantik* films then, Buttgereit is keen to expose the highly manipulative nature of the film medium – specifically in the second film's depiction of heterosexual pornography and the first's re-creation of the slasher horror genre. For all the implicit comment it offers on the cultural colonisation of German cinema in the years following the war, the hero of *Nekromantik 2* clearly sees nothing wrong with his job as a voice-over artist on imported pornographic films. But it is significant that Buttgereit draws a series of visual analogies between him and the sexually dysfunctional serial killer of Michael Powell's *Peeping Tom* (1960), another 'Mark' who repeatedly views the footage he has shot while murdering women. This would seem to point to a certain matrix of concerns to do with power, the gaze and subjectivity (specifically the ways in which objects of pornographic representation are fetishistically reduced to what Monika calls 'dicks and cunts up close') the encoding of discourses of power at the heart of the gaze and the potentially murderous consequences of such encoding. In *Nekromantik*'s take on the slasher film too we find ourselves in classic stalker territory, with audience point-of-view neatly matched to that of the knife-wielding monster who ties his victim's hands above her head, traces his knife from her shoe up her stockinged leg into her mouth as she stands, breasts exposed, screaming and moaning in a generically specific synthesis of terror and ecstasy. The sufficiently desensitised audience, which includes Buttgereit in left foreground, are predictably bored by such objectifying shenanigans – kissing, fondling each other, eating, talking – but never actually looking at the misogynistic hatred that for Buttgereit clearly underscores such images. For as Monika the necrophiliac asserts in *Nekromantik 2*, it is no more perverse to watch the dismemberment of animals for pleasure than it is to look at heterosexual pornography's reduction of people to their genitalia; it is simply more socially acceptable. The audience has become desensitised to the nastiness of such images, even while it is unable to look with any degree of clarity or good faith at the genuine horrors of the historic past. At the heart of Buttgereit's *oeuvre*, it seems, is an awareness of the politically problematic dimensions of visual pleasure, the ideologically expedient use to which that pleasure has been placed in the past and the legacy of that past in the present. There is no easy moralising here, none of the knee-jerkwill-to-censorship of the *Autonome Szene*, contemporary political activists whom Franz Rodenkirchen deemed practitioners of 'fascism from the left.'[14] Something far more complex is at work. It has a great deal to do with memory and, in Roland Barthes's formulation, counter-memory.

Buttgereit's consistent interest in the relationship between technologies of looking and the perpetuation of oppressive ideologies positions him at the heart of a range of theoretical debates relating to visual representation and memory predominant since the late 1970s. Like Edgar Reitz, the producer and director of *Heimat*, the eleven-part televisual chronicle of German domestic and communal life that itself engaged with the relationship between individual and communal remembering and the narratives of history, Buttgereit too is preoccupied with revealing what Eric Santer has termed 'the workings of history, power and socio-economic forces in the sensuous details of everyday life, intimate relationships, the face, the body.'[15] And like Reitz, he deploys a variety of representational media to do this – using Super-8, 8mm, 16mm and 32mm film, video, polaroids, stills-photography and television pictures in the construction of his representations of the dead and those who love them. Thus Buttgereit appears to affirm that the elegiac art of photography, in Susan Sontag's words, allows us not only 'to participate in another person's (or thing's) mortality, vulnerability, mutability' but in the medium's very will to 'testify to time's relentless melt.'[16] It is not simply, as John Berger has observed, that the photograph becomes even 'more traumatic than most memories or mementos' because it appears 'to confirm, prophetically, the later discontinuity created by the absence or death'[17] of the subject. In his depiction of Monika's photograph album of dead relatives, her frankly hilarious 'family photographs' of herself and her decomposing lover sitting innocently on the sofa and in her newspaper pictures of Rob prior to his suicide, as well as in Buttgereit's own depiction of the corpse as object of erotic desire, we can see an endeavour not only to record what has been and what is no longer (the living person now dead) but an attempt, in the very act of looking at such pictures, to inter-ject the absent dead into the living present – whereby they become not memories, but in Roland Barthes' sense counter-memories – a way of remembering otherwise.[18]

This is, of course, another aspect of Buttgereit's attempts to unbind the wounds of trauma by laying bare the wounded corpse of the past. For in making explicit the linkages between visual repre-sentation and memory, by predicating much of his thematic ma-chinery on the will to remember the otherwise absent and forgotten, Buttgereit once more draws our gaze back to that sense of horror that for New German Cinema underscored all representations of the German past. And he also forces us to look again at that dark irrationality that lies at the heart of the German subject. Akin to that of Claude Lanzmann in *Shoah* (1985) the nine-hour documen-tary consisting of interviews with survivors of the extermination camps of Auschwitz, Treblinka, Sobibor, Chelmno and Belzec, his task is to bring the past into the present; to indicate through visual representations that the past is never over and done with; that it is absurd to try to erase the trauma that called one's national subjectiv-ity into being in the first place. For such trauma must be looked upon before it can be healed. In all its viscerality, Buttgereit's is a project that forces the audience to look at that which they would rather avoid. And in so doing he offers both a counter-memory to Nazi cinema's elision of its own bloody deeds and a representation of human desire that rejects the power dynamics of heterosexual pornography and slasher-horror alike.

All of this, of course, makes Buttgereit a highly self-referential director – one who consistently references and re-configures the cin-ematic medium in his work. Monika and David of *Nekromantik 2*, for example, meet at an avant-garde film, a very funny parody of Louis Malle's *My Dinner With Andre* (1981). Entitled *Mon dejeunner avec Vera* it has a man and woman feasting on hard-boiled eggs while

sitting naked at a table on the roof of a block of flats; the relationship between the title and any notion of 'truth' remaining tangential
of course. Between the two *Nekromantik* films moreover, Buttgereit
made *Der Tödesking* (1990) in which, in the mind of the little girl
who introduces the piece, seven characters kill themselves: one for
every day of the week. Mulling upon the permeable membrane between lived reality and cinematic representation, *Der Tödesking* repeatedly deploys a Brechtian *Verfremdungseffect* whereby the
constructed nature of the repeated suicide-tableaux is foregrounded
through frequently amusing plays on the medium of film. The entire 'Tuesday' sequence, for example, including a man renting a film
at a video store and going home to watch it, turns out to be a horror
video that is screened in an empty room in which a dead body hangs
in the background. For as the foetal narrator figure who transmutes
into a decomposing corpse intimates, death is always implicit in
German life. Until a form of truthful looking can be found, it seems,
the two are locked in an endlessly repeated cycle, a Nietszchean return in which the tragedies of German history are endlessly enacted
and repeated in the most mordant ways possible.

   All of this comes to a head, so to speak, with Rob's suicide in
the final moments of *Nekromantik*. Lying on the bed he once shared
with Betty and for a brief interlude with their dead lover also, Rob
masturbates his memorably tumescent penis while slowly
disembowelling himself, coming in an impressively colourful splat-
ter of blood and semen, back-masked sound and chiaroscuro lighting. Far from being gore-for-gore's sake though, Rob's suicidal
masochism does seem to posit a traumatised subjectivity so wracked
by sexual dysfunction, existential despair and utter isolation that as
is the case for many of Fassbinder's ill-fated hero-protagonists, suicide is the only option. Populating his films, like Herzog, with characters that exist on the margins of society but nonetheless are not
simply freaks, but aspects of ourselves, Buttgereit thus appears to
propose that what lies at the heart of German subjectivity is a tragic
will to self-destruction. Born of the traumas of the past, and by a
premature binding of the wounds that the past inflicted, it is a will
that manifests itself not only in failed relationships with the living
but in a confused and desperate fetishisation of the dead.

It is this very paradigm that is embodied in Monika of *Nekromantik 2,* a film whose very credits are interspersed with another counter-memory: the grainy, monochrome re-running of Rob's suicide scene from *Nekromantik* itself. Disinterring Rob's corpse at the opening of the film and somehow managing to get it home, Monika thus embodies Caruth's model of traumatised subjectivity simultaneously aroused and repulsed by the corpse as originary site of trauma. Protractedly vacillating between her erotic pleasure in and visceral disgust at her sexual encounters with the corpse, Monica retains Rob's head and comically reduced penis while embarking on a relationship with the pornographic-voice-over artist Mark, who nonetheless bores her sexually and finds her liking of animal-dismemberment films obscene. Self-consciously echoing the marriage of Maria and Oswald in Fassbinder's *The Marriage of Maria Braun* and numerous other NGC (New German Cinema) renderings of similar models of emotional isolation, theirs is also a relationship founded on a shared loneliness, in a world where 'people can't live alone, but they cannot live together either.'[19] It culminates of course with Monika's decapitation of Mark during sex, her placing a tourniquet around his still erect penis and replacing his head with that of the exceedingly rotten Rob. Horrifically, the result of such congress with the living dead is Monika's pregnancy which for all it echoes the unnatural reproduction of *Hot Love* does seem to offer some model of authentic subjectivity emerging from a union with the dead, some kind of potentially meaningful inter-subjective relationship emerging from Monika's act of eroticised mourning. For without such an affirmation, all life once more is death and all becoming is an ending; a dynamic which Buttgereit so clearly wants to move on from in his films.

It is accordingly notable that such a cyclical model of life in death and death in life is built in to the very form of Buttgereit's film texts, most significantly in the infamous scenario in *Nekromantik* when, prompted by the television psychiatrist's desensitisation discourse, Rob appears to recall a distinctively disturbing episode from his past. Here another unpleasant father figure in decidedly unattractive blue knitwear, in a distinctively industrial setting and to the accompaniment of backward-masked industrial noise picks up and

slits the throat of a fluffy black and white bunny. Said rabbit is subsequently skinned, gutted and hung up by its legs, in a pose most
redolent of sadomasochistic porn, while inter-cut footage of the autopsy of a human corpse visually echoes the scene: the insides of
both creatures becoming their outsides as fur and skin are stripped
away and internal organs are removed in wet and gloopy chunks.
Once again it seems that Buttgereit is forcing us to look at something we would rather avoid – most pronounced being the industrial scene of slaughter and the protagonist's resemblance not only
to the *Heimatfilm* killer of Rob and Betty's beloved corpse but to the
director's own father in *Mein Papi*. But there is perhaps a further
historic reference being made here: the term 'rabbit films' or
Kaninchenfilme being the collective noun for the twelve films that
were banned in East Germany in 1965, films that were felt to be too
sceptical, nihilistic, relativistic or subjective to conform to statist
ideology. As Sabine Hake puts it:

> the directors' failure or unwillingness to develop a dialectical
> conception of reality, the argument went, had resulted in sto-
> ries, images and, perhaps most importantly, dispositions and
> attitudes that were irrelevant, if not detrimental to the self-
> definition of GDR society. [It was a move that] forced film-
> makers to retreat to uncontroversial topics and conventional
> treatments.[20]

Quite apart from its capacity to shock, what is most extraordinary
about the rabbit sequence though is the fact that it is replayed, and
replayed backwards, in the closing sequence of the film as Rob ejacu-
lates gallons of blood and semen on his bed of death. The rabbit,
once dismembered, is literally put back together again. The trauma
that lay deep in Rob's past is exorcised in death: 'what has been
destroyed is now restored; old wounds heal and bad things turn
good again.'[21]

Such redemptive sentiments were, of course, remarkably apposite to the buoyant reunification climate into which *Nekromantik
2* was released. But as was the case with a number of horror films
that emerged during this period, any optimism was tinged with an
awareness that in order to recover from the trauma engendered by
years of partition, the wounds partition had engendered must not

be prematurely bound up in the interests of an ideologically expedient sense of national cohesion.[22] Shocking in subject matter and
unflinchingly visceral in their portrayal of sex and death, Buttgereit's
films thus took as their very premise the horrors of a nationally specific trauma that had already been prematurely buried in the interests of social cohesion – the trauma engendered by National
Socialism. Thus deploying the conventions of body horror he would
work to expose the complicity of the film medium in acts of ideological manipulation of the subject who, unable to engage meaning-
fully with the psychological and socio-cultural trauma that lies in
the nation's past, remains critically wounded in the here and now. In
mounting a plea for a new form of historically and politically engaged looking at that past as a means of healing, Buttgereit thus
pointed to the ways in which the film medium in general and horror
cinema in particular can bring about not only a re-sensitisation to
the horrors of the past but a new means of conceiving of the future.
In this, he not only produced stylistically inventive and conceptually sophisticated works of modern horror cinema but offered a new
model of German subjectivity for a post-reunification age. It is a
considerable achievement for one whose films have been widely
banned, critically neglected and commonly viewed as low-budget
shockers of little artistic and intellectual merit. Such attitudes, need-
less to say, are entirely predictable responses from a still wounded,
still traumatised national culture unable yet to engage with Buttgereit's
unflinchingly radical stance.

Notes

1   M. Ward, 'Review of *Necromantic*' [*sic*]. *About Cult Film*.
    www.aboutcultfilm.com/reviews/nekromantic.html. Accessed 13 Sep-
    tember 2005.
2   M. Ward, 'Review of *Necromantic*' [*sic*]. *About Cult Film*.
    www.aboutcultfilm.com/reviews/nekromantic.html. Accessed 13 Sep-
    tember 2005.
3   *The Oberhausen Manifesto*, 1962. http://web.uvic.ca/geru/439/
    oberhausen.htlm. University of Victoria, Department of German Stud-
    ies, 2 November 2006.
4   *The Trend – Punk Rockers Speak About Their Lives* (1981–82) and

That Was S.O.36 (1984–85).

5   Jörg Buttgereit, quoted in David Kerekes, *Sex, Murder, Art: The Films of Jörg Buttgereit* (Manchester: Headpress, 1998), p. 52.

6   Thomas Elsaesser, *New German Cinema: A History* (London: Bfi/ Macmillan, 1989), p. 239.

7   Eric Santner, *Stranded Objects: Mourning, Memory and Film in Post-war Germany* (Ithaca, NY and London: Cornell University Press, 1993), p. 39.

8   A. Kaes, *From Hitler to Heimat: The Return of History as Film* (Cambridge, MA and London: Harvard University Press, 1989), p. 68.

9   In part, of course, one could argue that there is a tendency to critically ignore or marginalise all horror film from Germany, both the *The Companion to German Cinema* (London: Bfi, 1991) and the more recent *The German Cinema Book* (London: Bfi, 2002) omitting the genre entirely.

10 Films such as *Black Forest Girl* (1950) or *The Fisher Girl of Lake Constance* (1956).

11 Elsaesser, *New German Cinema*, p. 242.

12 P. Comar, *The Human Body: Image and Emotion* (London: Thames & Hudson, 1999), p. 87.

13 Caruth, 'Trauma and Experience,' in Levi and Rothenberg (eds), *The Holocaust*, p. 193.

14 Kerekes, *Sex, Murder, Art*, p. 40.

15 Santer, *Stranded Objects*, p. 58.

16 Susan Sontag, *On Photography* (New York: Dell, 1977), p. 15.

17 John Berger, *Another Way of Telling* (New York: Pantheon, 1982), p. 87.

18 Roland Barthes, *Camera Lucida: Reflections on Photography*, (trans) Richard Howard (London: Vintage, 1993), p. 79.

19 Rainer Werner Fassbinder, 'Six Films by Douglas Sirk,' in Laura Mulvey and J. Halliday (eds), *Douglas Sirk* (Edinburgh: Edinburgh Film Festival, 1972), p. 104.

20 Sabine Hake, *German National Cinema* (London: Routledge, 2002), p. 124.

21 Kerekes, *Sex, Murder, Art*, p. 39.

22 Thus, while horror film production had dropped to an all time low in Germany in the 1970s and 1980s, reunification led to a number of films being produced that deployed the generic conventions of horror to explore the sins of the past and look to future redemption. Hence Christoph Schlingensief's *The German Chainsaw Massacre* (1990) translated and relocated Tobe Hooper's 1974 Texan original to a

German setting, with a West German family of butchers slaughtering East Germans for meat as they travelled westwards in search of a better life. Such violent attacks on 'foreigners' was echoed in Andreas Schnaas's *Terror 2000* (1992) whilst a fear of death in life and life in death could be seen in both Ralph Heuttner's *Babylon* (1992) and Schnaas's *Zombie 90 / Extreme Pestilence* (1991). Romauld Karmakar's *The Deathmaker* (1995) pointed to the dark irrationality underscoring German self-perception by returning to the true story of 1920s Hanover serial killer Fritz Haarmann, the key protagonist in Fritz Lang's seminal *M* (1931). Thus, whilst Rainer Matsutani's *Over My Dead Body* (1995) allowed a man to return briefly from the dead to atone for his crimes in life, Peter Fratzscher's *Night Time* (1997) was premised on a putative werewolf searching for evidence of the night-time misadventures he was unable to recollect by day. Stefan Ruzowitsky moreover would return to the highly controversial subjects of medical experimentation on human subjects, institutional complicity and governmental sanction in his films *Anatomy* (2000) and *Anatomy 2* (2002). Both directly evoked the crimes of the Nazi past but within a contemporary reunification context.

2

Nihonjinron, women, horror: post-war national identity and the spirit of subaltern vengeance in *Ringu* and *The Ring*

Over the past fifteen years, as a post-9/11 United States has sought to increase its international influence over the strategically significant nations of Afghanistan, Iraq, Iran and North Korea, there has been an exponential increase in both the consumption of Japanese horror films and in American remakes of Japanese horror for an English-speaking international audience.[1] Most commercially successful and, it seems, culturally resonant, has been *The Ring,* Gore Verbinski's 2002 remake of Nakata Hideo's *Ringu* of 1998 (itself an adaptation of a Suzuki Koji novel of 1991), a film that has earned gross international revenues of over $229 million and become the seventh-highest grossing horror film in history.[2] Drawing on the Japanese *onryou* or vengeful ghost narrative, *Ringu* and *The Ring* are intimately concerned with traumatic dislocations to national self-image and the ways in which the media may promulgate ideologically dominant models of national identity for the internalisation of individuals who, as we have seen in the case of post-war Germany, nonetheless remain gravely wounded by the events of the historic past.[3] As this chapter will argue, the capacity of *onryou*-style narratives to undertake such culturally grounded explorations of national trauma is a product of the genre's history in Japan, specifically its implicit opposition to the right-wing militarism that led to the Pacific War. For since the 1960s, Japanese horror cinema has repeatedly had the female corpse return from the dead to demand retribution for the hitherto concealed wounds inflicted on the nation by unpunished historical crimes. In this, the *onryou* has granted compelling-yet-repulsive access to the political unconscious that lies beneath the psychological unconscious of individual characters, the film narrative as a whole and indeed the cultural life of the nation. For in both Japanese and American *onryou* narratives the vengeful ghost's target is not merely 'the living' but the repressive and totalising ideologies that they have internalised as a means of denying the dislocations to national self-image wrought by traumatic events such as war. As this chapter will illustrate then, the generic conventions of the *onryou* may be seen to undermine the imperialistic agendas of both twentieth-century Japan *and* the twenty first-century United States; calling into question both the value of the *bushido* code in Japan's past *and* contemporary US culturally conservative bellicose nationalism. For in each case the *onryou* sub-genre is effectively and affectively stalked by the spectre of vengeful alterity that haunts its bourgeois capitalistic hegemonies and the imperialistic ambitions they uphold, tearing away the bindings that dress the nation's war-engendered wounds, and exposing their full and bloody horror to public view.

Cinematically speaking, the *onryou* motif came into its own in the years following America's Occupation of the defeated Japan when, taking control of all aspects of Japanese social, cultural, economic and political life for a period of seven years' America exercised its 'desire to see the Japanese behave like Americans [which] by definition was good.'[4] Such an unabashedly colonialist agenda had encouraged the Japanese people to embrace American models of civil liberties and human rights, particularly those pertaining to freedom of religion, speech, the press and assembly. Abolishing Shinto as the state religion and forcing the Emperor to disavow his divinity, the Americans thus set out to 'destroy the wartime militaristic and xenophobic mentality'[5] that had started with the massacre of hundreds of thousands of Chinese in Nanking in 1937 and ended with the US atomic bombing of Nagasaki and Hiroshima in 1945. To accomplish such seismic alterations to Japanese cultural and social life the Americans had introduced the Showa Constitution which entailed the renunciation of war, promoted universal adult suffrage, the equality of the sexes and rights to property, work and trade union membership. Education meanwhile became a universal right regardless of race, creed, sex, social position or family origin. The constitution thus set out to enact the American Declaration of Independence's foundational assertion that the supreme aim of government was the promotion of 'life, liberty and the pursuit of happiness' in all its citizens. And to culturally reinforce such values, traditionally Japanese cultural products were heavily censored. Out went all traces of militarism, with sword-fight dramas and samurai films being initially banned, as were some ninety-eight *kabuki* plays. Poetry anthologies were scrutinised and even Mount Fuji, the object of Shintoist nature worship, became a forbidden subject for visual representation.[6]

Unsurprisingly, such a radical project of re-fashioning Japan in the image of the United States called into question what it meant to call oneself Japanese and how in turn Japanese cultural identity might be expressed artistically or transmitted through popular cultural forms. Certainly, the ways in which the Japanese people responded to this sense of cultural dislocation has a great deal to tell us about the deep ideological divisions that now lay at the heart of this deeply traumatised nation. For in one camp, aligned with the nationalistic right, were those proponents of the *bushido*- style militarism of the pre-war years; those who defended or denied the events of Nanking and justified the human rights atrocities perpetrated during the war years as a necessary part of military strategy. In the other camp, aligned with the peacenik left, were those who decried the militaristic past as a crime against the Japanese people who had been doubly victimised by the punitive dropping of American atom bombs on Hiroshima and Nagasaki. As Shindo Kaneto, director of *Children of Hiroshima* (1952) and later of two notable *onryou* films put it, in a rather clumsy translation:

> we might say the atomic bomb had been given to [the] Japanese as a revelation of science who preferred savageness, fanaticism and intolerant Japanese spirit to freedom, culture and science. The atomic bomb was an alarm to civilization and an awakening towards peace for [the] Japanese.[7]

What had brought Japan to ruin, intellectuals like Shindo argued, was the *bushido* code – a form of savage and intolerant fanaticism that exploited the weak, destroyed all that stood in the way of military supremacy and promoted an anti-intellectual and fundamentally irrational form of xenophobic patriarchy. And it is at this point in Japan's negotiation of its own historic past, that the figure of the abject woman familiar from a number of ancient storytelling forms would be cinematically resurrected by Shindo as a means of exploring *nihonjinron*, or post-war Japanese identity in the light of recent traumatic events.[8] Invariably possessing slow and spastic movements, long dark hair and one or more staring eyes, these vengeful ghosts kill all they see and incorporate those they kill into their community of the dead. Thus in Shindo's own *Onibaba* and *Kuruneko* and in Kobayashi Masaki's *Kwaidan* we can see an explicitly retributive feminine principle at work, one that explicitly targets the macho militarism of the *bushido* code while demanding from beyond the grave a form of justice that restores balance, or *Wa,* to Japanese social life. Encapsulating Bakhtin's sense of 'pregnant death, a death that gives birth,' the *onryou*'s 'decaying and deformed flesh' thus combines 'with the flesh of a new life, conceived but as yet unformed'[9] in order to present contemporary audiences with a historically and culturally specific abject. Here is 'the jettisoned object ... radically excluded,' the repulsive but compelling wound itself that draws the observer 'toward the place where meaning collapses ... on the edge of non-existence and hallucination.'[10] Terrifying, unappeasable, unstoppable, the *onryou* thus granted a highly resonant insight not only into Japanese cultural trauma of the post-war period but the culturally silenced horrors of the pre-war and wartime years. In time, as this chapter will illustrate, she would grant a similar insight into the terrors of the United States's own nationalistic warmongering.

Onibaba and *Kuroneko* are set in the socially turbulent fourteenth century when warlords (competing claims for control of the very identity of the Japanese people) tore the country apart and threw the peasantry into abject poverty. In the former film a mother and daughter-in-law live together in an area of towering reeds but tiring of their diet of vermin, and in the absence of their forcibly conscripted son and husband, take to murdering passing *samurai* and selling their arms for food. The corpses they throw into the hole of the film's title. As the opening titles indicate, this is a 'deep and dark' space whose 'silence has endured since ancient times'; a space, one surmises, wherein all aspects of Japanese culture and consciousness that cannot be assimilated into a balanced and harmonious world view must be ejected.[11] Thus dwarfed by their surroundings, buffeted by winds of ill fortune that blow evil for the nation as a whole, they do their best to survive while terrible portents that directly evoke the horrors of Hiroshima and Nagasaki abound: 'a black sun rose, the day was night. It's as if the earth was turned upside down.' Clearly, it is *bushido* that has brought them to such a pass and it is unsurprising that when a mask-wearing *samurai* appears, the mother-in-law openly asserts 'men like you killed my son' and must in turn be 'punished … for starting a war.' The mask that hides the masculine principle's dark desires to control and conquer is thus ripped away and the nation's wounds are unbound. But in placing the mask on her own face the mother-in-law makes a fatal error. Like the victims of Hiroshima and Nagasaki she becomes horribly mutilated by donning the mask of militarism and for all her shouted protests, 'I'm not a demon, I'm a human being,' she too is swallowed up by the hole. Shindo's realistically realised women, who eat like men and kill like men, refuse to be exploited while being comfortable with their own sexuality, have been corrupted by the *bushido* code. For this reason the mother-in-law will be cast out, being swallowed by the hole as convincingly as would be Yamamura Sadako, abject corpse woman of *Ringu*, some three centuries later.

Such concerns were echoed in Shindo's follow-up project *Kuruneko*, the tale of a mother and daughter-in-law whose son and husband has once again been carried away to fight in the service of an anonymous lord. In his absence this unfortunate pair are raped and murdered by a group of masterless *samurai* who wander from village to village in an endless orgy of theft, sexual violence and murder. Swearing vengeance on the warrior class 'for warring' and on a world that proclaims 'the weak will always starve,' the women enter into a demonic pact. Brought back to life in the guise of rich gentlewomen, they lead *samurai* through the forests to their ghostly home where, having given them the chance to redeem themselves, they transform into black cats and rip out the throats of the unrepentant. A generic relative of the *onryou*, this *bakeneko-monu* thus aligns the feminine abject with the verminous and untrustworthy figure of the cat, illustrating the hidden power and resilience of both. And once more the target is macho militarism. But the lost son Haichi whose loyalties are now divided between his family and his lord, his past and his present, makes a choice that damns him forever. He opts for loyalty to his master's destructive ideal and ends up with nothing; lying at the close of the film in the burned ruins of his family house as the snow falls upon him and the cries of a cat echo plaintively around him. Having turned his back on his family, having rejected the ideals of balance, continuity and stability embodied in the feminine principle he is left with nothing; as indeed was Japan following its wartime defeat. What is more, such a dynamic is repeated almost exactly in the 'Black Hair' episode of *Kwaidan*, whose *samurai* protagonist is haunted by the eponymous tresses of his loyal, self-effacing and cruelly abandoned first wife. His death, when it comes, is caused by a vision of his own horribly aged face; precisely that which kills the protagonists in the original Suzuki Koji novel *Ringu* from which Nakata Hideo's and Gore Verbinski's films would be adapted. [12]

Suzuki Koji's novel, which began the *Ringu / Ring* series is the story of a magazine reporter Asakawa Kazuyuki (the married father of a daughter) who enlists the help of an old college associate Takayama Ryuji (a philosopher and self-proclaimed rapist) to trace the origins of a killer videotape. It is a narrative that consistently deploys the metaphor of the virus to explore the politics of individual, gendered and national identity in an age of multi-media representation. Here Sadako is a genetically-male though feminine-seeming hermaphrodite killed by the last survivor of smallpox in Japan, a doctor who raped her and then killed her when he post-coitally glimpsed her abnormal genitalia; his recognition of and patriarchal horror at Sadako's balanced embodiment of masculine and feminine principles leading to her bloody and brutal murder. The video and its lethal potentiality is thus a product of Sadako's own telekinetic abilities mixed with the smallpox virus's will to survive by whatever means necessary. Sadako, as spirit of vengeance, therefore asserts her own right to survive and to reproduce by becoming both mother and father to a new breed of infected individuals, her meta-hybridity being echoed in the book's inference that her father was not in fact human but a water spirit summoned by the real-life ascetic En no Ozunu. Most notably though, Sadako's victims do not die because she emerges from the television screen (as is the case in later filmic adaptations) but as is the case in *Kwaidan* when their virally damaged hearts stop beating at the sight of a terrifying vision of themselves prematurely aged. Cast off and excluded by the social world of the symbolic order, its representations of itself to itself, its formulation and recognition of the ideologically interpellated subject, Sadako thus occupies a space of thirty-year silence before erupting into the eclectic incomprehensibility of the images captured on the cursed video: perspectivally distorted maternal hair-brushing, the bubbling eruption of Japanese characters, crawling damaged people, a pointing man, the character 'sada' reflected in a human eye, the corona of light peeping around the partially closed cover of a well. But because she illustrates the ways in which dominant ideologies assign a state of psychotic meaninglessness to the unheard and unrecognised who, because they are considered incomprehensible, are excluded from the material world, Sadako's video can also be seen to propose a new way of reconceiving and reconfiguring both the subject and his or her society. For as Slavoj Žižek (following Marx) would conceive of it, Sadako is the spectral apparition who returns to haunt the real that has excluded her. She is the wound that suppurates through the dressings, denying all claims that she is healed. It is therefore significant that the Sadako of the novel does not appear from the television set. Neither, as in the idiot-proof Hollywood version, does she rasp 'seven days' down the telephone to her victims. She says precisely nothing; her message lying in the length of her silence, the ostensibly incomprehensible nature of her video communication and the inexorability of her stumbling march to vengeance.

Nakata Hideo's *Ringu*, the first cinematic treatment of the novel, was made in 1998 as a recession-hit Japan's technology markets crashed, unemployment soared and the nation seemed plagued both by a rash of insurance-money killings and by a number of apocalyptic quasi-religious groups inspired by the Aum Cult who, in March 1995, had mounted a poison gas attack on the Tokyo subway system.

Significantly, Nakata's primary adaptation of the novel was to erase Sadako's hermaphroditism entirely and to replace the male Asakawa Kazuyuki with the female Asakawa Reiko who is also an investigative reporter but here the separated career-driven mother of a young son, Yoishi. Thus highlighting a residual cultural adherence to the doctrine of separate spheres of activity for the sexes, whereby women's biological destiny is to nurture the next generation and not compete with men on the job market, Reiko embodies the plight of the ambitious Japanese woman who is also a mother while Sadako becomes, even more explicitly than in the book, the thwarted potentiality of all victims of masculine aggression. Like Kazuyuki, Reiko is also investigating the recent urban myth of a lethal videotape when her niece Tomoko and three of her friends mysteriously die. As in the novel, the group have recently holidayed in a cabin on the Izu peninsula where they watched a mysterious videotape. Travelling to the log cabin in question, Reiko thus watches and subsequently copies the tape for Takayama Ryuji, who retains the name of the novel's protagonist but is now a mathematician and her ex-husband. Discovering that their son Yoishi has watched the tape, the two set out to save their child but unlike the US version there is no implication that their quest might restore their relationship. The preservation of the next generation is all important here and heterosexual romance, ostensibly obligatory in the United States, is deemed an irrelevance. As in the novel they travel first to Oshima, the birthplace of the dead psychic Yamamura Shizuko whom they have identified from images on the tape. Here they discover the story of Yamamura Sadako, Shizuko's illegitimate daughter who disappeared some thirty years before having, unbeknown to anyone, been murdered by her father. Sadako, it seems, has psychically created the video in an attempt to appease her will to avenge her father's crimes. Thus, although Reiko and Ryuji locate Sadako's bones in a well beneath the Izu cabin and as in the novel arrange for their burial, this does not prevent Ryuji's death – as the spectral Sadako emerges terrifyingly from his television screen seven days after his initial viewing of the tape. Realising that she saved herself by replicating the tape and passing it on, Reiko helps her son Yoishi to copy the tape and pass it to his grandfather who willingly submits to his own fate.

Located in a highly Americanised Japan, Nakata's *Ringu* is
nonetheless a major stylistic and political contributor to the *onryou*
tradition. This is a world of baseball games on television, western-
style homes, career-driven single mothers, advanced news media and
the sophisticated technological mediation of everyday life. But it is
also a Japan of far-flung islands, isolated villages, traditional rural
dwellings complete with *tatami* mats, futons and paper screens,
grandparental devotion to the family, incomprehensible regional
dialects and ancient folk superstitions. As is the case with the hermaphrodite Sadako of the novel or the abject Sadako here, to be
Japanese is to incorporate a range of seemingly irreconcilable
binarisms. On the one hand is the modern, rational, scientific, individualistic, liberal and democratic Americanised Japan of the Showa
Constitution. On the other is an older, irrational, superstitious Japan of the past, where the wronged woman returns for vengeance
on a world that has not only destroyed her but built leisure facilities
upon her unmarked grave. It is not that the technological mediation
of life propounded by *Ringu*'s video and stills cameras, VCRs, telephones and televisions is a product of 'the intrusion of "posthuman"
otherness into everyday life.' [13] It is more that the 'simulacral proliferation of information in a media saturated social sphere' [14] in evidence here evokes what Baudrillard, in *The Transparency of Evil*, would
deem the hell of the same, whereby certain pre-Showa forms and
models of individual, gendered and familial relations (the problematic Others to dominant social formations and modes of remembering the past) are effectively erased. This is, of course, a theme familiar
from the Japanese New Wave, specifically films such as Shohei's
Kuragejima: Tales from a Southern Island (1968) where the primitive
way of life of remote islanders is counterpoised to that of an urbane
engineer visiting from Tokyo and the culture of factories, air travel
and Coca-Cola that follows in his wake. The islanders, the film argues, may be savages. But they have the cultural homogeneity and
social harmony that is entirely lacking in the modern world. The
United States may have attempted to abnegate the alterity of the
Japanese people by first infecting them with its ideology of individualistic democratic progress and then absorbing them into the
international marketplace of nations. But in the form of Sadako's

video, the hitherto silenced voice of all that has been lost to this process erupts into life – or more accurately a form of remembering the dead that is death-in-life. Modern Japanese culture, in Baudrillard's formulation, is thus exposed as life 'after the orgy' whereby ostensible 'political liberation, sexual liberation, liberation of the forces of production ... women's liberation, children's liberation, liberation of unconscious drives, liberation of art'[15] ushered in by the American Occupation presents a simulacral ideal that champions a colonialist agenda by silencing the past. It is, of course, entirely illusory and Sadako exists to expose it as such.

Suzuki Koji has himself asserted that the vengeful female of the *Ringu* cycle was named for one Takahashi Sadako: a real-life psychic of the nineteen-teens, the protégé of Professor Fukurai on whom Ikuma Heihachiro, Sadako's father in the book, is based.[16] This real-world Sadako was said to possess the gift of *nensha* – the ability to project an image on to film or some other medium. But given the *onryou* tradition of which the film is a part, it must also be recognised that the name 'Sadako,' meaning 'chaste child' and now old-fashioned and little used, has a great deal of cultural resonance in Japan. Specifically, her naming evokes one Sasaki Sadako (or 'Sadako of the Thousand Paper Cranes'), a child of Hiroshima who died of leukaemia in 1955. In her attempt to escape her inevitable fate this Sadako had fashioned some 644 origami cranes, believing that if she folded 1000 the gods would make her well again. The remainder were made by her classmates and buried with her. Sadako's story would in time come to signify the destruction of innocence by war; her name becoming a kind of shorthand for all that was destroyed by Japan's territorial ambitions and the concomitant decision of the United States to unleash the nuclear menace upon the civilians of Japan. In 1958 a memorial to her and other child victims of the bombs was erected in Hiroshima Peace Park with the inscription 'This is our cry. This is our prayer. Peace in the world.'[17]

In her terrible vengeance on the living, manifesting itself as a will to replicate herself through the endless and exponential proliferation of cursed videos, Sadako can thus be seen to embody what the postcolonial theorist Spivak would call 'the kind of Power and Desire that would inhabit the unnamed subject of the Other.'[18]

Occupying the subaltern position of one whose history has been skilfully concealed and who thus 'cannot speak' for herself, she none-theless tires of 'lying in shadow'[19] and travels, in Nakata's vision, through the television screen into the real world of the present. Moving quite literally through the televisual medium, using it for the transmission of her own long-silenced voice, her own erased materiality, Sadako becomes that which will not be eradicated by US colonialism in Japan or by the Japanese refusal to acknowledge the sins of its own past. In keeping with her abject status her text is multiplicitous. She is the living corpse who collapses the boundaries between life and death, good and evil, the human and the inhuman, the natural and the supernatural. She throws old certainties into doubt. She calls into question normative conceptions of what it is to be human and what it now means to be Japanese. As such, her sub-jectivity becomes itself a form of elusive and allusive post-colonial text in which the hitherto silenced story of her people is told. And while her image and her message may be altered and adapted for a US audience, she retains the *onryou*'s ability to warn the bellicose neo-conservative United States of the horrors of war and to caution against an easy acceptance of militaristic ideology, however couched in the language of home, family, democracy, justice and peace.

Although made by different directors, *The Ring* and *The Ring 2* share a common screenwriter in Ehren Kruger. He is perhaps better known for *Arlington Road* (1998), the Mark Pellington directed ex-ploration of the competing claims to American selfhood proffered respectively by the US government (and its military, legislative and societal agencies) and the right-wing militias that form much of the nation's political underground. Locating ideals of national identity (loyalty, freedom, independence, self-reliance, hard work, etc.) within the family unit, Kruger's is a tense and frightening evocation of the political efficacy of terrorism, this time home-grown. The form and function of technologically mediated representations of terrorist atrocity (including video footage and stills photography) also come in for detailed consideration here as does the role and responsibility of the televisual and print media – both of which are mercilessly indicted for acting in service of dominant ideologies of national identity. An underrated classic, *Arlington Road* is thus intimately concerned with what it means to be an American at the very end of the twentieth century (though notably before 9/11) and specifically how a deeply divided nation nonetheless asserts and imposes an entirely de-problematised model of its own exceptional status on the world. Surprisingly perhaps, these are the very interests that Kruger brings to the screenplays of the remade *Ringu* films. In this, of course, he participates in a longstanding tendency to evoke Japanese alterity as a means of exploring American selfhood. But he also operates in keeping with the *onryou*'s history, warning against acceptance of totalising formulations of national identity, particularly those promulgated by the neo-conservative ascendancy.

US appropriation of Japanese history and its cultural products has clearly not been historically confined to the genre of cinematic horror, though. In the immediate post-war period Cold War films such as *Sands of Iwo Jima* (1949) or *Halls of Montezuma* (1951) had revisited the Pacific War for explicitly nationalistic purposes, thus asserting the superiority of US modes of social and political organisation in the face of the deindividuated alterity of the ruthless Japanese threat. This was similarly visible in more socially liberal and ostensibly anti-racist offerings of the Cold War, such as Joshua Logan's *Sayonara* (1957) – a Marlon Brando vehicle that criticised the post-war American policy of preventing GIs from marrying Japanese women by deploying the Japanese *shinju* sub-plot, whereby Red Buttons and his Japanese bride commit lovers' suicide in the face of their social exclusion. Giving up a promising military career and marriage to a General's daughter for his own forbidden love, Brando thus embodied all the rebellious individualism of his earlier characters, while Japan provided little more than an exotic backdrop against which he could explore what it means to be an American and a man. The process would be echoed in Hollywood's wholesale appropriation of film plots and characters drawn from Japanese cinema: Kurosawa Akira's *The Seven Samurai* (1951) becoming John Sturgis's *The Magnificent Seven* (1960) while the perilous transportation of a politically significant princess, the central plot device of Kurosawa's *The Hidden Fortress* (1958) being profitably transposed onto a highly American far away galaxy in George Lucas's *Star Wars* (1977). While more liberal offerings such as John Boorman's 1968 offering *Hell in the Pacific* mounted a doomed plea for common humanity in the face of national self-interest, Japanese culture and society was most commonly depicted by Hollywood as part of a shoddily schematic binarism, whereby the civilised, democratic and individualistic nature of American society was counterpoised to the savage, despotic and de-individualising tendencies of the Japanese.[20] It was a trend unfortunately visible in more recent films such as *Empire of the Sun* (1987) and *Pearl Harbour* (2001), while even ostensibly anti-racist products such as *Windtalkers* (2002) can be seen to evoke Japanese selfhood predominantly as a means of exploring American social attitudes – specifically US xenophobia and the vexed question of Native American rights. Thus, while it must be acknowledged that the increased popularity in the United States of distinctively Japanese genres (such as *anime* or *yakuza*) have put images of Japanese selfhood centre-screen, there remains a tendency to re-cast those images in ways that speak directly to American audiences about themselves.[21] Hence, for all the thermo-nuclear resonance of its title, Ridley Scott's *Black Rain* (1989) is less an American take on the social and psychological fallout of the US bombing of Hiroshima and Nagasaki (which is the subject matter of Imamura Shohei's film of the same name and date) than a formulaic gangster thriller set against an exotic Japanese backdrop. Even Quentin Tarantino's stylistically hybrid *Kill Bill* can be seen to participate in the trend. 'The Origin of O Ren' narrative of *Kill Bill Part One* (2004), much vaunted as an excellent example of the director's stylistic inventiveness, is little more than an English-narrated *anime* with a score drawn from the quintessentially American genre the Western: all brass, maracas and harmonica harmonies. All this, of course, leads up to the truly significant point in O Ren's narrative when, despite being surrounded by her *yakuza* henchmen and practicing the Japanese martial arts she has excelled at all her life, the hitherto indestructible assassin is despatched by our all-American heroine the Bride.

Given the history of American cinematic attitudes to Japan it is unsurprising that *The Ring* contains some significant alterations to its Japanese source material. The action is relocated to America's Pacific north-west, specifically the city of Seattle where, interestingly, a peace park named for the representative 'child of Hiroshima'

Seiko Sadako is located. Here the female reporter is Rachel Keller, single parent to the psychically inclined Aidan whose photographer father Noah has no contact with his son prior to the beginning of the narrative. This failed family unit is complemented by the Morgans, whose adopted pre-pubescent daughter Samara, herself possessed of malign supernatural powers, spends much of her short life in a psychiatric institution before being murdered by her adoptive mother and thrown down a well. Here she remains, increasingly decayed and decreasingly child-like, until her rage is projected upwards onto a video tape and the cycle of vengeance and retribution drawn from the Japanese originals begins again.

Evidently, the American remake of *Ringu* makes reference to its Japanese origins in terms of plot and the iconography of the vengeful *onryou* but these are very much in keeping with the US film industry's longstanding colonisation of Japanese cultural products. Having excluded the original's screenwriter Takashi Hiroshi and director Nakata Hideo from the credits of *The Ring* moreover, the film makers even opt in true colonialist style to evoke a certain 'Japaneseness' for atmospheric purposes. They even include repeatedly interpolated shots of the non-indigenous Japanese maple tree (the fruits of which are called the samara). But like the Japanese wallhanging at the Morgan ranch, the Japanese *anime* character in Aidan's room or the ways in which Noah's loft windows resemble Japanese paper screens, these references are merely decorative; playful touches akin to *The Ring 2* providing Aidan with a physician called Dr Koji. Evidently, and quite typically, what is of interest here is not Japan but the United States. And what is most significant is Kruger's decision to replace the adult Sadako with the pre-pubescent girl child Samara.

In death, Samara's appearance is most certainly drawn from the Japanese *onryou* tradition, all long hair and staring eye, spastic movements and decomposing flesh. But the fact that she is also depicted as a living child is highly significant within an American cultural context, providing a ready means of exploring the myths and deceptions that underpin the self-image of the United States. For ever since Mark Twain offered a coruscating indictment of the hypocrisy of the slave-owning Christian South in *Huckleberry Finn*

(1883), American literature has repeatedly evoked the perspective of the child or adolescent as a means of commenting on the failure of the United States to live up to its exceptionalist promise. Most recently, films as diverse as *Kids* (1995), *Gummo* (1997) and *AI: Artificial Intelligence* (2001) have continued this practice, depicting the uses and abuses of children and the families that raise them as a means of testing the nation's claims to moral as well as political and economic leadership of the world. So, if *Ringu* had called into question the whitewashing of the Japanese past by depicting the media-saturated 'hell of the same' that is the present, then *The Ring* undertakes a similarly sceptical treatment of dominant ideologies of identity in its critique of the nuclear family as a sustaining institution of advanced American capitalism.

Championed as the key means of transmitting social and ethical values by the neo-conservative right, the family is clearly a means of inculcating the child with a sense of self that is firmly embedded in the political necessity of the present while allowing for the transmission of property along dynastic lines. But as an excised scene from the film reveals, this cornerstone of neo-conservative rhetoric is seen to be in a perilous condition, a page in the Shelter Mountain Inn's guest book reading: 'I had a lovely vacation with my fat wife who I'm cheating on and who I'll divorce in a year before I get blood cancer and die.' This is, of course, the precise spot upon which the child Samara was murdered by her mother. Rachel Keller, even more preoccupied with her career than was Asakawa Reiko and even more dissatisfied, appears to have little contact with her own family. There are no self-sacrificing grandparents upon whom she can rely to save her son and her relationship with Ruth, her Republican elder sister who aggressively totes 'family values' while resenting Rachel's career, is understandably tense. She has even chosen to have a child with a photographer who participates in the simulacral proliferation of identities that haunts both films while describing his own father as 'a disappointment' and taking no interest in the life of his son. But it is Samara, the child psychiatrically institutionalised and finally murdered by her adoptive parents who best reveals the mediation of American family life by the machinations of the state; becoming the locus of a series of debates concerning the nature and culture of

American society that challenge the Republican right's totalising assertions and in so doing force the audience to confront all that is cast off and destroyed by the militaristic will to war.

Unlike Sadako, Samara is confined at the behest of her adoptive parents to a psychiatric institution where she is heavily sedated for the protection of the staff, confined under video surveillance to her room and subject to videotaped interviews while attached to heart and brain monitoring electrodes. The subject of rigorous observation that would not be out of place in Foucault's *Madness and Civilization* (1961), she is perfectly positioned, in all her ostensible irrationality, to expose the machinations of the supposedly rational society that so confines her. Hers is not what Marcuse would term the 'happy consciousness' that blindly accepts the status quo, but one that can be neither enticed nor compelled to conform. She feels no pain, needs no sleep, experiences no visible distress at her own isolation and calmly explains her own compulsion to harm. 'You don't want to hurt anyone', says her doctor. 'But I do,' the cherubic Samara retorts, adding politely: 'I'm sorry. It won't stop.' As CCTV footage and X-ray film indicate though, for all her doctors' attempts to mould her thoughts and behaviour, Samara resists her enforced silence in life and overcomes it in death. She can imprint images on X-ray film, on videotape and on the human psyche: 'Oh Christ!' declares her father immediately before his suicide, 'The things she'd show you.' Once again, it seems, the figure of the *onryou*, here as child, is to reveal that which is more usually hidden, to expose the wound to scrutiny and, in horrifying an audience, to promote its healing. In this, of course, she is considerably more honest than the US news media that at the time of the film's production was still shying away from showing their audiences anything that may have influenced public opinion against the war in Iraq; including the necessary return of dead soldiers' bodies to the United States for burial.

In life, then, Samara is viewed as a monster – one who not only mounts an attack on the supposedly sacred bond between a mother and her child by sending her mother mad, but one who destroys her father's livelihood by driving his horses to their deaths. The psychosurgery her father imposes upon her is clearly not enough to make her conform to the lineaments of the bourgeois family, however, and patriarchal revenge is swift. In an extraordinarily pastoral vision sequence her fate is depicted in saturated colour. In a verdant forest clearing, as horses run on the horizon and choral voices soothe the senses, Samara and her mother stand by the well. 'Isn't it beautiful here Samara', says her mother, evoking an ideal vision of land and family that is far removed from what is to come. Immediately and violently she covers the child's face with a black plastic bag, smothering her and throwing her ostensibly lifeless body down the well. Anna's act of retributive violence against one unable and unwilling to conform to the pastoral pretensions of this ideal America self-evidently encapsulates the political significance of the film's deployment of the *onryou* motif. Certainly, Anna's assertion, 'I know things will get better,' as the still living child topples into a watery tomb, rings very hollow indeed. What is most extraordinary though is the way in which the killing of children, an inevitability in any war, is both justified by the narrative logic of the film and internalised by its characters.

Resident on Moesko Island between 1970 and 1977 – years which overlap with the doomed US attempt to extend democratic individualism amongst the reluctant peoples of North Vietnam – Samara's name is that of a city of tactical importance in both George Bush's Gulf War and his son George W. Bush's sequel. As it also references 'The Appointment in Samarra' [*sic*] a folk tale famously retold by W. Somerset Maugham, a sense of America's appointment with its own destiny abounds.[22] It was clearly wrong to bring the feminised death that is Samara to the island that is an idealised United States. She was self-evidently destined to corrupt the retrospectively imagined pastoral perfection of this self-sustaining community just as the original white settlers defiled the fresh green breast of the new world in the sixteenth century. 'Some things aren't meant to be', the island's doctor remarks of Samara. 'My wife was not supposed to have a child', Richard Morgan echoes shortly before his rococo though fiercely-edited suicide. But if it was designed to conceal and excuse the Morgans' grotesque murder of Samara, such evocations of Puritan predestination theology fail utterly to convince. They serve moreover to remind us that alone amongst the nations of the developed world certain US states, most notably the Presidential home state of Texas, continue to deploy such arguments in their justification of the execution of those who fail to conform to social and cultural norms. If nothing else, the repeatedly justified murder of Samara illustrates how the United States, for all its pretensions to rationality, is itself motivated by an irrational will to vengeance on all who challenge its hegemonies; vengeance shored up where necessary by a highly selective deployment of Judeo-Christian thought. It is the kind of 'eye for an eye' thinking that saw the invasion of Afghanistan and Iraq as vengeance for 9/11 or even saw 9/11 itself as divine punishment for the secularisation of American society.[23] And as the tagline from the trailer excised from the film affirms, it is a way of thinking that ensures that 'everyone will suffer' and suffer justly if they step out of line.

If, then, the family offers no refuge from the horrors of advanced industrial capitalism and its militaristic territorial ambitions, then what is offered as means of alternative comfort, is a world of things and representations of things. The protagonists live in expansive rural ranches, trendy urban lofts and affluent suburban houses. They drive expensive cars. They are well dressed and enjoy engaging careers in the media. Their children are educated in well-funded and well-equipped schools. And everyone, apart from the domestic help and a convenience store proprietor, is both bourgeois and white. This is clearly the sanitised and safe world of fortress America, the artificiality of which is evoked by the blue filter that characterises the Seattle street scenes. What is more, it is a world endlessly refracted through an utter superfluity of electronic devices. At every turn, and even more intensely than in *Ringu*, *The Ring* illustrates the ubiquity of media-generated reproductions of identities and ideals. Anna Morgan's story is pieced together from print media archives; Noah's face appears distorted in the local store's CCTV even as he provides Rachel with access to his employer's sophisticated video-editing facilities. Television sets and VCRs abound; dominating family living rooms, appearing in hotels and hospitals. As a scene that directly references Hitchcock's *Rear Window* (1954) indicates, the rich diversity of lives and lifestyles of which the United States boasts has been replaced by a televisually mediated cultural homogeneity that at no point challenges the social and economic status quo. Quite extraordinarily, Richard Morgan's highly fetishistic suicide combines the water that is associated with his murdered daughter, a bridle from his own dead horses and, of course, a TV. Such is the state of American fatherhood! Rachel Keller, the modern American mother, is even knocked into the well that is Samara's final resting place by a television set. In a post-9/11 culture in which the horror of the World Trade Center's destruction is endlessly recycled as justification for curtailments of civil liberties at home and the invasion of Afghanistan and Iraq abroad, Richard Morgan's view of the media seems particularly apposite.[24] In a moment that would make Adorno and Horkheimer proud, he asserts that the media exists not to inform and empower but to 'take one person's tragedy and force the world to experience it; spread it like a sickness;' this, of course, as distraction from weightier matters on which the people's opinion is neither called for nor desired.[25] Thus permeated by the state-sponsored and media-disseminated capitalism that shapes the desires and identifications of individuals and social groups, the ostensible homogeneity of the United States is neatly exposed as a fiction predicated on the exclusion of those déclassé subjects who are denied or demonised by a media in thrall to dominant ideologies of nationhood. It is a culture built on wounds that the media work assiduously to conceal. And once again, it is the purpose of the horror film to unbind those wounds and to expose them to public view.

Dispossessed of the nation's fictive promises of equality, the medically abused and mother-murdered Samara becomes a peculiarly American form of *onryou*, an abstraction that identifies the horrors that emerge within the American family and hence American society, being that which cannot be entirely appropriated; an otherness that resists containment. Like Sadako before her, she is ideally positioned to expose the plight of those excluded and silenced by the forces, structures and formations of contemporary society and specifically by those subjects who, by virtue of their internalisation of dominant ideologies of nationhood, are more socially integrated than she. And as in *Ringu*, what horrifies most is the moment at which the silenced abject erupts into the social world: as thermographic X-ray, as the visions experienced by Anna Morgan and later Rachel Keller, as material emergence from the television screen and as the spectral video itself. Shown in full and in interpolated montages at significant moments of the narrative, Samara's video as conceived of by Verbinski is far more legible than that of Nakata's Sadako. Its expertly lit monochrome images, ranging from guts being ripped from a human mouth to scenes of Anna Morgan's suicide, are either allegorical of Samara's abuse or directly drawn from her life. And unlike Nakata's images, they display a unifying visual logic of assemblage that links them to the film as a whole – a series of images relating to circles and spirals, for example, creating a continuum between the ostensibly irrational world of the video and the purportedly rational world of the contemporary United States. Both by implication are grotesquely violent: images of maggots and crawling people, severed digits, bubbling blood, cancerous cellular division and child murder evoking a world of pain historically omitted from the US news media; specifically its coverage of events such as the bombing of Hiroshima and Nagasaki or the immense numbers of civilian fatalities in the wars in Afghanistan and Iraq. In this, Samara's eruption into speech differs radically from the official version of United States history. When she emerges from the television to take Noah's life she is decayed, vengeful and considerably less childlike than she appeared on the hospital video. She will not be silenced, she will not be infantilised. She will have her revenge.

In the Verbinski/Kruger adoption and adaptation of the *onryou* we can therefore see encapsulated the attempted project of cultural assimilation that has informed US attitudes towards Japanese cinema since the termination of the Pacific War. But equally visible are the ways in which the *onryou* motif is admirably suited to exploring the invidious effects of *all* unified or totalising models of national identity. The conventions of the *onryou* can thus be seen to undermine the imperialistic agendas of both twentieth-century Japan and twenty-first century United States – throwing into question both the value of the *bushido* code in Japan's past and the validity of the exceptionalist model of national identity so beloved of the American right; ideals of family stability, communal responsibility and democratic opportunity on which neo-conservative models of US cultural superiority rest. Contemporary Hollywood depictions of

Japan like *The Last Samurai* might, in other words, participate in the neo-colonialist agenda that has typified cinematic representations of Japan since the 1940s by glorifying the selfsame *bushido* mindset that led to the catastrophic militarisation of Japan in the 1930s. But films like *The Ring* operate rather differently, for to adapt a Japanese *onryou* is to invite subversion of all dominant ideologies. In the light of 9/11, the paranoia it has inspired within the United States and the scramble for international influence it has engendered abroad, the United States's re-engagement with Japan, its onetime colonial subject via the medium of cinematic horror, may be profitable, but it is also ideologically dangerous. Thus, for all its ostensible political conservativism, Verbinski and Kruger's re-visioning of *Ringu* insistently calls into question the mass-culturally mediated self-image of a nation that against all the evidence, daily asserts itself to be 'one nation, indivisible under God.'

Notes

1   Such a trend was apparent as early as the 1990s, with Tsukamoto Shinya's *Tetsuo: The Iron Man* (1991) and *Tetsuo 2: Bodyhammer* (1991) finding an enthusiastic art house audience. Crossing over into the cinematic mainstream have been Miike Takeshi's *Audition* (2001), Ishii Takeshi's *Freeze Me* (2002), Kitamura Ryuhei's *Versus* (2000) and Fukasaku Kinji's *Battle Royale* (2001) and *Battle Royal II* (2003). Meanwhile, Nakata Hideo's *Ringu* (1998), *Ringu 2* (1999) and *Dark Water* (2003) and Shimuzu Takashi's *Ju-On: The Grudge* (2002) and *The Grudge 2* (2005) have met with such large scale US interest that they have been profitably re-made in the US for an international English speaking audience.

2   In the period between its release and the time of writing (November 2005) *The Ring* has taken $229,100,000 at the box office and $20,670,000 in domestic rentals alone. See *The Numbers*, www.the-numbers.com/movies/2002/TRING/html. Accessed 9 September 2005.

3   '*Onryou* is the Japanese term for a vengeful ghost. *Onryou* are usually girls or young women and have slow and spastic movements. Male *Onryou*, though much rarer are much more violent and have hands that are always clenching into fists and unclenching. It is believed that these spirits are created when a person is very cruelly murdered. They

kill all they see, and the people they kill become one of them. These *yokai* are commonly associated with vengeance and violent justice.' From *Wikipedia, the Free Encyclopedia.* http://en.wikipedia.org/wiki/ Onryou. Accessed 9 September 2005.

4   David Lu, *Japan: A Documentary History, Volume II: The Late Tokugawa Period to the Present* (Armonk and London: East Gate Press, 1999), p. 459.

5   Hirano Kyoko, *Mr Smith Goes to Tokyo: Japanese Cinema Under the American Occupation 1945–1952* (Washington & London: Smithsonian Institution Press, 1992), p. 119.

6   See, for example, 'Chapter Two: Prohibited Subjects' in Hirano, *Mr Smith*, pp. 47–103.

7   Hirano, *Mr Smith*, p. 64.

8   Drawn from the *kaidan* or ghost story, such women were melded both with the demonic woman of *Noh* theatrical tradition such as the *kyojo-mono* or *shuven-mono* and the evil woman, *akuba* or *akujo*, of the *kabuki* theatre. In the *bakeneko-monu* she was part woman, part cat. Invariably she was an admixture of the living and the dead.

9   Mary J. Russo, 'Female Grotesques: Carnival and Theory,' in Katie Conboy, Nadia Mdiena and Sarah Stanbury (eds), *Writing on the Body: Female Embodiment and Feminist Theory* (New York: Columbia University Press, 1997), p. 325.

10   Russo, 'Female Grotesques,' p. 326.

11   It is a space iconographically and conceptually related to that of the subterranean prison of Teshigahara Hiroshi's *The Woman in the Dunes* (1964) and the deep dark well of *Ringu*.

12   Even before Gore Verbinski undertook his remake of *The Ring* for American audiences and long before Nakata was himself invited to direct its sequel, *The Ring 2* (2005), there have been numerous other filmic, television and manga versions of the *Ringu* story in Asia, and several sequels. In terms of novels, Suzuki's *The Spiral* or *Rasen* (1995) sees the pathologist Andou Mitsuo undertaking an autopsy on Ryuji, his former classmate, finding a viral code within his DNA and under-taking his own hunt for Sadako having read the now-dead Asakawa's narrative of events. In January 1998 and February 1999 Suzuki also published *Loop* and *The Birthday*, short stories on the same subject. He penned the manga version in 1996, with art by Nagai Kourjirou. This was, however, overtaken by manga versions of the *Ringu* and *Ringu 2*, written by Takahashi Hiroshi, art by Inagaki Miscio, and published in 1999. An English translation of *Ringu* by Naomi Kokubo appeared in 2003 and of *Ringu 2* by Steve Hoffman in 2004. There

have been television specials: *Kanzenban, Saishuushou* and *Rasen: The Series* and a prequel *Ringu 0* (2000) directed not by Nakata but by Tsuruta Norio. In 1999, a South Korean version *The Ring Virus* was released, directed by Kim Dong-bin. More faithful to the Suzuki novel, and containing the original rape/virus thesis it is nonetheless highly cinematographically derivative of the Japanese original.

13   Jay McRoy, *Japanese Horror Cinema* (Edinburgh: Edinburgh University Press, 2005), p. 41.

14   McRoy, *Japanese Horror*, p. 41.

15   Jean Baudrillard, *The Transparency of Evil: Essays on Extreme Phenomena*, (trans) James Benedict (London and New York: Verso, 2002), p. 3.

16   See *The Ring World*, www.theringworld.com. Accessed 9 September 2005.

17   Such echoes are doubly resonant, moreover, if we consider Imamura Shohei's film *Intentions of Murder* (1964), the heroine of which is also called Sadako – a country girl who refuses to commit suicide when raped and, in time, grows strong enough to dominate the upper-class household that once entirely controlled her. This Sadako thus encapsulates a pronounced feminine strength that overcomes all patriarchal attacks upon her, becoming eventually   'a matriarchal ruler ... the priestess archetype ... ruling over the tribe ... the ancient Shamaness of Japanese mythology.' David Desser, *Eros Plus Massacre: An Introduction to the Japanese New Wave Cinema* (Bloomington, IN: Indiana University Press, 1988), p. 126.

18   Gayatri Chakravorty Spivak, 'Can the Subaltern Speak? Speculations on Widow Sacrifice,' in Bill Ashcroft, Gareth Griffiths and Helen Tiffin (eds), *The Post Colonial Studies Reader* (London and New York: Routledge, 1995), p. 25.

19   Spivak, 'Can the Subaltern Speak?,' p. 28.

20   The apotheosis of this is, of course, Edward Zwick's *The Last Samurai* (2003) wherein the American hero adopts the *bushido* code, clothing, hairstyle and romantic inclinations of the disappearing *samurai* while retaining the star image of Tom Cruise. In the process he becomes less a hybrid of Japanese and US models of masculinity than an embodiment and enactment of US cultural imperialism in Japan. The *bushido* code and indeed all aspects of Japanese culture, is here of interest only in so far as it informs, influences or illuminates American self-image: in this instance by transforming an American in crisis into an ideal specimen of his race. As I will argue, this is not only entirely typical of the attitudes of the American cinematic mainstream towards Japan –

whereby Japanese culture is consistently deployed as a means of reaffirming, in highly conservative ways, the cultural superiority of American-style democratic individualism and the bourgeois capitalism it serves, but a causal factor in the cultural trauma inflicted upon the Japanese people by the US Occupation itself.

21 Popular *yakuza* dramas would include Kitano Takeshi's *Violent Cop* (1989), *Boiling Point* (1990), *Sonatine* (1993) and his LA-set crossover success *Brother* (1997) and Miike Takeshi's *Shinzuku Triad Society* (1995), *Dead or Alive* (1999), *Dead or Alive 2 – Birds* (2000), *Dead or Alive – Final* (2002) and *Ichi the Killer* (2001). Most popular *anime* would include Otomoto Katsuhiio's *Akira* (1988), Oshii Mamoru's *Ghost in the Shell* (1995) and Miyazaki Hayao's *Spirited Away* (2001) – the last the highest grossing Japanese film ever made.

22 W. Somerset Maugham, *Sheppey* (London: William Heinemann, 1933), quoted in Wesley C. Salmon, *Causality and Explanation* (New York: Oxford University Press, 1998), p. 27.

> The speaker is Death. 'There was a merchant in Baghdad who sent his servant to market to buy provisions and in a little while the servant came back, white and trembling, and said, "Master, just now when I was in the marketplace I was jostled by a woman in the crowd and when I turned I saw it was Death that jostled me. She looked at me and made a threatening gesture, now lend me your horse, and I will ride away from the city and avoid my fate. I will go to Samarra and there Death will not find me." The merchant lent him his horse, and the servant mounted it, and he dug his spurs in its flanks and as fast as the horse could gallop he went. Then the merchant went down to the marketplace and he saw me standing in the crowd and he came to me and said, "Why did you make a threatening gesture to my servant when you saw him this morning?" "That was not a threatening gesture," I said, "it was only a start of surprise. I was astonished to see him in Baghdad, for I had an appointment with him in Samarra."'

23 As the evangelical minister Jerry Falwell remarked on the religious chat show *The 700 Club* in the week of the bombing of the World Trade Center, 'What we saw on Tuesday, as terrible as it is, could be miniscule if, in fact, God continues to lift the curtain and allow the enemies of America to give us probably what we deserve … the pagans and the abortionists and the feminists and the gays and the lesbians … the ACLU, People for the American Way, all of them who try

and secularise America.' Quoted in Frances Wheen, *How Mumbo-Jumbo Conquered the World* (London: Harper Perennial, 2004), pp. 183–4.

24   As I will argue more fully in Chapter 5, by establishing an Office of Homeland Security beyond the scrutiny of Congress and introducing legislation that had major implications for Americans' legal rights in terms of freedom of association, information and speech, the right to legal representation and to trial by jury, the so-called PATRIOT Act has brought about a radical transformation to the relationship between the American people, their police forces and the US military; one that is highly reminiscent of President Nixon's wholesale surveillance of potentially damaging oppositional groups in the name of freedom, specifically freedom from the evils of communism. And as in the Nixon period, such developments have been reflected in film culture in general and in the genre of cinematic horror in particular.

25   Theodor Adorno and Max Horkheimer. 'The Culture Industry: Enlightenment as Mass Deception,' in Adorno and Horkheimer, *The Dialectic of Enlightenment* (London: New Left Books, 1979).

PART II

The traumatised 1970s and the threat
of apocalypse now

Introduction

> I think the nation was just repeatedly traumatised by the events of that time and still is mystified by the forces at work during those times also.[1]

On 20 January 1961, John F. Kennedy was inaugurated as President of the United States. He had won the election with the narrowest of majorities but came to the White House as the nation's youngest and first non-Protestant president, bringing with him the expectation of great change. Certainly Kennedy's election signified a certain optimism regarding the character of the United States and its role in the world that was unprecedented since the glory days of victory in the Second World War. Such confidence would come to be summed up in Kennedy's *Civil Rights Message* of 11 June 1963 where, appealing to a specific set of nationally specific foundational myths, he invited the American people to become pioneers on a new frontier of cooperative social endeavour; joining together to build a land in which poverty would be eliminated, discrimination of all sorts would be eradicated and the old order of the 1950s, with its Red-scare rhetoric and totalitarian proclivities, would be wiped away.[2]

For all his appeal to timeless and highly cinematic American myths though, Kennedy's United States was a very different place to that of pioneering days, being a global superpower purposefully set on drawing an additional frontier between its own civilized self and the perceived savagery of the communist world. Thus within four months of his inauguration Kennedy would attempt to topple Castro from Cuba and would send a contingent of Green Berets to train South Vietnamese troops engaged in a civil war against communist

North Vietnam. Narrowly avoiding plunging the world into thermo-
nuclear war with the Cuban Missile Crisis of 1962, Kennedy would
declare his solidarity with the people of West Berlin the following
year. But as Freedom Riders set out from Washington in pursuit of
civil rights for the southern states' dispossessed black population and
a newly integrated Alabama erupted into violence, Kennedy's pioneering endeavours would come to a rapid and violent close.

In November 1963, in circumstances that remain controversial, John F. Kennedy was assassinated in Dallas, only six months
after Medgar Evers, leading light in the NAACP, was murdered for
his own political activities. In 1965 Malcolm X, founder of the
Organisation for Afro-American Unity, would be killed by fellow
Islamic activists, while in 1968 Senator Robert Kennedy and Martin Luther King, both iconic figures of the Civil Rights and Black
Power struggles were murdered. Protesting at the assassination of
their leaders and the ongoing poverty and discrimination to which
they were subject despite civil rights legislation, black communities
in 124 cities across the United States exploded into open revolt.
Meanwhile the nation's universities became the scene of violent anti-
war demonstrations as students protested against the atrocities being perpetrated by the US military in Vietnam. For having been
given unlimited powers by Congress to stem the perceived Communist threat from North Vietnam in 1964, Lyndon B. Johnson
had radically escalated American military involvement in the region
so that by 1965, some 154,000 troops were up country, fighting a
massive land war against an indigenous guerrilla movement. As the
US military's saturation bombing, burning and deforestation of Vietnam in the name of freedom became public knowledge via the news
media, as thousands of American men were forcibly conscripted into
the military, many returning home in body bags, millions took to
the streets to protest at their own government's traumatic distortion
of the 'meaning' of American freedoms. As students were gunned
down on their university campus for defending rights enshrined in
their Constitution, the massive dislocations wrought to American
self-image by the Vietnam War abroad and civil strife at home became increasingly apparent.[3] And with the election of Richard Nixon
in November 1968, the gulf between the nation's foundational mythology and its contemporary realities perceptibly widened.

Cracking down hard on anti-war elements and engaging in wholesale wiretapping and file-keeping on hundreds of thousands of individuals and organisations across the United States, Nixon would roll back the civil rights legislation of the 1960s and forestall the implementation of measures designed to protect the American environment from destruction and the American people from poverty while guaranteeing enormous expenditure on the military. By 1973, however, it was all over: an official ceasefire being signed between the essentially defeated US and essentially victorious North Vietnam in January of that year, but not before American military atrocities were revealed at the court martial of William Calley, the First Lieutenant held responsible for his unit's murder of hundreds of Vietnamese civilians at the strategically irrelevant hamlet of My Lai in 1968. Many of these, it was revealed, were elderly, infants or non-combatant women – the latter being subject to gang rape and horrific sexual torture by American troops before being murdered along with their families. Broadcast across the news media, pictures of the massacre of Vietnamese civilians at My Lai and the murder of American students at Kent State provided the nation with haunting images of the utter degeneration of the American ideal of freedom. Meanwhile footage of burning buildings, assassinated activists, murdered children and civil rights activists set upon with dogs and water canon illustrated the entrenched racism of large sections of the American population for whom the prospect of genuine ethnic equality was a call to murder. By 1974, it was all over for Nixon too, the president resigning in August under the threat of impeachment while the oil crisis ate ever deeper into American productivity as national confidence stood at its lowest point since the Great Depression.

In the 1970s, directors such as George A. Romero, Wes Craven, Tobe Hooper and John Carpenter and special pioneers men such as Tom Savini pioneered a generically specific filmic lexicon which set out to expose the historically specific traumas engendered by the militaristic authoritarianism that had underscored American life from the accession of Kennedy to the resignation of Nixon, the civil rights violations of the latter's terms of office, the might of the government–business matrix and the plight of the poorest and most marginalised of the nation's citizens – particularly within the nation's run-down and dangerous 'stagflationary' cities. Chapter 3 will thus explore the films of the independent director who single-handedly transformed the zombie from undead Caribbean-dwelling slave to rapacious synecdoche for the United States' failure to live up to its originary promise.[4] In his films of the 1970s, Romero brilliantly allegorises the historical traumas of the present by engaging with the selfsame 'crisis of confidence' addressed in President Carter's 1979 speech of the same name. Thus he repeatedly poses the question as to how a nation so historically proud of hard work, strong families, close-knit communities and faith in God had fallen to worship self-indulgence and consumption in an attempt to fill the emptiness of lives made doubly meaningless by the nation's failed foray into South Asia. In so doing, Romero would pioneer a set of generically specific conventions that enabled the exploration of the disjunction between structural trauma, whereby the foundational dream of a perfectible nation, itself 'an anxiety producing condition of possibility related to the potential for historical traumatisation,'[5] is counterpoised to the concrete historical traumas of Dallas and My Lai, Watergate and Kent State. Thus, in Romero's horrors of the 1970s, 'the problematic relations between absence and loss (or lack) as well as between structural and historical trauma'[6] are explored, and in a way that appears to pre-figure and pre-empt the Reaganite eschatology of the following decade.

If public confidence in the Presidency had been shaken to its foundations by Watergate, Vietnam and civil insurrection, then when Ronald Reagan came to office on a landslide victory in 1981, his task was to restore the nation's self-belief. This he did by repeatedly encouraging Americans to forget Watergate and to view Vietnam less as a national defeat than as a failure of national confidence in the dream of American perfectibility. For like Nixon before him, Reagan would repeatedly claim that it was not North Vietnam that had defeated the United States, but unpatriotic countercultural and anti-establishment elements within the United States that had engendered a failure of the national will to win. His was, as James Berger has observed, an attempt to assert that 'what may be seen to be flaws, unspeakable traumas, and irredeemable tragedies can nevertheless be fit into optimistic and redemptive narratives' if one is prepared to assert that while 'America's history contains traumatic events and national crimes' these can nonetheless 'be assimilated into a narrative of national perfection'[7] if one denies all evidence to the contrary forcibly enough. This was, of course, another attempt at pre-emptively binding the unhealed wounds of the nation.

Chapter 4 thus extends my exploration of the historically trau-matic legacy of Vietnam to serial-killer horror, a sub-genre that came to prominence during the presidencies of Ronald Reagan and his neo-conservative successor George Bush. For it was in the figure of the serial killer that competing versions of essentialised American identity (themselves the figurations of structural trauma) would battle it out to the bloody end. Thus adopting foreign and domestic poli-cies that in Eric Hobsbawm's words 'can be understood only as an attempt to wipe out the stain of humiliation'[8] imparted by the United States' ideological and military defeat in Vietnam, Reagan would repeatedly make 'gestures of military power against sitting targets: like the invasion of the small Caribbean island of Grenada (1983), the massive naval and air attack on Libya (1986) and even the more massive and pointless invasion of Panama (1989).'[9] For in so doing, the president set out to demonstrate 'the unchallengeable supremacy and invulnerability of the USA'[10] to a nation that so clearly felt itself challenged, inferior and deeply wounded by historical events. What is more, Reagan's crusade against the Evil Empire of the Soviet Union was matched by a domestic crusade no less vehement: as the ageing movie actor fought it out with all forms of liberalism (deemed 'the "l" word') including the welfare state legacy of Franklin D. Roosevelt's New Deal and Kennedy's dreams of civil rights for all. Thus vacillat-ing between a tacit affirmation of the trauma that lay at the heart of the United States self-image (figured as the exceptional and perfect-ible nation now lost) and a premature denial of the historical trau-mas inflicted on the nation by his Republican precursors, Reagan's policies and persona would manifest themselves in a tendency to-wards what James Berger would term 'repeated apocalyptic purgings, both real and imaginary, as if *this* time [the United States] will fi-nally get right what was always right, and somehow never was right.'[11]

Naturally, Reagan's reactionary political programme, under-scored by denial and the will to apocalypse, would come to be re-flected in cinematic production: in films such as *Rambo: First Blood*

Part Two (1985) and in an entire slew of movies like Robert Zemekis's
Back to the Future (1985) which were nostalgically set in the picket-
fenced suburbia of Eisenhower's 1950s – long before the events of
Vietnam and Watergate, economic collapse and civil insurrection
had repeatedly wounded the Republican right's ideologically expedient vision of the nation. Relying heavily on his cinematic persona,
Reagan thus set out to deny, decry or conceal a historically vital
component of American self-image – the will to consensual and
cooperative social endeavour; now denigrated publicly as 'the "l"
word' – as if liberalism itself had become an obscenity.[12] As a means
of evading the challenges wrought to national self-image by recent
events and asserting the perfection of the nation in the face of all
available evidence, Reagan could be seen to mobilise and counter-
poise two mutually contradictory impulses within American society
– the imperative to democratic conformity on the one hand and the
cultural fetishisation of self-seeking individualism on the other. Thus,
in an attempt to deny that the United States was either wounded or
traumatised by recent historical events, Reagan would attempt to
bind up his nation's injuries with inflated rhetoric, down home homi-
lies and repeated appeals to his erstwhile cinematic persona. But as
Chapter 4 will explore, such ideological obfuscation would be con-
tiguous with a mass cultural obsession with the figure of the serial
killer who, for over twenty years, would pick and hack and slash
away at any attempts to so conceal the nation's wounds. And no-
where was this more presciently, entertainingly or popularly encapsulated than in the figure of Hannibal Lecter, serial-killing
cannibalistic psychiatrist.

Thus, as Chapters 3 and 4 will explore, it was out of the horrific events of the 1960s and 1970s that some of the United States'
greatest horror films emerged. Functioning as allegories of American involvement in Vietnam, as prophesies of doom for a socially
irresponsible and sybaritic population and as enactments of mutually contradictory ideologies of national identity that were contem-
poraneously deployed in an attempt to conceal the nation's ongoing
trauma, US horror of the 1970s and beyond was often shocking in
its viscerality and despairing in its vision of mankind. In this, the
genre not only reflected the historical trauma done to Kennedy's
inaugural idealism by Vietnam and civil strife, but provided what

the director Wes Craven would term a kind of 'boot camp for the psyche' where audience members could strip away the ideological bindings that concealed the nation's psychological wounds and engage with the historically traumatic legacy of what had been done and what continued to be done both in the name of America and freedom.[13]

Notes

1 Wes Craven, interviewed in the documentary *American Nightmare*. Adam Simon, 2000.

2 John F. Kennedy, *Civil Rights Message*, 11 June 1963. *Historical Documents*. www.historicaldocuments.com/JohnFKennedysCivilRights Message.htm. Accessed 2 November 2006.

3 Most infamous was the events of 4 May 1970 when members of the Ohio National Guard opened fire on protesting students, killing four and wounding nine.

4 As Tony Williams has illustrated at length, prior to Romero's 1968 reinvention of the zombie as cannibalistic corpse in *Night of the Living Dead* the figure had been cinematically modelled on Haitian folk tales of chemically enslaved field workers risen from a death-like sleep to carry on their agricultural duties. Such figures can be seen, for example, in Jacques Touneur's updating of *Jane Eyre*, *I Walked with a Zombie* (1943) where the first Mrs Rochester is depicted not as mad but as the victim of a voodoo spell.

5 LaCapra, 'Trauma, Absence, Loss,' in Levi and Rothberg (eds), *The Holocaust*, p. 202.

6 LaCapra, 'Trauma, Absence, Loss, in Levi and Rothberg (eds), *The Holocaust*, p. 203.

7 James Berger, *After the End: Representations of Post-Apolcalypse* (Minneapolis, MN: Minnesota University Press, 1999), p. 134.

8 Eric Hobsbawm, *Age of Extremes: The Short Twentieth Century*. (London: Abacus, 1994), p. 248

9 Hobsbawm, *Age of Extremes*, p. 248.

10 Hobsbawm, *Age of Extremes,* p. 248.

11 Berger, *After the End,* p. 135.

12 As I argue in Chapter 3, it was this will that not only underpinned the nation's pretensions to social democracy but informed the earliest settlers' covenant with their god.

13 Craven, *American Nightmare* (2000).

3

'Consumed out of the good land': George A. Romero's horror of the 1970s

It's not over with – it's going to come in through another door.[1]

One wonders if it's worth saving.[2]

In 1630 the religious radical John Winthrop, recently appointed Governor of New England, delivered a rousing sermon entitled *A Model of Christian Charity*.[3] Here he outlined the hopes and fears of the community of men and women who had left Europe in search of religious freedom and warned of the dangers that imperiled the success of their mission to redeem the sins of the old world in the new. For not only were there the challenges of a harsh climate, unwelcoming landscape and hostile Native Americans to contend with, but in order to found a society whose express purpose was the spiritual salvation of the world, the pilgrims must continually fight against their own selfish and transient desires. Only if they were 'knit together in this work as one man,' he warned, only if they considered each other as 'members of the same body,'[4] could their venture succeed. Thus entering into a 'near ... marriage'[5] with their God, the community could only hope to survive and prosper if it unquestioningly obeyed the injunctions of the creator. For if the settlers chose to place their selfish desires over the common good, should they 'fall to embrace this present world and prosecute [their] carnal intentions, seeking great things for [themselves] and [their] posterity' then, Winthrop warned, the Lord would 'surely break out in wrath'[6] against them. They would be 'consumed out of the good land.'[7]

The long-dead figure of John Winthrop is resurrected here for a number of reasons, primarily because close consideration of

his words provides a salutary reminder that the foundational historical documents of the United States, as is the case with all nations, are continually open to ideological manipulation in the service
of competing interest groups; not least those who wish to minimise,
conceal or deny historical trauma. In the 1960s, for example, when
it still seemed possible to win both the war in Vietnam and the
approval of the American people, it is notable that a range of United
States presidents as diverse as Kennedy, Johnson and Nixon actually
sought to justify successive domestic and foreign policies, specifically in South Asia, by re-mobilising for themselves some of
Winthrop's most potent images and ideas. Most common was the
rhetorical mutation of Winthrop's vision of the nation as a shining
'city on a hill,'[8] by which the preacher had meant a redemptive community of the faithful, into a latter-day allegory of contemporary
political struggles, whereby the United States became a beacon of
democratic freedom whose light illuminated the oppression inherent in all non-American ethical, political or economic systems, specifically of course that of the communist world. As early as 20 January
1961, for example, John F. Kennedy's *Inaugural Address* had openly
evoked this image in welcoming the United States' mission to defend freedom in its hour of maximum danger. He had argued that
the energy, faith and devotion that Americans brought to this endeavour would illuminate the country and all who served it; adding
that the glow from this fire could truly light the world.[9] Some two
years later, addressing the people of West Berlin, Kennedy had further evoked Winthrop by describing that city as a defended island of
freedom, a stockade surrounded by the evil system that was communism.[10] Extending the metaphor further, Kennedy's successor
Lyndon B. Johnson would compare the plight of the peaceable and
agrarian South Vietnamese to that of Winthrop's early colonists and
would align the barbaric savagery of North Vietnamese forces with
hostile seventeenth-century Native Americans who had frequently
besieged the pilgrims within their stockades and overrun their settle-
ments.[11] So evocative was this appeal to foundational myths of nationhood that Richard Nixon himself was keen to get in on the act,
his rousing *First Inaugural Address* of 1969 outlining the United
States' mission to build a great cathedral of the spirit by leading the

world out of the valley of turmoil on to the high ground of peace.[12] Thus the covenant theology of a seventeenth-century puritan who believed the New World could offer spiritual salvation to the old was selectively deployed by a number of presidents at the height of the Cold War as a means of bolstering American territorial and ideological ambitions that were far removed from those of the nation's early white settlers. Thus a cunning and highly selective refashioning of Winthrop's warnings against self-interest, greed and exploitation facilitated a specious validation of United States ambitions abroad; the traumatic legacy of which could be ably concealed by appeals to a quasi-mythic Puritan past, here filtered through the post-enlightenment discourse of manifest destiny.

It is nonetheless significant that by the 1970s, the decade in which Vietnam was lost and the twin spectres of economic collapse and presidential corruption threatened to douse the shining city's illuminations for ever, Winthrop's imagery would be effectively reclaimed – as a new generation of activists, writers, artists and particularly film-makers looked to the nation's foundational mythology as a means of understanding why and how things had gone so terribly wrong in the present.[13] So, throughout the 1970s, in the face of traumatic dislocations wrought to American self-image by the failure of Civil Rights at home and the spectre of neo-imperialist militarism abroad, the apocalyptic consciousness that had informed Winthrop's egalitarian, cooperative and pronouncedly spiritual vision of the nation would undergo something of a resurgence; being redeployed conceptually and visually as a means of revealing the ideological obfuscations of political rhetoric and exposing the wounded self-image of the nation. And no single film maker would address himself more single mindedly to the project than the small-scale, low-budget, independent writer and director George A. Romero, a man acutely aware that Americans were in grave danger of being 'consumed out of the good land' not by any external threat but by the nation's failure to live up to its originary promise and by its leaders' subsequent refusal to look upon the psycho-social wounds inflicted upon the people by that failure. Romero does not simply depict the traumatic ramifications of historic events, as a number of critics have observed, but undertakes a highly self-conscious exploration as to the ways in which the generic conventions of horror cinema might expose the ways in which dominant ideologies of nationhood work as a means of repressing that trauma. Thus George A. Romero, like Jörg Buttgereit before him, can be seen to strip away the layers of ideological obfuscation that have prevented the people from acknowledging their traumatised status. And in so doing, he can be seen to lay the United States' socio-cultural and psychological wounds bare to public scrutiny and, potentially, to healing.[14]

Between 1973 and 1978 then, Romero wrote and directed three uniquely pessimistic masterworks of horror cinema that exposed the historically-specific injuries of the decade while drawing on the conceptual vocabulary of the nation's foundational texts as a means of exploring the ideological function of national identity discourses. These films were *The Crazies, Martin* and *Dawn of the Dead*. Deploying the conventions of contagion horror, supernatural horror and body horror respectively, Romero here explored the darkest nightmares of the nation's earliest European settlers as a means of investigating the traumas of the present age. For in waging war against a small though strategically significant Asian nation, the United States had clearly reneged on its originary covenant with God and was in danger of bringing the entire American enterprise tumbling about its ears. Thus besieged from without by governmental forces of authoritarian right-wing militarism, and from within by the rapacious self-seeking individualism that the economic policies of successive administrations had so shamelessly promoted alongside a homogenising consumerism that gave the lie to any notion of independent or autonomous American selfhood, it was clear (to all but the nation's political masters) that the citizens of 1970s America existed in an ongoing state of historical trauma. Theirs was a nation in which the social body was either infected, murderously divided or rapaciously decaying, an America in which the family existed in an unending state of disintegration, all cooperative endeavours appeared condemned to fail and the individual seemed destined to live and to die alone. Strictly speaking then, it is not simply as Robin Wood has argued, that:

> Romero has shown us the failure of tradition and religious faith;
> the incompetence of the federal government, civil defense

authorities, and the news media; the inadequacy of communal
action and romantic love; the self-consuming destructiveness
of familial ties; and the vulnerability of the family home.[15]

More accurately, for Romero, Americans are now forced to inhabit a
United States in which faith in god, in government and in the institutions of advanced American capitalism as well as faith in one's
fellow human beings has been perverted in service of class-bound
and economically-driven hegemonies. This is, in other words, a
United States of Winthrop's 'carnal intentions,' a culture of frenzied
acquisitiveness, entrenched racism and class divisions, a nation devoid of liberality, cooperation and the will to equality. It is a place in
which the civic body is in such poor shape that the nation's claims to
the moral leadership of the 'free' world are exposed as the hypocriti-
cal fantasies of a degenerate superpower in the final moments before
its timely collapse. For in Romero's graphically realised eschatology,
the Promised Land has become once more a wilderness, populated
now by flesh-eating zombies and serial-killing rapists; fitting testament to the wounds inflicted on the national's self-image by the
previous decade.

Released in 1973, the year in which the United States effectively lost the Vietnam War, *The Crazies* is very much a product of
Nixon's first term of office. Set in Evans City, a small town in West
Pennsylvania just north of Pittsburg, the film explores the legacy of
an administration that had steadily rolled back the civil rights legislation of the 1960s, cracked down hard on anti-war elements and
other dissident groups and engaged in the wholesale wiretapping
and file-keeping on hundreds of thousands of individuals and
organisations across America. Exploring the might of the government–business matrix that had forestalled implementation of measures designed to protect the American environment from destruction
or the American people from poverty while guaranteeing enormous
expenditure on the military, the film has the citizens of Evans City
accidentally exposed to a bacteriological weapon developed by their
own government and presumably destined for Vietnam.

First encircled and then invaded by the faceless agents of the
military–industrial complex (as once the New England Pilgrims had
felt themselves encircled by hostile Native Americans) the town's

inhabitants either die immediately or go 'incurably mad,' entering into an orgy of murderous destruction whereby men bludgeon their wives to death and incinerate their children; fathers and daughters indulge in acts of consensual incest and grey-haired grandmothers employ knitting needles as assuredly as Leatherface of *The Texas Chainsaw Massacre* ever wielded a chainsaw. As the American family is itself consumed by murderous desires, a very Nixonesque President sanctions the 'accidental' dropping of an atom bomb on the town. It is an act designed to consume townspeople and virus alike in a conflagration of flame, flame reminiscent of the US military's wholesale napalming of Vietnam and the earlier nuclear holocausts of Hiroshima and Nagasaki and highly redolent of the purging fires of divine retribution that (according to Winthrop) would signal the death of the civic body and the failure of the pilgrims' endeavour in the New World. That the virus and the personnel who have developed it are codenamed 'Trixie' is, of course, a classic piece of Romeroesque humour – linking such socially destructive and frankly inhumane activities directly to the president of the time: 'Tricky Dicky' Nixon. That the President is so willing to slaughter the native-born Americans of Evans City should not, of course, surprise us. *The Crazies* was released, after all, in the year in which members of the Sioux nation gathered at the historic battle site of Wounded Knee, South Dakota to protest against earlier administrations' crimes of genocide, broken treaties and civil rights violations. The 'real Americans' of the 1970s have become so alienated from their elected representatives (and from the twisted version of the nation's past that is the politicians' stock in trade) that they now have a great deal in common with those their ancestors dispossessed. Robbed of their liberty by a freedom-toting administration that purposefully infects them with its poisonous lies (as once it infected the Native Americans with smallpox), ordinary Americans seem to have only two options: insanity or death. As the doomed scientist remarks: 'The whole thing's insane, how can you tell who's infected and who isn't?'[16] The entire civic body, it seems, has been infected by a murderous will to mutually assured destruction. And the role of Romero's horror is to look unflinchingly on the sickness and, in looking, to reveal the persistent lies of an administration that persists in asserting that all is well.

It is notable though that the one community member ostensibly immune to the virus is David, the town's only green beret: a man who validates Winthrop's cooperative ideal of American social life through his work with the town's Volunteer Fire Department and who thus offers up a totemic challenge to the coercive strategies of the present administration. A veteran of the Vietnam War who uses the skills he acquired up country in an attempt to breach the government-imposed perimeter with his best friend Clank, a regular army veteran, and his pregnant girlfriend Judy (neither of whom survive), David is the typically ambiguous Vietnam figure of Romero's 1970s horror. A killer by training if not disposition, David in many ways prefigures Peter of *Dawn of the Dead*, just as the gung-ho Clank prefigures Roger. Unable to repress the memories of murderous deeds he has committed in his country's name, David illustrates the utter irreconcilability of the two versions of American identity proffered to young men by the dominant ideology. He is trapped between those worlds; haunted by visions of the past, which he seems destined to experience again and again as the horrors of Vietnam seep into small town American life. Standing on the dividing line between foreign war and domestic peace, social cohesion and anarchic chaos, individual rights and totalitarian government, a wounded nation and that government's denial of its wounds, David may survive the virus but he is unable to escape its social ramifications. Utterly traumatised by the wartime experiences that appear to bleed into his hometown world, David is utterly alone; a loneliness that is further exacerbated by the degeneration of his community, the loss of his best friend and the death of his fiancée. The radical individualism that Americans have so long prized, the individualism that imprinted the figure of the lone frontiersman, the gunslinger and the biker-outlaw upon the national consciousness (and which, as we will see, would re-emerge in the 1980s' obsession with the serial killer) is found to be a sorry substitute for cooperative social endeavour. Of all the townspeople herded into the gymnasium at the movie's close, only David is in possession of his faculties. He may offer a solution to the epidemic but the authoritarian demagogues of the military are so wrapped up in their macho power games that they are unable to recognise it. In the figure of the veteran, destined by

virtue of his past experiences to always stand alone and in that soli-
tude be destroyed, Romero thus encapsulates the traumatised isolation of the American subject at the end of the Vietnam War. And as
Martin and *Dawn of the Dead* further demonstrate, this atomised
and solitary subjectivity is entirely symptomatic of the trauma
wrought to the American civic body by the events of the previous
ten years.

   The Crazies is then a film that beats to the rhythm of the military drums that furnish much of its soundtrack, playing taps for a
community that has been infected by the *zeitgeist* of the Nixon era.
Thus Romero evokes the ongoing futility of the already lost but yet
to be concluded Vietnam War by his insertion of documentary footage of bombers in flight, his depiction of a priest dousing himself in
petrol and setting himself alight with a Zippo and by having the
military incinerate the bodies of the infected with flame-throwers,
even as the townspeople of Evans City impose massive damage on
their technologically superior enemy. As such, he offers a coruscating indictment of America's ongoing love affair with the gun. Certainly, the gun may be associated with the gas-masked, white-suited
soldiers who invade the peaceful environs of family homes in the
manner of the Latin-American murder squads armed and financed
by Nixon. But within these ostensibly peaceable familial spaces
Romero's *mise-en-scène* includes gun cabinets, mechanical machine
guns for children to play with, toy soldiers and framed prints of
fathers and sons in the military uniforms of their respective eras'
wars. The martial law that is imposed upon Evans City from without and which makes 'every damn civilian weapon in the entire perimeter' subject to confiscation is thus echoed from within by the
townspeople themselves, whose home-made weapons and personal
fire-power affirm their own intrinsic adherence to the culture of the
gun. It is, of course, an adherence that enabled their ancestors initially to appropriate the wilderness by force and subsequently to
dominate the world through military and economic might. In this
context it is also notable that Judy, the hero's love interest, is shot
not by agents of the state but by gun-wielding teenagers guilelessly
asserting their constitutional right to bear arms against a force that
seeks to curtail their vision of freedom American-style. It is no

coincidence, in other words, that when the infected Clank is outnumbered by faceless gunmen (in winter woodland that is itself reminiscent of deforested jungle) his gaze falls on a snake making its way
into the hollow of a fallen tree. The garden of the New World, the
Eden of mankind's new beginning, is thus shown to harbour a viper
in its bosom: a viper that has tempted Americans away from the
straight and narrow path of cooperative social justice 1960s-style
into the despondent economic slough of the 1970s present, a viper
whose very existence is continually denied by the nation's leaders. As
Winthrop once warned, the nation has fallen into a state of corruption. So, as Judy dies with her unborn child still kicking inside her,
her hopeless desire to name the baby after its father leaves us with
the sense that both Evans City and the nation itself have no meaningful future, both being haunted by memories they are unable to
understand or assimilate. For all the hopes of the original settlers,
the New World has become a nation that can only bring forth death.
The virus has already made it to Louisville. The destruction of the
Union is already under way and the only response the average American can make (in the words of Carole Bayer Sager's mawkish protest
pop that accompanies the film's closing credits) is to cry 'Heaven
Help Us.' It is a most Winthroppian prayer, an entirely apposite
symbolisation of the loss of the dream of freedom.

This sense of a blighted future engendered by the sins of the
past and repressed cultural memory of those sins is most fully explored in *Martin,* a film Romero released in 1976 as Gerald Ford
unconditionally pardoned Nixon's Watergate transgressions and the
previous year's fall of Saigon finally sank in to the American consciousness. This was a point in time in which the gulf between public opinion and official policy, the people's reality and that of their
rulers, had never seemed wider and the state of the nation had never
appeared more divided or unashamedly corrupt. Filmed against the
background of America's most severe economic crisis since the Depression (an earlier national trauma that is repeatedly memorialised
in the derelict urban iconography of the film), *Martin* is a strange
tale of modern vampirism set in Braddock: a decaying suburban
district east of Pittsburgh. Here is a city subject to galloping infla-
tion, staggering levels of unemployment and imminent economic

collapse, a city of urban decay and radio talk shows, car graveyards and bottle-hugging derelicts, consumer durables, marital ennui and meaningless sexual encounters. Into such a world comes the epony-mous hero, an individual who is either a psychotic teenage serial killer who drugs his victims prior to drinking their blood or, as he and his cousin believe and as the intercut monochrome homages to Universal horror classics show, an 84-year-old vampire from the old country adrift in the modern American world.

Throughout the film, Martin's social contacts admirably evoke the social stratification and communal fragmentation of mid-1970s America. A single woman on a train heading for New York, a man engaged in extra-marital sex with the adulterous wife of a business-man away from home and a derelict who subsists in the abandoned warehouses and factories of the dying steel-town all provide Martin with a meal of blood. More importantly, they also grant Romero a chance to play upon the huge disparities of wealth and power that characterised America during this period. While biker gangs ram-page across the neighborhood, drug dealers meet in secret confer-ence and young men harass and abuse shopping housewives, Romero again establishes a dividing line, perimeter or fortress wall between opposed and competing sectors of the American public. Outside stand the dispossessed, the disgruntled, the disposable byproducts of American consumer capitalism, their lives symbolically encapsu-lated in the strip show and porn shops of Braddock's less than salu-brious side streets. Within this perimeter are the tastefully furnished homes of the bourgeoisie – homes like that of Mrs Santini, with its white walls and framed reproductions of Goya and the early Mondrian; homes like that of Martin's adulterous victim, with her glass walls and concealed doors, leather sofas, remote controlled ga-rage and myriad electrical goods. Both outside and inside the for-tress it seems that sad, sordid and self-regarding lives are being lived. Mrs Santini has compensatory sex with Martin in his capacity as grocery boy, as do Martin's cousin Christine and Martin's adulter-ous victim. And the futurity implied by children is altogether absent from both worlds. For as Martin observes of his own sterile isola-tion: 'I shouldn't have friends, not even for the sexy stuff.'

It is possible to argue that *Martin* is somehow 'about' the family's pernicious reinforcement of the conformist norms of a conservative society in a state of imminent collapse.[17] Many critics have claimed, for example, that the teenage Martin is a victim of a personality disorder brought on by his family's insistence that he is *nosferatu*, a vampire whose soul must first be saved prior to his bodily destruction. And there is clearly something to this argument. Throughout the film, Romero insistently highlights Martin's cousin Cuda's obsession with 'the family curse, the family shame,' the old man's penchant for the external symbols of religious superstition (the cross, the Madonna, the wreath of garlic) and his insistent belief that the decline of 'the old ways' has inexorably led to the social collapse of the present. Certainly, this is a world of useless objects and meaningless *mise-en-scène*, with dolls and statues, windows and vases, books and soft toys panned portentously but lacking any ostensible significance or order. This is a static world of down-at-heel veterans exposed to public view in public washrooms, a debased chorus offering only banal platitudes in a world in which repeated shots of cars being crushed to blocks of metal in a wrecking yard mark the utter disposability of American culture, American dreams. In such a world as this, it may be argued, Martin becomes conveniently symbolic of all that ails his cousin Cuda: all the chaos, disorder and darkness that once lay outside the pilgrims' stockade and still lies out there both in the Pittsburg night and within the breast of the American citizenry. According to such a reading, then, the interpolated Universal scenes in which Martin's vampiric identity is re-cast in the cinematic language of the silver screen may intimate the pervasive effects of family life, family drama and family trauma on the individual subject. Martin, one may argue, has constructed such fantasies in order to live up to the image of him projected by his family. He has internalised their belief system and found a way of making it relevant to himself.

That said, the film is rather more ambiguous than this reading allows and contains rather more potent and disturbing ideas. For throughout the movie not only does Romero repeatedly invite us to countenance the possibility that Martin's vampirism is actually real, but in so doing encourages us to explore the ramifications of what Dominick LaCapra would term 'perpetrator trauma' for a culture recently shown to have committed large-scale human rights abuses both on its own citizens and on the people of Vietnam. Lacking the conceptual vocabulary in which to house his experiences of the past then, Martin re-fashions his memories in the cinematic lexicon of Universal horror movies, the mass cultural monsters of which appear to offer him a heroic subjectivity absent from his dependent and infantilised present life. In such filmic fantasies he is positioned first as the romantic-hero-vampire offering his compliant and complicit victims a kind of 'haemosexual' release: a picture far different from the spirited resistance put up by the anonymous housewife or by the woman on the train who bites, kicks and wrestles with the 'freak rapist asshole' and necrophiliac that Martin actually is. As the present-day sections of the narrative make clear, such fantasies (or re-constructed memories if you will) have more to do with Martin's present-day predicament than one might initially suppose. Here erratic low angle shots and extreme close-ups of tormenting Latinate priests and silently complicit family members present Martin as both perpetrator of his crimes and victim of his memories; the representational strategies of classic 1930s horror evoking the 'crazy life full of crazy people' that Martin acknowledges is his lot. His problem, of course, is that he is unable to negotiate the trauma of the past and move on for lacking the conceptual vocabulary with which to make sense of his experiences: Martin remains trapped in a perpetual present, haunted by endlessly recycled memories of a logically impossible past.

And so, deploying the technology at his disposal in the form of sedative drugs, hypodermic syringes and remote control devices, Martin attempts to live out his vampiric destiny in the modern world. Rejecting the existence of magic and well aware that the cloak and fangs of mass cultural representations of the vampire are 'only a costume,' Martin thus synthesises ancient desires and new world technologies. He is a hybrid of forbidden lusts and contemporary consumer capitalism, the interpolated Universal scenes thus being less a testament to the family's invidious effects on the individual than a representation of the ways in which the individual internalises their own traumatic experience in a world only too ready to profit from their horror. This is, after all, a world of banal radio phone-ins that position Martin as 'The Count,' 'a real live honest to goodness vampire' whose personal confusion is seen as little more than a means of increasing audience ratings and improving the returns for the show's sponsors.

So, far from being a unique aberration Martin is a rather rococo example of the pernicious effects of traumatic events on the subjectivity of the American individual as victim of a kind of nationally-specific schizophrenia. At this point in the nation's history it seems that every American contains within themselves a series of irreconcilable contradictions: Mrs Santini with her fine house and unhappy marriage, Christine with her yearnings for freedom and her regressive love of her family, Arthur with his strong work ethic and utter inability to find a job and Martin with his thwarted will to social interaction and human warmth but so damaged by past events, of which he may have been the perpetrator, that he can only drift through the harsh, abrasive and punitive world that he inhabits. All of these bespeak a nation divided. On the one hand is the will to believe in a range of government-sponsored American dreams of equality, opportunity, freedom and democracy. On the other is the awareness that contemporary America is a land of military atrocity, social stratification, economic stagnation, civil liberties violations and corrupt government. On the one hand is the ideal of essential and immutable selfhood (whether one be an American, a vampire, or both). On the other are the distorted renderings of that identity promulgated by mass culture. On the one hand is the spiritual faith that led religious radicals to the New World and underpinned their mission to tame a continent. On the other is a self-reflexive awareness of the history of oppression and exploitation practiced by human beings in the name of god, democracy and nationhood. What emerges is a sense that spiritual faith has become an irrelevance in the modern world of cancerous old priests and their shallow, sybaritic successors. In the manner of Winthrop, such priests may urge parishioners to work together and sell off their surplus goods to rebuild the church anew, but such exhortations fail comprehensively to heal the wounds of the past, rejuvenate the community or integrate our vampire hero into it. Two hundred years after the Declaration of Independence the idealistic visions of the past are pitted against the consumer durables of the present and both appear empty and devoid of promise. Two years later, Romero would release his 1978 masterwork *Dawn of the Dead*.

In *Dawn of the Dead* the controlled, contained or foreshadowed mayhem of *The Crazies* and *Martin* explodes into global apocalypse as the United States not only loses its right to claim moral leadership of the world but shows itself, in the light of wartime atrocities, student protests, urban riots and countercultural condemnation of all branches of government, to be entirely incapable of handling the national disaster that faces it at home.[18] For during the three weeks that precede the narrative's inception the dead have returned to gorge themselves on the still-living flesh of their compatriots who in turn arise again to kill. While, as in Vietnam, the disintegrating media continues to feed the populace on a diet of 'moral bullshit' and false information that in actuality leads many to their deaths, representatives of the state such as the SWAT team sent to round up the dissident poor either kill themselves, abscond or are driven murderously mad by what they see. This is a society at the point of utter disintegration, where martial law has been declared and citizens have been forbidden from occupying private residences, in a move echoing the US policy of forced relocation in Vietnam and the earlier dispossession of Native Americans throughout the South and West. For as Romero indicates in his own novelisation of the film, even at the beginning of the narrative 'the administration in power didn't have the faith and confidence of the people.'[19] In the City of Brotherly Love, where once the Declaration of Independence was signed, the civil order has collapsed, with citizens actively disobeying the government's injunctions to turn over the bodies of their dead to specially equipped divisions of the National Guard; and in so doing fuelling the fires of their own destruction. As Winthrop once warned, the people of America are being consumed out of the good land from within; the rest of the film delineating precisely which sins have brought them to such a pass.

That much of the remaining action occurs in a large shopping centre that is also a Civil Defense bunker obviously enables Romero to embark on a protracted parody of the highly militarised consumer society that America of the late 1970s had become.[20] In so doing, of course, he illustrates in considerable detail the ways in which Americans are complicit in their own destruction – becoming in the process both victims and perpetrators of the traumatic injury to national self-image inflicted by the events of the 1970s. For as the macho SWAT member and Vietnam veteran Roger indicates, this self-sufficient and windowless place is 'fat city,' a veritable 'gold mine' of consumer delights. Like the wilderness before the white man came, this is an 'important place' in the lives of its original inhabitants who nonetheless have no use for many of its material resources. Thus aligning the zombies with the dispossessed Native Americans, Romero terrifies us with his grotesque juxtaposition of untouched consumer goods and ambulant corpses in workaday clothes. The sheer banality of their plaid shirts, flared jeans and wide-lapelled suits, kaftans, sportswear and fashionable ethnic-chic only underscores our awareness that these people were very recently ordinary Americans of the late 1970s. Distinguished by their clothing (most memorably including a nurse, a baseball player and a Hare Krishna devotee) yet homogenised by their deadness and their insatiable appetites for living human flesh, the zombies not only embody Winthrop's fear of being 'consumed out of the good land' but operate as perfect and rather pitiful allegories of the American self under capitalism: children of the military-industrial complex whose lives and deaths have been underwritten by the gun. Like media-generated images of the individual as consumer they are alike and interchangeable, lacking any interior consciousness, simply driven to consume. Such a notion is emphasised, for example, when Roger and Peter turn on the power in the mall. Led by the swannee whistle that accompanies the comically cartoonic muzac in the mall, jaunty cutting between the dials in the control room, the fountains, automated shop displays, turning mannequin heads and the zombies themselves allows the film to convey a distinct sense that our consumer selves are consistently manipulated by the environments that we inhabit. For like the zombies we too wander through corridors of consumer delights with arms outstretched, banging at the windows and attempting to lay our hands on the goodies inside until we tire of those baubles and move on to the next transient object of our passing desire. That the camera moves unmolested amongst the zombies as they stagger and stumble, bump and bounce upon their way merely heightens this impression, as do the frequent point-of-view shots that allow us to see directly through the eyes of a zombie about to be dispatched. Thus we are encouraged to denounce the insistence of the film's government that the zombies are not of our species. For as the film posits and its contemporary audience knew, the citizens of 1970s USA were as dead as their dreams of national perfectibility. It was the trauma engendered by the all too visible failure of the nation's foundational ideology and the subsequent political denials of that trauma that had reduced the nation to this.

In the light of this it is notable how much our hero-protagonists have in common with the hostile forces that surround them. Both humans and zombies are attempting to survive, both are capable of reproducing themselves and both must destroy the enemy in order to do so. All that really distinguishes the groups is their choice of weaponry and tactics: the many hands and teeth of the very many zombies versus the military hardware of the small band of survivors. It is a paradigm, of course, that once again echoes the ill-fated technological superiority of American forces in Vietnam and, earlier still, that of white settlers against the Native Americans. Unsurprisingly, in the light of this, the gun is an important means of social bonding in this movie. The helicopter pilot and weatherman Stephen increasingly participates in the macho camaraderie of the two Vietnam veterans as his shooting skills improve. The pregnant journalist Fran's dependent femininity transmutes into a highly autonomous parody of the female outlaw as she becomes increasingly attached to the guns that begin as an erotic accessory and end up as a means of survival for herself and her unborn child. But as Romero is keen to emphasise, a fetishisation of such weaponry is every bit as lethal as a zombie's bite. It is the SWAT man Roger's gun-wielding machismo that brings about his end while Stephen's decision to take pot shots at the invading bikers gets him killed and returns the mall to zombie hands. Only Peter, one of a series of African-American hero protagonists in Romero's films, seems immune from the effects of such weaponry. He chastises both Stephen for his dangerous shooting at the airstrip and Roger for his reckless antics in the truck. It is Peter who urges Roger to trade arms for survival by relinquishing his weapon to a zombie and Peter who, at the movie's close, passes his own gun to the selfsame zombie who holds it aloft like a cross, an icon, a totem of all that America has become.

Clearly this is not to argue that the four key protagonists function like avenging angels immune from the sins of the nation, redeeming America through their high-minded creation of a new 'New World' from out of the ashes of the old. Such a piece of intrinsically reactionary apocalypticism, as James Berger has reminded us, is far better suited to the political machinations of a Reagan than to Romero's own political project. Accordingly, timely reminders of the sins of the forefathers are embodied in the dangerously macho Roger and the superficial and greedy Stephen. The former whoops like a cowboy in victory and groans 'we whipped 'em, we whipped 'em good' (in the manner of a dying Indian killer) in defeat, the intermittent western-style musical crescendos that accompany each of our heroes victories on Romero's soundtrack further echoing the frontier motif. And in the figure of Stephen we can see encapsulated the further dissolution of such intrinsically destructive American dreams at the hands of consumer capitalism. Here is a man who builds himself a penthouse apartment in the bunker, furnished with state-of-the-art electrical goods, tasteful furniture and top-of-the-range tableware while proclaiming 'it's ours, we took it' before plunging himself into the world of the dead and his companions into ruin.

Notably, both Roger and Stephen function more as echoes of the outlaw biker gang that brings about an end to their empty idyll than as ideological or moral repudiations of it. Like the zombies themselves, both groups are quintessentially American and each encapsulates disparate fragments of American history and its attendant myths, thus providing a range of perspectives on the trauma wrought to ideas of American identity by recent historic events. Clad in a range of western regalia and sending forth US cavalry bugle calls, the gang that has survived so long on the open road clearly embodies many of the skills and values of the men that tamed a wilderness. Here is murderous strength and the utter absence of any moral scruples. Here is playful sadism and childish greed. Here is the cooperative familiarity of a hard-pressed group who 'don't like people who don't share' and who thus warn each other to look out for the welfare of the whole. Here are echoes of US infantry in Vietnam or US cavalry on the prairies of the West, soldiers who destroyed Native American culture as assuredly as their descendants unleashed napalm and Agent Orange on the innocent civilians of Vietnam. Moreover in the bikers' astonishing theft of rings and jewelry from an African American zombie who screams and slashes in outrage, we can see the historic institution of American slavery re-enacted as a crime that must somehow be punished. In the gang's ultimately destructive will to plunder we can see the fate of the American people writ large. Pillaging an eclectic selection of non-essential items from the stores, goods that echo the watches and rings, fur and leather coats, luxury foodstuffs and branded liquor previously coveted by our heroes, the bikers effectively re-enact the progressive degeneration of the pioneer ideal in time. Hypnotised by the spectacle of so many goods so readily attainable the group thus comes to share the desires of the undead and, in so doing, to invite their own destruction. Only the African-American Peter and the pregnant Fran, it seems, can see beyond the spectacle that mesmerises the others. Only they can acknowledge that like all Romero's 1970s Americans 'we're the thieves and the bad guys' and that for all its ostensible delights, the mall, the nation, is 'a prison too.' In so doing this they can be seen to offer a vision of a future United States that has negotiated its long history of racism and sexism, has healed the trauma of the 1970s and has moved on.

The final re-taking of the mall by the zombie hoard nonetheless marks the end of the American endeavour as Winthrop originally conceived of it. The entrenched social divisions that lie at the heart of American society, that pit Puerto Rican immigrant and dispossessed African-American against the government, biker gang against urban-professional-thirty-something can only be healed by death; a death that transforms each into a tottering parody of 1970s US citizens. Alongside the Johnstown National Rifle Association types who, as Stephen observes, 'are probably enjoying the whole thing,' each group has internalised the pervasive violence of the American endeavour to the extent that they have become inseparable from it. 'I'm a Man', plays Romero's soundtrack over the rednecks' zombie-hunting scenes, replete with group photos of the military and men in hunting shirts picking off the undead while popping open another beer. And with the exception of Peter, whose own future is highly uncertain, this model of beer-drinking, woman-abusing, easy-killing manhood appears to be not only culturally pervasive but obligatory. Here the cooperative and communal ideal that Winthrop espoused for the New World is shown to have been eviscerated by an overweening if entirely illusory individualism symbolised at the movie's beginning and end by the spectacle of ravenous zombies fighting over dead meat. The Puerto Rican priest may warn Americans to 'stop the killing or … lose the war' but at this movie's very inception that war has been lost; not to any outside enemy, but to the enemies within. And like Winthrop before him, Romero seems to argue, the loss of that war has been America's longtime fate.

In the light of this it is entirely unsurprising that Romero's subsequent zombie films (*Day of the Dead*, 1985 and *Land of the Dead*, 2005) offer an ongoing elaboration on these themes as a means of exploring the specific socio-cultural context of each film's production and accordingly the psychological, cultural and social legacy bequeathed by the 1970s to subsequent generations. *Day of the Dead* thus provides an updated vision of national decay in the midst of the Reaganite 1980s by which time the living are outnumbered by the ambulant dead by some four hundred thousand to one while *Land of the Dead*, set 'Some Time' after the zombie apocalypse, illustrates how the society that rises from the ashes of the old world is every bit as corrupt, exploitative and segregated as that it replaces. In both films, however, there is a significantly enhanced individuation of increasingly vocal zombies who are purposely extracted from the faceless horde as a means of updating Romero's ongoing critique of America's contemporary malaise. In the bellicose 1980s, a decade addressed more fully in Chapter 4, Romero's target is the military-industrial complex as personified both by the belligerently sexist Captain Rose and by Bub, the elegiac zombie GI, the first of his breed to remember daily tasks such as saluting a superior and firing a gun. Intriguingly, the zombies are here conceptually aligned with victims of Nazi science experimented upon in the concentration camps of the Second World War. Such alignment of the Republican right and fascist totalitarianism calls into question not only the total bankruptcy of the American endeavour but points to the gullibility of 1980s Americans who, like the zombie lab rats, have been tricked into 'being good little girls and boys … on the promise of some reward to come.' The only reward on offer here, however, is the just punishment of an angry god. For, as the Jamaican helicopter pilot John asserts, it is all too obvious that Americans are 'being punished by the creator' for their militaristic ambitions and utter lack of humility in the face of his creation. Certainly, it is an eschatological paradigm that, as we will see in more detail in Chapter 4, was admirably suited to Reagan's apocalyptic conceptualisation of his nuclear struggle with the 'Evil Empire' of the Soviet Union.

In either case, as *Land of the Dead* confirms, Winthrop's dream of cooperative social endeavour remains an elusive one, particularly when the living are so easily duped, manipulated and coerced by economic and social elites. Bearing the tag line 'The dead shall inherit the Earth,' *Land of the Dead* thus centres on Fiddler's Green, an ethnically restricted luxury condominium bordered on three sides by water, protected by a fascistically-styled private army and supplied with the luxuries of the old world by a collection of outlaw middlemen. Thus, while these outlaws are seen to distract the zombies with powerful fireworks in order to pillage their towns' salvageable supplies, the living are kept in line by more familiar diversions. For 'if you can drink it, shoot it up, fuck it [or] gamble on it,' it belongs to the appropriately named Kaufman, the progenitor of Fiddler's Green who runs the settlement and the shanty town that surrounds it like a cross between Wall Street and Guantanamo Bay. From within the settlement he is opposed by a collection of socialist radicals and by Riley, the mercenary who wants to escape his enslavement to Kaufman's world and head north into Canada where his pioneering vision of a depopulated world without fences might be realised, Most notably, Kaufman is challenged from without by the gas-pumping Big Daddy, the latest black Romero hero who leads his zombie army on Fiddlers Green, breaks through its defences and destroys Kaufman's world in a conflagration of petroleum and flame.

Having reneged on their covenant with god on not one but two occasions, Kaufman is destroyed and a new future of peaceful coexistence of the living and the dead is implied. It is an uncharacteristically hopeful ending for Romero but one that again reiterates the necessity of national adherence to Winthrop's vision of cooperative social endeavour if Americans are not to be 'consumed out of the good land.'

Through a hugely creative deployment of the conventions of contagion horror, supernatural horror and body horror, the films of George A. Romero thus provide some of the most visually arresting political challenges to the low, dishonest decades from which they emerged. Each offers the viewer a haunting series of images, akin to those that plague traumatised survivors of cataclysmic events and in so doing each reminds us that while perpetrator trauma may be quantifiably different to survivor trauma, it is trauma nonetheless. Like the church bells that ring out their ode to joy at *Martin's* end, each of these films is thus an elegy to the dreams of the nation's founders, a mode of memorialising the hopes of each generation of American selves while reminding us that the American civic body is now utterly dissolute; an infected, divided and corrupted corpse fit only for the fires of perdition.

Notes

1 Tony Williams, 'Wes Craven: An Interview,' *Journal of Popular Film and Television*, 8:3 (1980), 10.

2 Spoken by Dr Foster, the thwarted scientist of George A. Romero's *Dawn of the Dead* (1978).

3 John Winthrop, 'A Model of Christian Charity,' in Ronald S. Gottesman, Laurence B. Holland, David Kalstone *et al.* (eds), *The Norton Anthology of American Literature* (New York: W.W. Norton, 1979), pp. 11–25.

4 Winthrop, *Model*, p. 23.

5 Winthrop, *Model*, p. 22.

6 Winthrop, *Model*, p. 23.

7 Winthrop, *Model*, p, 24.

8 Winthrop, *Model*, p. 24. This is, in fact, an image drawn from Matthew 5 (14–15): 'Ye are the light of the world. A city that is set on a hill cannot be hid. Neither do men light a candle, and put it under a

bushel, but on a candlestick and it giveth light unto all that are in the house.'

9   John F. Kennedy, *Inaugural Address* (20 January 1961). www.bartleby. com/124/pres56.html. Accessed 2 November 2006.

10 John F. Kennedy, *Ich bin ein Berliner* (26 June 1963). www.historyplace. com/speeches/berliner.htm. Accessed 2 November 2006.

11 Lyndon B. Johnson, 'Address at Johns Hopkins University: Peace Without Conquest' (7 April 1965). www.lbjlib.utexas.edu/johnson/ archives.hom/speeches.hom/650407.asp. Accessed 2 November 2006.

12 Richard M. Nixon, *First Inaugural Address* (20 January 1969). www.bartleby.com/124/pres58.html. Accessed 2 November 2006.

13 There is, of course, a substantial body of critical and theoretical work on the socio-cultural function of 1970s American horror cinema, Robin Wood's 'An Introduction to the American Horror Film,' beginning this particular strand of politically engaged enquiry. Intriguingly, Wood himself would characterise Puritan attitudes to Native Americans as a classic case of projection on to the other of that which was repressed within the self, and would trace the key repressions that underpin American society across the history of horror cinema in the United States. He would convincingly illustrate, moreover, the ways in which the generic conventions of horror may simultaneously allow for the inevitable, and liberating, return of the repressed even as those self-same conventions may be differently deployed to inflict a secondary repression on audiences through simplistic reaffirmations of dominant ideologies. Robin Wood, Introduction to *The American Nightmare: Essays on the Horror Film*, Robin Wood and Richard Lippe (eds) (Toronto: Festival of Festivals, 1979).

14 To my knowledge, very little if any work has been done on this specific area, even Adam Lowenstein virtually omitting consideration of Romero from his critique of trauma, horror and national identity. There has, however, been a tradition of exploring Romero's work in the light of the Vietnam conflict, most notably by Robin Wood in *Hollywood From Vietnam to Reagan* (New York: Columbia University Press, 1986) and Sumiko Higashi in 'Night of the Living Dead: A Horror Film about the Horrors of the Vietnam Era,' in *Hanoi to Hollywood: The Vietnam War in American Film*, Linda Dittmar and Gene Michaud (eds), (New Brunswick: Rutgers University Press, 1990), pp. 175–88. Kendall R. Phillips, in *Projected Fears: Horror Films and American Culture* (Westport, CT: Praegar, 2005) has set Romero's work against its (counter)cultural context, while Gregory A. Waller has adopted a broadly Freudian lexicon to explore the zombie as projection

of archetypal anxieties in *The Living and the Undead: From Stoker's Dracula to Romero's* Dawn of the Dead (Urbana and Chicago, IL: University of Illinois Press, 1986) . The recent full- length study of Romero's work, Tony Williams's *The Cinema of George A. Romero: Knight of the Living Dead* (London and New York: Wallflower, 2003) provides a wealth of contextualised close readings of the films in the light of the cultural centrality of discourses relating to literary naturalism in the United States, a focus that echoes the similarly structural reading of the films' aesthetic identity proffered by R.H.W. Dillard in '*Night of the Living Dead*: It's Not Just a Wind that's Passing Through', in Gregory A. Waller (ed.), *American Horrors: Essays on the Modern American Horror Film* (Urbana and Chicago, IL: University of Illinois Press, 1987). Thus, while Romero criticism has ranged from the textual through the contextual there has not, as yet, been a sufficiently fulsome focus on the relationship between trauma, national identity and the horror genre, and it is precisely this that this chapter sets out to address.

15   Robin Wood, quoted in Waller, *The Living and the Undead*, p. 296.
16   David Crawford, rehearsing his very similar role in *Dawn of the Dead*.
17   See, for example, Tony Williams, *Hearths of Darkness: The Family in the American Horror Film* (London: Associated University Press, 1996).
18   It is a dynamic spookily redolent of George W. Bush's inability to offer effective assistance to the flood-hit residents of New Orleans in 2006, having under-funded the city's flood defences and Civil Defense agencies in the interests of military expenditure in Afghanistan and Iraq.
19   George A. Romero and Susanna Sparrow, *Dawn of the Dead* (London: Sphere, 1979), p. 15.
20   Actually the Monroeville Mall, close both to Braddock and to Evans City.

4

All hail to the serial killer: America's last frontier hero in the age of Reaganite eschatology and beyond

Buffalo Bill's
defunct
      who used to
      ride a watersmooth-silver stallion
and break onetwothreefourfive pidgeonsjustlikethat
                                    Jesus

he was a handsome man
      and what I want to know is
how do you like your blueeyed boy
Mister Death[1]

Reflecting the hunger of American audiences for further misadventures of the cannibalistic serial killer Hannibal Lecter, Ridley Scott's film *Hannibal* took a record-breaking $58,000,000 on its opening weekend in the United States.[2] Despite the critics, who compared it unfavourably to *The Silence of the Lambs* its final domestic gross stood at an impressive $200,000,000, itself an American box-office record for any non-action movie.[3] Such massive public interest in Lecter had of course begun with his appearance in Thomas Harris's best-selling novels *Red Dragon* (1981), *The Silence of the Lambs* (1988) and *Hannibal* (1999). It had been consolidated by earlier filmic adaptations of these works: Lecter being played by Brian Cox in Michael Mann's *Manhunter* and by the Oscar-winning Anthony Hopkins in *The Silence of the Lambs* and *Hannibal.* It was a role Hopkins would reprise the following year in Brett Ratner's *Red Dragon* (2002), a further adaptation of the novel of the same name.

As semiologically identifiable as the earlier serial killers Jason (of the nine *Friday 13th* movies, 1979–93) or Freddie Krueger (of the five *Nightmare on Elm Streets*, 1984–89) whose quasi-comic crimes dominated multiplexes across the 1980s, Lecter leavened his monstrosity with a mordant wit; so much so that his claim to have eaten a victim's liver 'with some fava beans and a nice Chianti' was voted the twenty-first most famous line in cinema history by the American Film Institute.[4] But as this chapter will argue, the iconic Lecter's true significance lay in the ways he allowed contemporary audiences to engage psychologically and socio-culturally with the historic traumas of the Reagan years while exposing the ideological mediation of that trauma by all aspects of the culture industry. It would be a mistake though, to believe that the cultural iconicity of Lecter is without precedent, for as this chapter will further indicate, the violent murderer has been a recurrent figure in the mass cultural imagination of the United States since the earliest days of the republic. He has come to the forefront of the popular imagination at times of political, social or economic dislocation; and his outrageous deeds and fantasies have allowed for a timely re-examination of one of the core paradoxes of American social life. For in the serial-killer narrative we can see two mutually contradictory yet simultaneously affirmed aspects of American self-image fighting it out quite literally to the death. On the one hand is the conformist will to consensual and cooperative social endeavour that formed the basis of Winthrop's covenant with God and which underpins the nation's pretensions to social democracy, being that which informed Franklin D. Roosevelt's introduction of the New Deal as means of social and economic recovery from the trauma of the Great Depression. On the other is the culturally vaunted doctrine of radical individualism that throughout the neo-conservative 1980s imbued American social life and American cultural products with an overweening sense of atomised and isolated subjectivity; whereby alienated individuals appear reluctant, unwilling or unable to cohere into a cooperative and democratic social group. In horror cinema's preoccupation with the figure of the serial killer throughout the 1980s and beyond we can see, therefore, a further means of negotiating the culturally dislocating legacy of the previous decade, a period that as we have seen in Chapter

3 had left Americans pronouncedly confused as to what now constituted 'American-ness.' [5]

Intriguingly, mass cultural representations of mass, multiple
or serial killer as a means of exploring the contradictions that lie at
the heart of culturally pervasive models of American national identity have a long history in the United States, being apparent as early
as 1798 when the emergent republic cast itself free of British colonial rule and set about healing the wounds of the Revolutionary
War while attempting to forge a cohesive judicial, political and constitutional identity for itself in the process. It was at this point that
Charles Brockden Brown, America's first professional novelist, wrote
Wieland (1798) a tale that set out to explore ideas of murderous
criminality as a psychological dysfunction predicated on the
individual's inability to reconcile his personal perceptions, motivations and desires with the democratically agreed empirical norms of
the cooperative and conformist society that surrounds him. The
eponymous Wieland is thus driven mad by voices in his head that
lead him first to question his hitherto idealistic vision of American
social life and then to act out the murderous impossibility of his
position as American citizen by taking a carving knife to his wife
and little children. Much later, and contemporaneous with the rash
of revolutions that in the 1840s interrogated and challenged the
meanings and modes of contemporary life in Europe, a range of
home-grown 'miseries and mysteries' writers would produce titillating exposés of the potentially murderous quality of modern American life in the emergent cities of the period.[6] Focusing more on
social deprivation and the violent crime that it engendered than on
individual criminal psychology, such stories introduced a mass American readership to sociologically-based criminological theories while
underscoring the dangers posed to the law-abiding public by deviant individuals who refused to be constrained by society's legal or
moral norms.[7] Hence, long before the very invention of celluloid,
the threats posed to the cohesiveness and integrity of the American
civic body by traumatic events such as war had been symbolically
located in the figure of the mass or serial murderer. Viewed through
the lens of quasi-sociological, quasi-psychological speculation that
itself prefigured the detection strategies of our own era (and the

detective, gangster and police procedural films that ritualistically re-enact them) such murderers would invariably be presented as morally deficient social malefactors worthy only of public condemnation and judicial execution.

It is nonetheless notable that while respectable writers were keen to participate in a rhetoric of moral condemnation and judicial vengeance, a mass reading audience were thrilled by the plethora of 'dime novels' that had been published by Gleason and Ballou in Boston since the 1840s and which pre-empted the conceptual concerns, iconography and narrative machinery of the later filmic Western. Quasi-heroic in stature, quasi-aberrant in their deeds, the protagonists of such mass-produced popular fictions, like the celluloid cowboys that would follow them, rejected the constraints of civilised society and instead located their insistent individuality in the wild regions of the western territories, beyond the control of state law or the injunctions of consensual morality. Thus aligned with the discourses of rugged pioneering individuality familiar from the Leatherstocking tales of James Fenimore Cooper[8] or the socio-cartographic explorations of William Byrd,[9] both of which will be more fully explored in Chapter 5, the singular self on the frontier of national experience became an American archetype, being one who 'had to make his own law because there was no other to make it,' and who 'had to defend himself and protect his rights by his force of personality, courage and skill at arms'[10] in a country where 'law was carried in holsters rather than books.'[11] Thus, while popular newspapers of the 'yellow press,' precursors of publications like the *National Tattler* of the Lecter films, were keen to demonise the murderers of the settled and civilised territories, men like Anton Probst (who hacked to death a family of five in Philadelphia in 1866) or Lydia Sherman (hanged in 1871 for poisoning up to forty-two family members and associates in New England) there remained a certain association in the popular media of violence and heroism, murder and an essential American self, all conceptually located 'out there' at the frontier of national experience, that archetypally American spot defined by the historian Frederick Jackson Turner as the 'meeting point between savagery and civilization.'[12] It is notable, of course, that Turner's seminal paper 'The Significance of the Frontier in

American History' (1893) effectively erased the mass slaughter that had facilitated the birth of the nation in favour of a sentimental pastoralism that championed the farmer over the gunslinger while attempting to erase the nation's origins in violence and expansion through chattel slavery, industrial exploitation, genocide and ecological decimation. With Turner, the figure of the murderer-as-frontier-hero was erased from the official account of the nation's coming-into-being, an erasure that would be replicated in the classic Western's insistent sanitising of the history of the frontier. Only in the late 1960s would a number of 'revisionist' genre movies reassess the ideology of the classic Western and find it a deceptive distortion of the nation's past, covering up the United States' material origins by denying the acts of bloody violence on which the nation rested. Such Westerns of course offered a potent critique of the nation's current involvement in Vietnam and the struggle for Civil Rights at home while deploying the traditional iconography, plot lines and characters of the genre to provide a sustained assault on establishment ideology, specifically notions of class, race and gender.[13] Now questions as to who actually owned the nation and its dreams were being transported back into the Old West to ask a range of questions: Who can be said to define or constitute a nation? Who really owns the land? Who decides what it is to be an American? And what rights and responsibilities may that entail? And in its revivification of the figure of the lone outlaw on the frontier of consensual morality, these were exactly the questions that the serial-killer narrative would pose.[14]

Certainly, from the 1960s onwards, as longstanding American ideas of individual identity and its interface with mechanisms of state control were interrogated and re-formulated, the figure of the serial killer has come to occupy an increasingly prominent and problematic position at the heart of popular culture. From the beginning of the decade, when Alfred Hitchcock adapted the crimes of the notorious Ed Gein for the screen and gave us Norman Bates of *Psycho* (1960) and Richard Fleischer cinematised Albert de Salvo's murder of thirteen women in *The Boston Strangler* (1968), the multiple murderers of the United States have provided the nation with a demonised vanguard, standing at the interface of real-life atrocity and the American culture industry. And just as the popular culture of this period drew upon real-life crimes perpetrated across the US, so too did a range of American murderers proactively seek to engage with the culture industry in a variety of ways: as a means of attaining personal renown or notoriety, as a means of refashioning the media's response to the phenomenon of multiple murder in their own image, or even as a tactic designed to precipitate the social revolution they saw as both necessary and inevitable. In the case of Charles Manson and his followers, of course, this took the form of an all-out attack on the icons of contemporary popular culture, as 'the family' quite literally invaded the Hollywood dream palace, beheaded stuntman Donald Shea, butchered the heavily pregnant actress Sharon Tate, three of her friends and two of her neighbours and daubed the walls of her home with words drawn from The Beatles' *White Album* (1968). As the idealistic hopes of Woodstock lay broken at Altamont, as the assassination of King, Evers, the Kennedys and Malcolm X gave the lie to the promise of Camelot, Civil Rights and Black Power, as the Vietnam War raged abroad and at home Chicago, Watts and New York exploded in race riots and as each of these were covered unremittingly on the news media, the serial killer, like Romero's zombies before him, came to function as a kind of conceptual shorthand for the degeneration of American dreams of cooperative endeavour into the atomised alienation of the present. The right-wing press, of course, blamed the moral relativism, sexual promiscuity, family breakdown and drug-raddled criminality of the 1960s for this, *The Washington Post* being typical in its presentation of the serial killer as icon of the permissive age, the product of America's 'slavish devotion to individualism, mobility, the right to buy smut, the right to ignore one's neighbors even when they seem weird'.[15] As Alvin Toffler commented, 'the old ways of integrating a society, methods based on uniformity, simplicity, and permanence, [were] no longer effective [for] a new, more finely fragmented social order [was] emerging.'[16] Outside the horror genre, it was a social order that had been encapsulated in films such as Martin Scorsese's *Taxi Driver* (1976), whose emotionally damaged and sexually dysfunctional Vietnam veteran Travis Bickle updated the archetype of the frontier hero; being himself the product of the ideological divide that America had attempted to draw between the 'savagery' of the perceived communist threat and the 'civilisation' embodied in American capitalism's militaristic democracy. Thus, while bands like Talking Heads provided a soundtrack to the murderous obsessions of the 1970s, with numbers like 'Psycho Killer,' true-crime books like Mel Heimer's *The Cannibal* (1971) or John Gurwell's *Mass Murder in Houston* (1974) offered detailed and ostensibly factual reportage of the life and crimes of men like Albert Fish and Dean Corll who had been the objects of extensive media speculation when at large. Clearly the same paradox that had informed young Wieland's descent into familial slaughter in the late eighteenth century was still very much at work in the United States. Democratic conformity and the individualistic drives of an implicitly violent culture could not be readily reconciled, particularly in the face of traumatic social dislocation engendered by the unique events of the decade.

It was out of this self-reflexively disintegrating society that two titanic cultural figures emerged. The first was Ronald Reagan, the former actor and television personality who swept to victory in November 1980, becoming the first elected Republican President since Nixon. The second was Hannibal Lecter. Inheriting a nation whose confidence in Presidency had been shaken to its roots first by Watergate and Vietnam and then by the economic crises of the oil-starved and stagflationary 1970s, Reagan wasted no time in capitalising on his own star image. He had after all spent a large part of his acting career in Westerns, a genre that simultaneously fetishised the radical individualism of the frontier tradition while celebrating those cooperative virtues of hard working, frugal neighbourliness that, for historians like Frederic Jackson Turner, had civilised the wilderness. But as we have seen, such binarisms were not easily synthesised outside the generic conventions of the Western. As the tragedy of Brockden Brown's Wieland has illustrated, the insistent individualism of American culture championed by the Republican right and the democratic imperative to cooperative social conformity have been in conflict since the coming into being of the United States. And since that time, as already argued, their irreconcilability has manifested itself at times of social crisis in the form of mass-cultural fetishisation of the murderer. That mass culture's most memorable serial killer to date should have emerged from the era of economic stagnation and bellicose nationalism that under Reagan threatened the world with the mutually assured destruction of thermonuclear war should therefore come as no surprise at all.

Accordingly, each of the books and films to feature Hannibal Lecter is underpinned by a range of cultural contradictions that have lain at the heart of the American murder industry for over two hundred years; binarisms that pit the transgressive individual against the common good, the lone frontiersman against the machinery of urban-industrial life under capitalism and the autonomy of the American self against the judicio-moral imperatives of the state. It is utterly apposite in other words that the plots and characters of *Manhunter*, *Red Dragon* and *The Silence of the Lambs* rest upon such oppositions – in each case the wit, wisdom and superior knowledge of Lecter being counterpoised to that of Special Agents Will Graham and Clarice Starling as they attempt to capture a second serial killer who, for all the efforts of the FBI's Behavioural Science Unit (BSU), has so far evaded justice. On the one hand, then, is the figure of the FBI crime-fighter utilising the tools of forensic pathology and behaviourist psychology to re-inscribe social order at the heart of the filmic text, a social order that is decreed by federal agencies and conceived of in the language of popular culture. Tirelessly hunting their own particular quarry and asserting throughout the process that psychological comprehension of the killer through behaviourist taxonomisation is a prerequisite of his judicial apprehension and the termination of his crimes, these agents are defenders of American civilisation establishment-style, conceptual descendents of the Seventh Cavalry, the white-hatted or star-emblazoned sheriffs of the frontier era or the Untouchables of Prohibition times. On the other hand, though, is the serial killer – one who compulsively endangers the cohesion of the nation through his unspeakable desires and outlandish actions; specifically his repetitive assaults on an innocent citizenry. He is the enemy of social cohesiveness, familiar from popular culture as the Indian, the black-hatted gunslinger or the urban gangster of European origin. Thus the conflict between the two interest groups is not simply an issue of public safety, but a fight to the death over the nature and meaning of America itself. It is a fight entirely appropriate to Reagan's own struggles against the 'Evil Empire' abroad and against 'the "L" word' or all aspects of social liberalism at home.

Certainly, in his origins, his high cultural tastes and in the actors chosen to depict him Lecter is not insistently American in anything but his will to total freedom. Although the films excise his ancestry as the child of a titled Lithuanian father and an Italian mother whose family heritage stretched back to the Florence of Dante, his unapologetic rejoicing in the decadence of the old world is most certainly a large part of his charm. Fond of cordon bleu cuisine, the music of Bach and the art and architecture of the Renaissance, Lecter's surname is Italian for 'scholar,' his given name being that of the Carthaginian general who took on the might of the Roman Empire in utterly individual fashion by crossing the Italian Alps on elephants. Lecter's academic and high-cultural tendencies can thus be seen in his intimate familiarity with the work of T.S. Eliot and John Donne, Marcus Aurelius and Shakespeare, the paintings of Duccio and the motions of the stars. Alongside his utter sadism then, this serial killer is notable for his intellectual acuity, his taste and his sophistication. A medical doctor and psychiatrist still eminent in his field, Lecter is what the BSU of the FBI would term a highly 'organised' offender, selecting his victims in advance, engaging in elaborate planning and executing his crimes and his victims with utterly ruthless efficiency. As such, he is what the BSU would term a 'hedonistic power/control killer' whose acts in the novels (though excised from the films) have included the purposeful release of violent criminals into the community; the murder of an ex-patient and the arrangement of the victim's body as a tableau representing the sixteenth-century 'wound man;' originally illustrating the mishaps the human frame is prone to on the field of battle. In the films these acts have included the infamous consumption of a census taker with legumes and a decent Italian red and the administration of hallucinogenic drugs that cause a paedophile ex-patient to feed his own face, in slivers, to two hungry dogs. In none of the films, however, do we receive any easy or reductive explanations as to Lecter's motivations. Thus the FBI may be keen to explain the motivations of a Tooth Fairy or a Buffalo Bill, but they are entirely unable to offer either a clinical or sociological explanation for Lecter's crimes. Certainly, Lecter himself provides no explanation as to his own nature, preferring to revel in the infamy of irrational evil rather than participate in the behaviourist rationalisations of second-rate therapists such as the asylum head Dr Chilton, whom Lecter subsequently hunts down and kills. Most notably, the films choose to excise the information concerning Lecter's childhood that is provided in the novel *Hannibal*, where he is depicted as the orphaned child of dispossessed Eastern European aristocrats struggling for survival in the winter of 1944 as German soldiers escaping from the collapsed Eastern front murder his parents and dine on his little sister Mischa.[17] Lecter may have physically and intellectually survived such horrific trauma but there is no hint of it in the films, where his previous life, past actions and present psychology remain utterly enigmatic. Like the frontier bandit Deadwood Dick who survived his own hanging and 'came back to life a free man whom no law in the universe could molest for past offences'[18] Lecter stands above explanation, apology or justice, becoming, in the process, a site at which the traumatic legacy of the 1980s is itself inscribed.

As such, Hannibal Lecter can be plausibly seen as the embodiment of the very paradox that has informed America's mission into the wilderness since the seventeenth century. He is cultured, intellectually brilliant, witty and charismatic. He is, to all intents and purposes, 'civilisation' incarnate. And yet, like the harbingers of American civilisation who tamed a wilderness through slaughter of its native people, the decimation of its ecosystem and the wholesale enslavement of the African-American race, he is capable of acts of enormous and seemingly barbaric savagery. But whereas the actuality of this savagery may have been suppressed by frontier historians like Turner, who transmuted the nation's westwards imperative into a peaceable search for available farming land, the enormously popular Lecter films play insistently upon the barbarism that lay at the origin and lies at the heart of American conceptions of society, and hence of the American individual as a constituent element of it.[19] Significantly, the very names of Harris's serial killers, men such as Francis Dolarhyde (of *Red Dragon/ Manhunter*) and Buffalo Bill (of *The Silence of the Lambs*) evoke their flight from the imperatives of urban-industrial capitalism towards the frontiers of human experience. Frances Dolarhyde is, after all, a 'visionary' serial killer who seeks to transcend his human corporeality in becoming the Red Dragon of William Blake's *The Great Red Dragon and the Woman Clothed with the Sun*. In such a guise he strikes at the American nuclear family under cover of darkness, slaughtering fathers, mothers, children and family pets and arranging their bodies as a passive audience to witness his transformation. It is unsurprising, moreover, that the anonymous flayer of women of *The Silence of the Lambs* is nicknamed 'Buffalo Bill,' a soubriquet that overtly aligns Jaime Gumb's flaying activities with the exploits of the real-life William Cody, frontier hero and progenitor of the Western film, while retaining the merest suggestion of the camp that led to fierce condemnation of the film as socially irresponsible in its overt homophobia, the killer's patronymic echoing of course that of Judy Garland, born Frances Gumm.

Buffalo Bill Cody gained his name from slaughtering some 4,280 head of buffalo in Kansas in the 1860s, ostensibly to feed railroad crews forging a mechanised path across the state but also as a means of wiping out Native American resistance to the encroachment of civilisation American-style. It was for such activities, alongside scouting for the cavalry and shooting uncounted 'unfriendly Indians,' that the original Buffalo Bill was awarded the Congressional Medal of Honour in 1872. Intriguingly, Cody would go on to publish a best-selling autobiography, would himself become a hero of a whole new generation of 'dime novels,' would establish a troupe of 'Wild West' performers who brought the excitement of the disappearing West to an increasingly civilised audience and, as we have seen, would even star in one of Thomas Edison's early cinematographic experiments. The killer Jaime Gumb is not, in other words, aligned with Buffalo Bill simply because, in the words of the Kansas Police Department, 'he skins his humps.' He receives the name because it allows an evocation of the vanished frontier and of men like William Cody who stood at that point in history when the murderous adventurers of the old west were transmuted into stylised simulacra of their former selves, exchanging bullets for blanks and genocide for a generous fee. In the words of ee cummings that opened this chapter, the Buffalo Bill of the past is now 'defunct.' The

'blueeyedboy' of the frontier has been consumed by the selfsame
'Mister Death'[20] who inspired his murderous career, a career legiti-
mated (in a very 1980s fashion) by the expansionist policies of Washington and validated by the American culture industry in the form
of the Wild West show, the cinematograph and later the movie Western. The serial killer who has come to replace our archetypally American hero may, in short, be a monster. But he is a monster who evokes
the complicity of the American people with the nation's history of
genocidal slaughter while retaining a certain aura of individual freedom existing putatively beyond the bounds of civilised life. It is
conceptually gratifying then that in the 2002 film *Red Dragon* Will
Graham captures a pony-tailed Lecter first by stabbing him with
arrows and then shooting him with a gun. His is a very American
way of bringing to heel an exceptionally maverick renegade.

In keeping with the conceptual logic of the serial killer sub-
genre, each of Lecter's twin nemeses are outsiders like himself. They
may be employees of the state, but within their respective
organisations they are marginalised on psychological and sociological grounds. Moreover, it is Lecter's firm conviction, and that of the
National Tattler, that Graham's acuity as a profiler is born of the
repressed desires of his serial-killing American self; desires that allow
him to enter the minds of his murderous quarry, make sense of their
actions and, like those who watch the activities of such killers via
the mixed media of popular culture, derive a certain scopophiliac
delight from the process. As Lecter remarks to Graham in both
Manhunter and *Red Dragon*, 'the reason you caught me Will is that
we're *just alike*,' a belief that is insistently born out by the repeated
use in both *Manhunter* and *Red Dragon* of point-of-view shots that
align Graham's perspective with that of the family-stalking serial
killer Dolarhyde. It is further echoed in the fact that while Graham
hunts the Tooth Fairy he is himself stalked by Freddy Lounds of the
Tattler. For Lecter, Graham is little more than a government-
sponsored serial killer, a man who has taken lives himself and who is
able to inhabit the mind of the monster with (admittedly uncomfortable) ease. The same, perhaps, could be said of those consumers
of serial-killer culture who participate in the vicarious thrills of the
killer and even accrue a certain erstwhile sense of individuality for

themselves in the process. Either way, it is argued, the hunter and the hunted have considerably more in common than is initially implied by the rhetoric of moral revulsion or the taxonomising strategies of behaviourist psychology. Both, after all, are Americans and both participate, alongside their audience, in a range of American dreams.

In the case of Clarice Starling of *The Silence of the Lambs* and *Hannibal*, of course, these are dreams of 'advancement:' the archetypally American will to recreate oneself in the image of the purportedly perfectible nation. A small, female Appalachian who as an undergraduate 'grilled' the BSU head 'pretty hard on the Bureau's Civil Rights record in the Hoover years,' Starling has a BA in Psychology and Criminology (Magna if not Summa) and has completed a postgraduate internship at an eminent psychiatric clinic. But still, as Lecter observes in a manner entirely apposite to the study of hillbilly horror in Chapter 5, she is 'not more than one generation away from poor white trash.' Subject to forms of sexist abuse from the prisoner Miggs and her own FBI colleagues that differ only in degree, Clarice has displayed since her own traumatised childhood – in which she lost her father and witnessed a grotesque act of mass animal slaughter – an eminently civilised desire to save the weak and helpless and thus to attain the eponymous silence of the lambs. But wherein lies that silence, Lecter tacitly asks? Is it attained, as Clarice believes, by the individual assuming responsibility to end that suffering? Or does it come, as Lecter seems to believe, when one not only ceases to feel responsible, but begins to take an active pleasure in the suffering of others? Such questions are, of course, of key interest to trauma theorists and significantly, it is on this point that the novel and the film versions of *Hannibal* part company.

The film *Hannibal* was released some ten years after *The Silence of the Lambs*, with Ridley Scott, director of *Alien*, at the helm and Juliet Lewis as Starling after Jody Foster refused to be involved with the project, having been utterly horrified by the ending of the book. And *Hannibal* the film does display marked deviations from its predecessors in the trilogy in that Lecter is no longer a prisoner and the FBI, far from seeking his help in the investigation of another serial killer, has placed him on its Ten Most Wanted Fugitives list alongside Usama bin Laden [*sic*] and others whose savagery threaten United States pretensions to a cultural and political monopoly on 'civilisation.' The rookie agent Starling has transformed moreover into an introspective and emotionally defensive thirty-something who rebuffs all signs of sexual interest or emotional engagement and pursues her career with a single-minded intensity that has led her to become 'the female FBI agent to have shot and killed most people.' But to Lecter, now working as a curator at the Uffizi Library in Florence, she is still 'tornado belt white trash' and all the better for it. Certainly, Starling is still subject to abuse within the FBI, this time by the grotesquely sexist and institutionally corrupt Krendler whose personal ambition makes him accountable only to those rich or powerful enough to further his political career. Only Lecter, it seems, can understand or celebrate her uniqueness. As he asserts most forcibly:

> You fell in love with the Bureau, the institution, only to discover after you'd given it everything you'd got that it does not love you back … It resents you more than the husband and children you gave up to it … you serve the idea of order Clarice. They don't. You believe the oath you took. They don't. You feel it is your duty to protect the sheep. They don't … You're not like them. They hate you and they envy you. They are weak.

In Lecter's mind of course, he and Clarice are united by both their strength and their joint repudiation of a corrupt establishment that seeks to reduce those individuals it ostensibly exists to serve into ovine nonentities. But for all Starling is prepared to defy her bosses and to rescue Lecter from the sadistic paedophile Mason Verger, she does so not to join him on the run but to bring him to justice. In this she differs radically from the Starling of the novel. For having being healed of her physical and psychological wounds by Lecter, novelistic Starling turns in her badge, exhumes her father's body in a gesture of farewell and throws in her hand with the serial killer. Her final actions are in fact startlingly reminiscent of Steinbeck's proletarian *pietà* in *The Grapes of Wrath* (1939), that tribute to New Deal liberalism and social cooperation where the dispossessed Rose-of-Sharon Joad, abandoned by her husband and recently delivered of a dead child, offers her milk-filled breast to a starving man in confirmation of their shared humanity and as an assertion of ordinary Americans' ability to endure. As Starling's dreams of public service and personal advancement fall dead from her body, the novel's heroine also offers her breast to a starving man – this time Hannibal Lecter – who himself grieves for the sister he lost as a child. Their union thus evokes the foundational myth of American populism: that of the heroic resilience of the American self in the face of corporate oppression and the indifference of the 'big government.' It is predicated, moreover, on a quintessential American will to flee the forces of oppression that would destroy them, the selfsame impulse that informs the Western's archetypal ride from civilisation into the sunset.[21] And in this it points to a mode of healing for the traumatised American self.

In the ostensibly improbable novelistic union of Hannibal Lecter and Clarice Starling we can thus see a range of popular cultural discourses coming together in a deliciously satisfying synthesis. Here the dispossessed orphans of European war and Appalachian poverty join forces against the judicial machinery of the state that threatens their very existence as autonomous individuals of rarefied tastes. Repudiating the strategies of taxonomisation and control deployed by the FBI man Krendler, the meat baron Verger and the politicians Verger's money has purchased, they set out for a new frontier of cooperative endeavour and mutually sustained individuality. In so doing, this most unlikely couple bring about the union of the monster and the manhunter, the bad guy and the good guy, the everyday American and his aberrant, disruptive and destructive other that has been implicit in each of the earlier films. It is arguably a means of synthesising a range of cultural binarisms thrown into sharp relief by the traumatic dislocations of the post-Vietnam period, binarisms that are still apposite in the neo-conservative post-9/11 War on Terror. The tragedy of the filmic *Hannibal*, of course, is that it fails to recognise the cultural logic of their union. Fleeing from unpalatable aspects of American self-image, the film thus opts for a symbolic self-castration of the serial killer: as Lecter hacks off his own hand to escape the handcuffs with which Starling has chained them together in order to await the arrival of the police. Certainly, a theological reading would be possible here, were one to see Lecter's actions as echoing those of the similarly self-castrated Christian mystic Origen who in the third century argued that in time even the devil could purge himself of evil to recover the forgiveness of God. But the film's subsequent scene, in which Lecter feeds a portion of brain to a child on an aeroplane, offers little scope for a redemptive reading of the film or its hero. As Lecter flies alone into the sunset, the film's critical stance on the corruption of the American judicio-political establishment simply evaporates in the manner of Watergate, 'Irangate,' 'Contragate' and more recently 'Osamagate.' All that is left is a rather tired laissez faire acceptance of the hegemonies within American society that the film has purported to condemn all along. For if the book's proposed union of hunter and hunted allowed for a radical interrogation of what it means to call oneself an American, then the 'amputation-escape plot' merely reinscribes the necessary inevitability of the status quo. America emerges as a politically and judicially corrupt nation whose institutions exist only to further the interests of the class-bound, racist, sexist and sexually perverted economic elite. And there's nothing Americans can do about it. It is not merely, as Daniel Shaw has argued, that 'Lecter acts as a tonic in an emasculated culture that requires us to apologise whenever our lusts or ambitions are all too obviously showing.'[22] It is that lust and ambition are the preserve of America's social and economic masters and however loud ordinary Americans might scream, nobody will come to help. Thus contrary to the pretensions of George W. Bush, popular horror cinema explains that America is not the avatar of civilisation. Instead, as Lecter remarks at the end of *Red Dragon* 'we live in a primitive time ... neither savage nor wise.' Such qualities are, of course, those of the iconic serial killer in his ongoing struggle against the conformist imperatives of a purportedly democratic state.

Notes

1   ee cummings, 'Buffalo Bill,' *ee cummings: Selected Poems 1923–1958*. (Harmondsworth: Penguin, 1960), p. 4.

2   Daniel O'Brien, *The Hannibal Files* (London: Reynold and Hearn, 2001), p. 158.

3   Daniel Shaw, 'The Master of Hannibal Lecter,' in Stephen Jay

Schneider and Daniel Shaw (eds), *Dark Thoughts: Philosophic Reflections on Cinematic Horror* (Lanham, MD and Oxford: Scarecrow Press, 2003), p. 10.

4   http://en.wikipedia.org/wiki/Hannibal_Lecter. Accessed 1 March 2006.

5   A comprehensive study of the origins and development of the filmic serial killer clearly lies beyond the scope or interests of this chapter but it is worth noting an observation by the critical historian of the genre, Adam Rockoff, which links the socio-cultural function of the serial killer in United States cinema with that of the *onryou* in Japan; the killer most commonly being 'an ordinary person who has suffered some terrible and sometimes not so terrible trauma (humiliation, the death of a loved one, rape, psychological abuse). It is because of this past injustice that he, or in a few cases, she seeks vengeance – and the bloodier the better.' Adam Rockoff, *Going to Pieces: The Rise and Fall of the Slasher Film* (Jefferson, NC and London: McFarland, 2002), pp. 5–6. Thus in the films such as *Friday 13th, Prom Night* (1980), *Happy Birthday to Me* (1981), *My Bloody Valentine* (1981), *The Burning* (1980) and *Terror Train* (1979) the gender- ambiguous murderer is provided with a historical back story that goes some way to explaining their crimes as a response to historical trauma. Similarly, in films such as *I Spit on Your Grave* (1978) a violent sexual assault on the protagonist provides her with justification for her subsequent crimes. In the case of Hannibal Lecter, however, things are rather more complex than a simple vengeance paradigm or a working through of personal trauma; for here the very meaning of what it means to call oneself an American is at stake.

6   See Joseph Holt Ingram, *The Mysteries of New York* (1842), Osgood Bradbury, *The Mysteries of Boston* (1844), Harry Spofford, *The Mysteries of Worcester* (1846) and George Lippard's best-selling *The Quaker City* (1844).

7   It was at this point in time, of course, that Edgar Allan Poe gave America the figure of August Dupin, whose semiologically grounded detective work resulted in the restoration of social order through the apprehension of those exceptional individuals, like the tricolour-wearing orang-utan of 'Murders in the Rue Morgue,' (1841) who sought to overthrow the status quo through socially disruptive acts of bloody murder.

8   *The Pioneers* (1823), *The Last of the Mohecans* (1826), *The Prairie*, and *The Pathfinder* (1840) and *The Deerslayer* (1841).

9   William Byrd, *History of the Dividing Line Betwixt Virginia and North*

Carolina, W.K. Boyd (ed.) (Raleigh: n.p., 1921.)

10   Walter Prescott Webb, *The Great Plains* (New York: Grosset and Dunlap, 1931), p. 496.

11   Ray Billington, *The Far Western Frontier 1830–1860* (New York: Bloat, 1996), p. 251.

12   Frederick Jackson Turner, 'The Significance of the Frontier in American History,' *The Early Writings of Frederick Jackson Turner* (1893. Madison: Wisconsin University Press, 1938), p. 187.

13   I am thinking here of anti-Vietnam Westerns such as Ralph Nelson's *Soldier Blue* (1970) and Arthur Penn's *Little Big Man* (1970), social realist Westerns such as Robert Altman's *McCabe and Mrs Miller* (1971) and romantic comedy Westerns such as George Roy Hill's *Butch Cassidy and the Sundance Kid* (1969) and Elliot Silverstein's *Cat Ballou* (1965).

14   As Jonathan Lake Crane has observed, there is a notable transition from the slasher protagonist of early films such as *My Bloody Valentine* to the 'canny, and always intriguing, serial killer or indefatigable psychostalker.' Jonathan Lake Crane, *Terror and Everyday Life: Singular Moments in the History of the Horror Film* (Thousand Oaks, London & New Delhi: Sage, 1994), p. 166. It was an evolution that would not merely allow the killer a greater range of prey but point to a greater realism in the genre, the murderous protagonist being less a supernatural bogeyman than a human being, admittedly one of rare gifts and insight. Hannibal Lecter is, of course, the apotheosis of this trend. More recently, such realism has been supplanted not only by the arthouse self-referentiality of films such as Neil Jordan's *In Dreams* (1998), the Belgian *Man Bites Dog* (1992) and the truly terrifying *Henry: Portrait of a Serial Killer* (1986) even as Oliver Stone has explicitly linked serial slaughter with sensationalist media coverage in *Natural Born Killers* (1994), a text that itself draws heavily upon Malick's *Badlands* (1974). More recently still there has been a frequently comedic, postmodernisation of the genre instigated by *Scream* (1996), *I Know What You Did Last Summer* (1997), *Scary Movie* (2000) and their sequels, by remakes such as Gus Van Sant's *Psycho* (1998) and updates like John Carpenter's *Halloween H2O* (1998). Thus, while 'serial-killer cinema' can be seen to have undergone a marked generic evolution that is itself worthy of consideration, the commercial success of the Lecter franchise and the eponymous anti-hero's cultural longevity has encouraged me to focus on his status as nexus of a range of distinctively American debates concerning national identity and trauma.

15   Joel Achenbach, 'Serial Killers: Shattering the Myth,' *Washington Post* (14 April 1991), p 17.

16   Alvin Toffler, *Future Shock* (London: Pan, 1981), p. 274.

17   Some six years earlier than the 1950 birthdate given for him in *The Silence of the Lambs*.

18   Edward L. Wheeler, *Deadwood Dick's Dream; or, The Rivals of the Road. A Mining Tale of Tombstone*. Beadle's Half Dime Library, 572 (1888), p. 2.

19   In this, of course, Hannibal Lecter can be seen to echo the murderer whom Mark Seltzer and others have named as the prototypical pro-genitor of the modern serial killer, one Henry Howard Holmes. Ap-prehended in Chicago, the nation's animal abattoir, as a period of mass pioneering, settlement and Indian slaughter in the lands of the South and West came to an end and the American Frontier was offi-cially closed, Holmes operated close to the site of the Columbia Expo-sition of 1893. With its trapdoors, chutes and hiding places, gas pipes, torture machines and surveillance devices, the house had been specifi-cally designed to facilitate Holmes's sexually motivated murder of young women who were either visiting the fair or working in its ancillary industries: gassing or torturing to death anything between the twenty-seven officially recognised victims and the two hundred or so that has been claimed by commentators such as Robbins and Arnold. In his ostensible omniscience and murderous omnipotence, Henry Holmes laid down a set of characteristics that would later come to be embod-ied in subsequent iconic serial killers such as Hannibal Lecter. Here was a scientifically and socially sophisticated urban man, a modern American archetype who keenly used the modern world's technologi-cal resources to pursue his murderous vocation while deploying the machinery of the United States' burgeoning culture industry to dis-seminate the story of his life and crimes.

20   Cummings, *Poems,* p. 4.

21   It is a will to flight encapsulated in literature, moreover, in iconic Ameri-can characters such as Captain Ahab of Herman Melville's *Moby Dick* (1851), Huck Finn of Mark Twain's *The Adventures of Huckleberry Finn* (1884), Dean Moriarty of Jack Kerouak's *On the Road* (1957) and Randal McMurphy of Ken Kesey's *One Flew Over the Cuckoo's Nest* (1962).

22   Shaw, 'Hannibal,' in Schneider and Shaw (eds), *Dark Thoughts*, p. 24.

PART III

From Vietnam to 9/11: the Orientalist other and the American poor white

Introduction

On 11 September 2001, two hijacked aircraft were flown into the twin towers of the World Trade Center, a third into the US Department of Defence's Pentagon building while a fourth, seemingly aiming for the Capitol in Washington, crashed in rural Pennsylvania. Self-evidently, as commentators such as Noam Chomsky have argued, this was a massive symbolic attack on the Western world – most specifically the military-industrial complex of American corporate capitalism.[1] But while the sheer ambition of Al-Qaeda's assault was entirely without precedent, the seismic media event that was 9/11 was, in fact, the culmination of a number of attacks on American interests that throughout the previous decade had indicated a growing disparity between American self-image and the ways in which certain elements of the international community perceived the United States.[2]

Having been assailed from within its own national boundaries for the first time since 1812, and in a manner so utterly spectacular as to appear logically impossible, one might imagine that the United States, a nation now locked in the post-traumatic loop of endlessly recycled images of the falling towers, would enter into a period of national self-examination as a means not only of bearing witness to the events of 11 September but of understanding why they had occurred in the first place. In terms of the United States' political establishment, however, such an examination was entirely unforthcoming. Instead, in a manner decidedly reminiscent of Nixon's wholesale demonisation of anti-government elements, and Reagan's revisionist perspective on the events of the 1970s, the

Republican right opted to exacerbate domestic paranoia and hence to avoid a detached and non-partisan examination of the situation. Repeatedly it was said that forces antithetical to expansionist American 'interests' abroad were at work within the nation's borders, threatening the very foundations of both social cooperation and democratic individualism American-style. Thus fostering a climate of introspective paranoia highly evocative of the 1970s, the Bush administration insistently emphasised the unconventional nature of the enemy which, being divorced from an individual state or an ideology of nationhood, became in Žižek's words 'an illegal, secret, almost virtual worldwide network'[3] that invidiously and invisibly challenged everything an exceptionalist America stood for. For as the President so bombastically put it in his January 2002 *State of the Nation Address*, what America stood for was 'freedom':

> Our enemies send other people's children on missions of suicide and murder. They embrace tyranny and death as a cause and creed. We stand for a different choice, made long ago on the day of our founding. We choose freedom and the dignity of every life ... We have known freedom's price. We have shown freedom's power. And in this great conflict, my fellow Americans, we will see freedom's victory.[4]

Such an ideologically saturated appeal to mythic national origins, a rhetorical and conceptual strategy that we have already encountered in the political rhetoric of a number of American presidents from Kennedy to Reagan, clearly illustrates the conflation of structural absence and historical loss that for thinkers such as Dominick LaCapra lies at the heart of all fundamentalist ideologies of nationhood.[5] But equally notable here is the way in which the president conceives of the terrorist threat in starkly Orientalist terms, adapting the repressive, retrograde and primitive image of the Orient constructed by colonialist Europe as a means of justifying its own economic interests and territorial ambitions in the East to his own particular ends.[6] Bush's attempts to 'control, manipulate, even incorporate [the] manifestly different world,'[7] that had attacked the United States would thus rest on a conceptual opposition of the post-Enlightenment rationality of the United States with its attendant (and as we have seen, highly contradictory) ideology of democratic individualism, and the older, darker, more primitive and fundamentally inferior religious culture of the undemocratic and anti-individualistic East. It was of course a reductive, simplistic and fundamentally misleading opposition, echoing that applied to Japan during and after the Second World War, but it offered a highly attractive assertion of national cohesion and political supremacy at a time of great confusion.

This occlusion of the political context of the events of 9/11 has been effectively echoed in mainstream cinematic production, the key exception of course being Michael Moore's *Farenheit 9/11* (2004), a film roundly coruscated as anti-American by the political right. Most recently, the tendency has been to focus on the heroic deeds of ordinary Americans in the face of terrorist atrocity, films such as Oliver Stone's *World Trade Center* (2006) and Peter Markle's *Flight 93* (2006) omitting the political context of the day's events entirely while promulgating an entirely deproblematised vision of freedom-loving American individualism in opposition to the totalitarian facelessness of the alien terrorist threat. As Chapter 5 of this study will illustrate though, such nationalist essentialism would be repeatedly challenged in the months and years following 9/11 by the resurgence of hillbilly horror, the 30-year-old cinematic horror sub-genre that had originally emerged from the political paranoia and flag flying Orientalism of the Vietnam years, being intimately concerned with the meanings of American freedom.

In Chapter 3 I explored George A. Romero's sense that it was in the 1970s that the United States acknowledged, for the first time since the Great Depression, the nation's ongoing inability to realise the dreams of its anti-materialist, spiritually-driven early settlers. At the hands of the authoritarian militarism of successive governments and the rapacious self-seeking consumer fetishism of individuals, the nation for Romero had broken its foundational covenant with God; condemning itself to the crass materialism and paranoid jingoism so powerfully encapsulated in the zombie apocalypse. But as I will illustrate in Chapter 5, zombie horror was not the only sub-genre deployed by American film makers to explore and revise ideas of national identity in the light of the traumatic events of the recent past. From the 1960s onwards, in response to the Vietnam War, the

generational, ethnic and regional conflict engendered by the impo-
sition of Civil Rights in the South and the rise of the counterculture
across the United States, a new kind of horror cinema, exclusively
located in the backwoods of the American psyche had emerged as
films such as John Boorman's *Deliverance* (1972), Tobe Hooper's
The Texas Chainsaw Massacre, Wes Craven's *The Hills Have Eyes* and
Walter Hill's *Southern Comfort* consistently pitted the representatives of urban-industrial capitalism and its cultural products against
a savage, intrinsically hostile and putatively subhuman threat: the
inbred, murderous and often cannibalistic denizens of rural white
communities of the American South.

Chapter 5 will thus explore the remarkable cinematic resurgence of hillbilly horror in the years since 9/11. For as George W.
Bush pits the ostensible civilisation of the US against the oriental
barbarism of the terrorist threat, providing himself in the process
with justification for both the invasion of Afghanistan and Iraq and
the introduction of a range of 'homeland security' measures that
have restricted US civil liberties with an effectiveness that would
have made Nixon proud, a new generation of horror film makers
have brought the next generation of hillbillies to cinema screens.
This time round, the hillbilly offers a self-reflexive repudiation of
the ways in which establishment ideology has attempted to deploy
mass culture to homogenise and assimilate the ethnic, class and regional diversity of the American people against the Oriental 'other'
and hence to present an ostensibly transparent, mimetically realised
and hence 'true' picture of American national identity. Engaging
with the traumatic inheritance of 9/11 though the new hillbilly horror, like Trauma Studies itself, is concerned with the complex relation between knowing and not knowing the truth, seeing and not
seeing the wounds inflicted on the national psyche by recent events.
In their graphic preoccupation with wounds and wounding, deformity and mutation, horrific physical violence and deep psychological horror, films such as Eli Roth's *Cabin Fever*, Rob Schmidt's *Wrong
Turn*, Marcus Nispel's remake of *The Texas Chainsaw Massacre* and
Alexandre Aja's remake of *The Hills Have Eyes* (2006) as well as
smaller-scale productions such as *The Undertow* (2003), *The Ruining* (2004), *Shallow Ground* (2004) and *The Attendant* (2004) can

thus be seen to operate in ways similar to Dominick LaCapra's 'traumatic realism' in the arts. Setting out to engage with and hence illuminate the social reality with which they have 'a mutually provocative relation ... exploring its problems and possibilities, testing its norms and conventions, and in turn being tested by it,' the representational strategies deployed by these genre texts can thus be seen to differ from 'stereotypical conceptions of mimesis,' enabling in their thematic machinery and visual lexicon, as well as their narrative drive, 'an often disconcerting exploration of disorientation, its symptomatic dimensions, and possible ways of responding to them.'[8] And in so doing, they can be seen to proffer a critique of ideologies of liberty American-style by asking the most taboo of all questions: whether, in the age of the PATRIOT Act, 'extraordinary rendition' and Guantanamo Bay, Americans can continue to claim a national association with the cause of freedom at all.

Notes

1   Noam Chomsky, *9/11* (New York: Seven Stories, 2002).
2   These were the 1993 attack on US marines in Mogadishu, the truck bombing in Riadh in 1995, the bombing of the Khobar Towers in Dahran in 1996, the bombing of US Embassies in East Africa in 1998 and the attack on the *USS Cole* in 2000.
3   Slavoj Žižek, 'Are we in a war? Do we have an enemy?,' *London Review of Book* (23 May 2002), p. 24.
4   George W Bush, *State of the Union Address* (29 January 2002). www.whitehouse.gov/news/releases/2002/01/print/200020129–11.html. Accessed 2 November 2006.
5   Dominick LaCapra, 'Trauma, Absence, Loss,' in Levi & Rothberg (eds), *The Holocaust*, pp. 199–206.
6   Edward Said, *Orientalism: Western Conceptions of the Orient* (London: Penguin, 1991).
7   Said, *Orientalism*, p. 12.
8   Dominick LaCapra, 'Conclusion: Writing (about) Trauma,' in LaCapra, *Writing History, Writing Trauma*. (Baltimore and London: Johns Hopkins University Press, 2001), p. 186.

5

'Squealing like a pig': the War on Terror and the resurgence of hillbilly horror after 9/11

In a manner intriguingly reminiscent of President Bush's Orientalist vilification of the terrorist threat in the months following the horrific events of 9 September 2001, the United States has a very long history of representing the inhabitants of its own isolated rural places or backwoods communities as monstrous, grotesque, diseased and polluted. Emerging as it did from the trauma of the Revolutionary War the foundational study of Colonial period self-image that is Hector St John de Crèvecoeur's *Letters from an American Farmer* (1782) can be seen to participate enthusiastically in this trend. Here Crèvecoeur stresses the enormous disjunction between the backwoodsman and those good country people whose adherence to protestant virtues of sobriety, thrift, Christian morality and hard work was transforming the ancient, hostile and potentially unknowable American wilderness into a utopian land of 'happiness and prosperity [with] hospitality and kindness and plenty everywhere.'[1] But far 'beyond the reach of government' and closely aligned with the dark irrationality of his habitat, warned Crèvecoeur, there was the backwoodsman; one who had turned from peaceful and exhausting agriculture to a life of hunting in the game-rich forests, a practice which led not only to 'drunkenness and idleness ... contention, inactivity and wretchedness'[2] but to a kind of socio-biological degeneration; a falling away not only from the ideals of the new republic but from humanity itself. Thus, for all the hopeful, forward-looking qualities of the age, the backwoods community became in Crèvecoeur's words 'a mongrel race, half civilised and half savage.'[3]

In their deviant hybridity it is nonetheless possible to see how the backwoodsmen proffered a radical challenge to exceptionalist models of American identity that continues to resurface in the popular imagination when historic trauma encourages the citizenry, if not their rulers, to national self-examination. For the backwoodsman was most certainly not an American Adam, building a democratic Eden in the amply legislated garden of the new world, being instead one who inhabited the physical and conceptual margins of the nation, the abject territory of 'outlaws, outcasts and paupers.'[4] Resisting cultural assimilation by dominant expansionist ideologies, and thus illustrating how those who had settled down to a life of hard work on the farm or in the emergent city had tacitly acquiesced to the limits placed on their freedoms, the backwoodsman thus established his own vision and version of America. His freedom was not mediated by its conceptual embodiment in a constitution. His independence was asserted not by its declaration or by its validation in law; but in his refusal to be subject to that law. In his monstrous physicality, all rotten teeth and rapacious sexuality, the backwoodsman thus repudiated any subordination of his material body to his cognitive self. And in turn he was cast off and disavowed by the civilised mainstream that itself was simultaneously attracted to and terrified of his unspeakable desires and unimaginably grotesque acts. As Jack Nicholson's alcoholic lawer George puts it shortly before being beaten to death by angry small-town conformists in Dennis Hopper's *Easy Rider* (1969):

> talking about [freedom] and being it – that's two different things … I mean, it's real hard to be free when you're bought and sold in the marketplace. Course, don't ever tell anybody … that they're not free, cause they're gonna get real busy killin' and maimin' to prove that they are.

As we have seen then, it was entirely appropriate that in the 1970s, as the United States sought to bring the light of freedom to the misguided orientals of North Vietnam, as the battle for civil rights raged across the nation and as a host of countercultural philosophies of oriental origin challenged American capitalism's white Anglo-Saxon protestant hegemony, that the hitherto repressed figure of the backwoodsman made a spectacular cinematic return, arguably functioning as a means of negotiating the increasingly traumatic disjunction between the aspirations of a 'civilised' society and the acts of savagery perpetrated in its name. In films such as Hershell Gordon Lewis's *Two Thousand Maniacs* (1964), John Boorman's *Deliverance*, Tobe Hooper's *The Texas Chainsaw Massacre*, Wes Craven's *The Hills Have Eyes* and Walter Hill's *Southern Comfort* amongst others, the monstrous alterity of the historically-embedded backwoodsman thus enabled film makers to address not only American foreign policy in South Asia but the ongoing desecration of American ecology, the paranoid militarism of American life, the degeneration of the frontier ethos at the hands of consumer culture and the ramifications for workers of the decay of America's industrial base. With his congenital abnormalities, rococo sexuality, appalling dentistry and in the case of Cajun backwoodsmen perverse insistence on speaking French, the horror hillbilly broke free of the mechanisms of social, cultural and psychological repression that attempted to contain his deviant repudiation of dominant norms and values. In so doing, of course, he not only enabled audiences to share in his vicarious pleasures, but provided horror cinema with an iconic means of peeling back ideologically expedient dressings that other branches of the culture industry had applied to the wounds of the period: specifically the damage done to national self-image as the war in Vietnam raged abroad and protests against it at home informed all aspects of United States social life. It is doubly appropriate, moreover, that since the bombing of the World Trade Center, the subsequent 'War on Terror' and instigation of an effective suspension of many long-prized civil and political rights in the United States, the cinematic hillbilly should return to cinema screens as a timely reminder to that nation that the wider world does not necessarily acquiesce to the United States's self-proclaimed mission to save it from itself. Hillbilly horror, in the conceptual vocabulary of Trauma Theory, can thus be seen as part of a 'process of acting out, working over, and to some extent working through' recent events, 'giving voice to the past'[5] and comprehending an unsettling and disorienting present.

Released in 1964, *Two Thousand Maniacs* was written, directed and photographed by the legendary cut-price cult film maker Hershell Gordon Lewis who also wrote and sang its memorable theme-tune

'Oh the South's Gonna Rise Again.' Set in the entirely fictional town of Pleasant Valley, Georgia – a redneck Brigadoon whose inhabitants awake after a hundred years to avenge their Civil War extermination at the hands of renegade Union troops – the film traces the unsavoury misadventures of three Northern couples cunningly forced to detour through the town and then stay as 'guests of honour' at its centenary celebrations. Oddly contemporary in speech and inhabiting a mid-1960s-styled town that possesses automobiles, electricity, telephones and other modern accoutrements, the 'maniacs' come straight from hillbilly central casting. Here is all the Confederate flag waving, banjo plucking and dungaree wearing one could possibly desire, while the loud, fat, autocratic Stetson-clad Mayor Buckman is the apotheosis of Southern patriarchal law. Interestingly, there is not a single black character: African-Americans being absolved here of both the crimes of the North and of the South that had so long enslaved them. As four of the victims are respectively dismembered with an axe, pulled apart by horses, rolled down a hill in a nail studded barrel and crushed beneath an exceedingly large rock, the maniacs enjoy various 'traditional' Southern pastimes: including a barbecue of human flesh, numerous choruses of 'Dixie' and, for the children, the torture and mutilation of small animals! In keeping with the will to freedom beyond the law that has been historically embodied by the rural poor white moreover, the maniacs escape the legal and indeed moral consequences of their actions, simply disappearing at the end of the film; though not before wondering whether space ships and rockets will be a reality when they next emerge.

But while Lewis's cult classic is very much a tongue-in-cheek parody of regional stereotypes and their mass cultural appropriation, the idealistic counterculture that emerged around this period would seriously champion the folk traditions of rural poor whites as a means of challenging the totalising culture of the American establishment they believed to be fascistic. Thus, while Bob Dylan's collaboration with Johnny Cash gave the nation the hybrid of hippy counterculture and American folk roots that was *Nashville Skyline* (1963) films like Arthur Penn's *Bonnie and Clyde* (1970) set about heroising the lawless Southern poor of the Great Depression. So, for all the hippie heroes of Dennis Hopper's *Easy Rider* are blown from their motorcycles by two archetypes of redneck intolerance, the sense remains that such acts of lawless 'killin' and maimin'' are a direct result of the encroachment of America's economic, political and legal systems on the autonomy of poor white country-dwellers. In *Easy Rider*, the hippies' refusal to be 'bought and sold in the marketplace' thus functions as a reminder that the rhetoric of freedom espoused by conservative Americans in justification of the war in Vietnam (and later Afghanistan and Iraq) is a means of social control, a rhetorical strategy designed to curtail liberty and stifle opposition while conveniently binding the physical, material and psychological wounds inflicted on the nation and the nation's enemies by war. The small-town poor whites who murder our heroes Wyatt and Billy are not simply symbolic agents of Nixon's silent majority then, but victims of America's historically lost possibilities and ongoing denial of that loss. They act in traumatised outrage against the establishment's marginalisation of them. And in so acting they not only repudiate the 'tamed' image of the southern poor white promulgated by television shows such as *The Beverley Hillbillies* as a means of smoothing over the sectional divisions of the nation, but purposefully highlight both the brutality of American life and the limits placed on liberty post-9/11.[6]

Adapted by James Dickey from his popular novel of 1970 and directed by John Boorman, *Deliverance* tells the tale of four Atlanta professionals who set out to travel a stretch of the Cahulawassee River in North Georgia before the area is flooded by the construction of a hydroelectric dam.[7] This is 'just about the last wild, untamed, un-polluted, un-fucked-up river in the South,' a landscape so comprehensively ravaged by urban life and encroaching suburbanisation that the degraded mountain dweller and his world are presented as 'the end of the line' where humanity and indeed the nation 'finishes up.' This is a world of 'rust and dust' where mountain people, naturally suspicious of outsiders, embody a range of distinctively eighteenth-century stereotypes. Here is the congenitally disabled *idiot-savant* on the banjo, his peculiarly bald head and pallid skin made even stranger by the low angle, side-lit shots that capture his aged and inscrutable face. Here is the spontaneously dancing

gas man, with his child-like enjoyment of music and wildly unfash-
ionable hat. Here too his ancient, hunched kinswoman babysitting
a contorted child whose own disability consigns her to a mound of
pillows, and her family line to probable extinction. As Bobby the ill-
fated insurance man puts it, 'talk about genetic deficiencies ... ain't
that pitiful?'

But while Dickey's novel embodied a yearning sense of a cultural valorisation of the backwoods tradition, offering as it does a
sustained critique of urban modernity and an insistence that for all
their shortcomings the mountain people possessed a cultural cohesion and personal integrity lost in the modern world, then Boorman's
film has no such ambitions. Other than Burt Reynolds's ridiculous
wetsuit, all that really sticks in the mind here are two elements that
do not appear in the book: the insistent refrain of the 'Duelling
Banjos' theme and the humiliating anal rape of the patronising insurance man Bobby by two of the most invidiously stereotyped hillbillies imaginable.[8] Proclaiming that the decidedly porcine Bobby
looks 'just like a hog,' our toothless rapists become rather pitiful
allegories for the degeneration of ideal American masculinity and
community.[9] What is more, their actions lead our ostensibly civilised
city-dwellers into retaliatory atrocities of their own, including murder and conspiracy to conceal that crime. For as Carol Clover has
observed, the encounter with the mountain men on which the narrative rests amply illustrates that 'civilisation sits lightly on even the
best bred amongst us' and hence that we are one step away from
becoming monsters ourselves.[10]

The contiguity of savagery and civilisation is, of course, most
fully explored in Wes Craven's *The Hills Have Eyes*. Coming in the
middle years of Tom Wolfe's 'me decade,' when an unprecedented
one in five American marriages ended in divorce and one in five
children were raised in single-parent households,[11] *The Hills Have
Eyes* took the hillbilly horror's ability to undermine all totalising
conceptions of national identity via rhetorical appeals to myths of
national origins to new heights.[12] Specifically, it proffered a gruesome challenge to the affirmation of the American family embodied
in the hugely popular ABC series *Roots* that in this year traced the
ancestry of Alex Haley back to the enslavement of his ancestor in

1750s Ghana.[13] For if *Roots* spoke to a mid-1970s audience's ideal-istic yearning for continuity and community (as well as ethnic equal-ity in an increasingly segregated society) then *The Hills Have Eyes* presented a necessary corrective to the series' conservative valorisations of the family as core unit of peaceful and consensual social organisation. Inspired by the legend of Sawney Bean, a Scot-tish cannibal of eighteenth-century myth said to have lived in a Galloway cave with his incest-begotten brood, the film elaborates on many of Craven's earlier preoccupations: specifically *Last House on the Left's* (1972) extension of horror into the heart of the Ameri-can family home.[14] In a world in which the military-industrial com-plex has destroyed the land with radiation as surely as it has infected the American family with its lies, a vengeful parody of the patriar-chal family emerges in the form of Papa Jupe, his sons Pluto and Mars, his daughter Ruby and unnamed wife, a former prostitute. And it is into their territory that the ironically named Carter family, agents of the urban-industrial complex itself, ill-fatedly come.[15] Following the retirement from the Cleveland police force of their own patriarch, the impatient, intolerant and openly racist Big Bob, the Carter clan is relocating to California, deviating somewhat from their journey to search out an abandoned silver mine willed to them by an aged aunt. Tightly knit, inventive and surprisingly tough, the Carters may fall victim to being hunted, raped, murdered and cannibalised but their surviving members display all the ingenuity of their pioneering ancestors in their overweening will to survive. Deploying their mother's corpse as a decoy, the family dog as a weapon, the technological resources of their vehicles, and wielding knives and axes as necessary, the middle-class Carter children prove themselves more than a match for the ravening desert-dwellers. At the cost of their own pretensions to 'civilisation' they therefore sur-vive – but not before a deeply shocked audience is forced to look once more on the degeneration of yet another cornerstone of mythic America.

Such a degenerate vision of the American family clearly owed a great deal to the fearsome clan of dispossessed abattoir workers of *The Texas Chain Saw Massacre*, released some three years earlier, which one critic has delightfully described as the '*Gone With the Wind* of meat movies.'[16] Hyperbolic humour aside, parallels with David O. Selznik's 1939 Depression-era reworking of Margaret Mitchell's romance of the fall and rise of the South are not as far-fetched as they may seem. Both films assert a sense of the permanence of the land in opposition to the transience of human endeavour in commerce, politics or war. Both illustrate the invidious effects of the large-scale industrialisation of the South that really took off with Reconstruction and both are sensitive to the class-based determinants of Southern identity. However, while Scarlet O'Hara does indeed return Tara to its former glory in the sure belief that 'tomorrow is another day,' for 'Sally Hardesty and her invalid brother,' as the opening titles indicate, 'an idyllic summer afternoon drive became a nightmare.' By the mid-1970s, it seems, no return to the ancestral home is possible. The family house built by the siblings' grandparents is abandoned and rotting while the industrialisation of the land, symbolised by the pervading stench of the slaughterhouse, is itself in decline. With no new mode of productive economic endeavour to replace it, unemployed slaughterhouse workers turn from killing for profit to killing for pleasure. It is perhaps unsurprising that while *Gone with the Wind* won some ten Academy Awards *The Texas Chainsaw Massacre,* like Buttgereit's *Nekromantik 2,* was widely banned and censored, gaining massive cult status for itself in the process.[17]

Released in the year America finally withdrew from Saigon and against the backdrop of Nixon's resignation, *The Texas Chainsaw Massacre* is pervaded by an apocalyptic climate of utter despair. From the opening, shots of the desecrated dead are accompanied by a radio news broadcast outlining a series of cataclysmic or horrific events: the collapse of a sixteen-storey building in Atlanta with 'sabotage suspected,' the discovery of two sexually mutilated corpses in Gary, the arrest in Dallas of a couple whose baby daughter was found chained in the attic and indications of ongoing violence in the Upper Amazon. The Americas appear to be on the point of collapse as an atmosphere of failure and loss pervades the sun-baked *mise-en-scène* of abandoned houses, desecrated graveyards and road-killed armadillos. As our protagonists move further away from the town, the good country people they have encountered are replaced by a birth-marked and dentally challenged hitchhiker with a penchant for self-mutilation, pyromania and acts of random violence. That his family has 'always been in meat' does not bode well for the future of our group or their nation. America may pride itself on its 'melting pot' credentials but here the pot makes only 'head cheese' – a disgusting concoction that can only be enjoyed 'if you didn't know what's in it.' This will be echoed in the hitchhiker's family home, that site of total cultural and evolutionary degeneration where bones, feathers and teeth are organised in enigmatic quasi-religious, quasi-psychotic formations. Here, in a hugely ironic echo of the creed of necessary violence espoused by the frontier-era cowboy hero of the silver screen, Father exclaims that while he cannot personally take any pleasure in killing 'there are just some things you gotta do; don't mean you gotta like it.' The rural white family has come to this. Grandma is a corpse, Grandpa nearly so, Father 'nothin' but a cook' who sells barbecued people at his roadside store and the sons a grave-robbing inbred and a chainsaw-wielding maniac dressed in the skins of the dead.

In all these deployments of the poor white or backwoodsman it is nonetheless notable that the Vietnam War, wellspring of so much of the decade's dislocation of self-image, is only tangentially present. Lacking a conceptual framework in which to locate the trauma of Vietnam it was not until 1981 that film makers would deploy the sub-genre as explicit commentary on the arrogant folly of America's second Cold War foray into South Asia. Such was Walter Hill's *Southern Comfort*, a film set some eight years earlier in 1973, the year of the Paris ceasefire agreement and the withdrawal of US troops from Vietnam: mid-way between the re-election of Nixon and his resignation. Thus, in critic Jack Sargeant's words, the film was made in the full awareness that

> the soldiers at My Lai were not some legion of the lost; they were the fathers, brothers and sons of ordinary American families. The horror was everywhere; it lay in the ordinary, in the general populace, thinly disguised by the veneer of civilisation.[18]

Thus opening with the M16-wielding soldiers of Bravo Team, a unit of the Louisiana National Guard, streaming out of a truck in full camouflage gear, it is only the matted-on title 'Louisiana 1973' that indicates that the locale is not in fact Vietnam but the Cajun bayou country. This setting is nonetheless used to admirable effect, not merely to evoke the Rousseauesque oneness with the landscape on which the culture of the Cajun hunters rests, but to illustrate how utterly incongruous American soldiers and their firepower are in this strangely alien landscape. The conflation of jungle and bayou in one great primordial swamp is echoed in Ry Cooder's haunting, melancholy score: a mixture of Delta blues, Cajun folk and oriental flute brought to the film by the musical consultants Marc Savoy and Kazu Matsui. As the one-armed Cajun pronounces close to the end of the film and as the Vietnamese had made amply apparent by 1973: 'It's real simple. We live back in here. This is our home. And nobody don't fuck with us.'

Self-evidently and self-reflexively involved in the establishment's 'beating up college kids and tear-gassing niggers' this is where the military tradition of the American South has ended, for as Spencer, one of the two survivors, says to the other, Hardin the Texan: 'Down here in Louisiana, when we don't carry guns, we carry ropes ... We're not too smart but we have a real good time.' That good time is nonetheless short-lived, for as we have seen in *Two Thousand Maniacs* and *The Hills Have Eyes* and will see again in *Wrong Turn*, the hillbilly horror rests upon the metaphor of the path lost or Rubicon crossed. And our protagonists are only one foolish act away from terror. Arrogantly cutting the fishing nets that stand in their way and taking a number of Cajun boats to avoid the tiresome trek around deep water, the team first insult the Cajuns who appear behind them on the shore, outraged at such acts of vandalism and theft, and then Stukey (described consistently as a 'dumb redneck') opens fire on the angry hunters with blanks. Retaliating with live ammunition, the Cajuns shoot Sgt. Poole in the head and in the confusion all three boats overturn. Parallels with the totemic shooting of President Kennedy in Dallas in November 1963 are obvious here. Like the nation itself our troop is without a leader, a directionless and ramshackle mob prepared to assert in frontier-savage mode '[t]here comes a time when you have to abandon principles and do what's right.' But for all the soldiers' assertion of self-evident truths, their acts are irrationally vindictive, Coach emphasising such manly assertions by stripping to the waist, painting a large red Crusader-style cross on his chest and throwing a petrol bomb into an innocent fur-trapper's home. Once more, the allegory of American military atrocities in Vietnam could not be more obvious. And as in Vietnam, the Cajuns fight back. Like the Viet Cong they display an intimate familiarity with their environment that enables them to move silently and invisibly through it, using its resources to pick off the troop in a number of gruesome ways. And in so doing, they assert their claim to ownership of that land and the determination of its fate.

In the light of all this, it is entirely unsurprising that the subgenre of hillbilly horror has experienced a renaissance since the bombing of the World Trade Center and George W. Bush's subsequent 'war on terror' which for all its recent re-branding as a 'struggle against violent extremists' has had major implications for civil liberties within the United States and human rights beyond its borders. Establishing an Office of Homeland Security beyond the scrutiny of Congress and introducing legislation that has had major implications for Americans' legal rights in terms of freedom of association, information and speech, the right to legal representation and to trial by jury, the so-called PATRIOT Act has brought about a radical transformation to the relationship between the American people, their police forces and the US military; one that is itself highly reminiscent of President Nixon's wholesale surveillance of potentially damaging oppositional groups in the name of freedom, though in Nixon's case freedom from the evils of communism. And as in the Nixon period, such developments have been reflected in film culture in general and in the sub-genre of hillbilly horror in particular. For a new generation subject to oppressively normative conceptions of what it means to call oneself a citizen of the United States, hillbilly horror thus offers its audience a means of critically engaging with the nation's territorial ambitions, allowing for an interrogation of the implications of the President's Orientalist demonisation of the terrorist as deviant other and of asking the most shocking of questions: whether, in the age of the propagandistically named PATRIOT Act, the concentration camp that is Guantanamo Bay and the judicially sanctioned form of kidnap and torture that is 'extraordinary rendition,' Americans have the right to speak of liberty at all. For all the President's protests that 'What is at stake is not just America's freedom. This is not just America's fight. This is the fight of all those who believe in progress and pluralism, tolerance and freedom,'[19] it is for hillbilly horror to remind us that repetition of the word 'freedom,' (however reinforced by 'killin' and maimin'') is no substitute for liberty itself. Thus, as the 1970s and the opening years of the new millennium coalesce – as Iraq becomes Bush's Vietnam and a new generation of civil rights campaigners emerge, it is entirely unsurprising that films such as Eli Roth's *Cabin Fever*, Rob Schmidt's *Wrong Turn*, Marcus Nispel's *The Texas Chainsaw Massacre*, Rob Zombie's *House of 1000 Corpses* and *The Devil's Rejects* and Alexandre Aja's remake of Wes Craven's *The Hills Have Eyes* all pay stylistic and conceptual homage to their 1970s predecessors in their exploration of the will to social and cultural heterogeneity demanded by the War on Terror as it was earlier demanded by the Vietnam conflict.[20]

The parallels between the generations is perhaps most clearly seen in Eli Roth's *Cabin Fever*, a highly self-reflexive homage to the horror cinema of the past thirty years, and one that that references amongst others *Night of the Living Dead, Deliverance, The Texas Chainsaw Massacre, Dawn of the Dead, The Hills Have Eyes, Psycho, The Birds* (1963), *The Evil Dead* (1982), *Alien, The Exorcist* (1973), *Cujo* (1983) and *Donnie Darko* (2002). Its most notable influence though is *The Crazies*, that allegory of Nixon's involvement in Vietnam I considered in Chapter 3, a film that itself explored the invidious effects of propaganda on the American psyche and underscored the utter ruthlessness of the American war machine in the pursuit of its politically supremacist ends. As in *The Crazies*, the source of horror is a virulent virus, but in keeping with the nebulous and invisible nature of the current terrorist threat, its origins remain unknown: evoking a sense of paranoid uncertainty amongst those infected that one could argue is not dissimilar to the PATRIOT Act's legitimation of sweeping curtailments of American civil liberties at home. Paranoia would, after all, be a logical response to a political climate in which it is perfectly legal for the government to covertly monitor any religious or political organisation they choose; when those suspected of terrorist involvement may be held without charge, denied lawyers or have their conversations with their lawyers recorded; when the authorities can search and seize personal effects without probable cause and when American citizens may be subsequently jailed without charge or trial. A self-seeking hedonism blind to the political realities of the time would of course be an alternative.

Thus, *Cabin Fever* addresses itself to the misadventures of five spoiled, selfish, rude and morally incompetent young middle-class-student types who celebrate their college graduation by taking a trip to the woods. Bleakly, for a genre that usually has a traumatised survivor or two to tell the tale and in so doing to address the trauma itself, none of them come through – as one by one they are attacked by a flesh-eating virus, an insane dog and local country people unhappy at the unplanned but purposefully concealed murder (*Deliverance*-style) of one of their number by these twenty-first-century city kids, conceptual descendants of the ill-fated Carter family of *The Hills Have Eyes*. As tends to be the case with the best of the recent refashionings of the genre a sense of homage here abounds. The local country store has a blond child sitting on the porch, who rather than play the banjo (as per *Deliverance*), is prone to surreal fits of slow-motion karate. Like Papa Jupe's family of *The Hills Have Eyes,* he also bites. As in *Southern Comfort* there is a plaid-shirt-wearing, pickup-driving vigilante execution squad and a country store-come-gas-station familiar from *Texas Chainsaw Massacre* onwards.

If the dream of the backwoodsman has here degenerated into the Bunyan Mountain Getaway Agency that rents out cabins as temporary refuges from the pressures of the modern world, so too have our protagonists, the brightest and the best of urban youth, degenerated into creatures so entirely vile that when their demise comes it is a welcome relief to the grateful audience. Driven by a series of infantile desires for beer and cigarettes, cannabis and candy they are entirely unprepared to accept moral responsibility for their actions. And whether those actions be sexual infidelity, shoplifting or murder it is clear that people like this will hide behind their ostensibly politically correct credentials with regards to race and gender while unequivocally proclaiming their own class and regional superiority. They claim freedom as a right, yet display no awareness whatsoever as to the responsibilities of liberty. Unsurprising then, that in their self-delusion these ideal specimens of American youth are readily reduced to a mob mentality, setting about an infected local in an entirely uncontrolled and frenzied fashion when faced with the slightest challenge. What is more, as tends to be the way with degenerate urban types in this sub-genre, their relationship to the natural world is deeply compromised. They are squeamish about necessary country practices such as the slaughter of the animals they eat for food but in the case of the particularly despicable Bert at least see nothing wrong with using the family pet as an aid to masturbation! Each seeks individual survival; being more than willing to condemn a sick friend to a lonely death in an isolated fruit cellar some distance from the cabin. Significantly for a post-9/11 film, a sense of spoiled but helpless children getting everything that's coming to them abounds. So, although it was castigated on its release as a rather dull and predictable work of self-important and derivative horror, *Cabin Fever* can also be viewed as an extremely forceful indictment of the ignorance and complacency of a generation that has managed to graduate college without learning a single thing about the world, their country or themselves. Such individuals are far removed from the countercultural activists of the 1970s who in the name of freedom campaigned against their government's actions at home and abroad and in so doing brought their own dreams of liberty to life. In the present world it is no surprise that the Deputy that our victims implore to protect them is too busy partying to serve. It is entirely apposite that the film closes with the infected 'Down Home Spring Water' moving out into the wider American world; this being a nation requiring no external threat to bring about its destruction. In its greed and personal ambition, in its isolated and self-obsessed subjectivity, it is quite capable of destroying itself.[21]

Such a sense is equally apparent in the Canadian production *Wrong Turn* – a text that mimics the generic and stylistic traits of the 1970s United States backwoods so convincingly that it forges an exceptionally pointed critique of the American present from beyond the nation's northern border. Set in 'Greenbriar Backcountry, West Virginia' a spot some 'fifty miles from anybody,' *Wrong Turn* is an unashamedly derivative piece of cashing-in on the genre's profitability with youth markets. It is in this, however, that its mode of engagement with both the history of the genre and its own historic moment becomes clear. In a title sequence highly reminiscent of

David Fincher's *Se7en* (1995) we are thus showered with images that evoke the barely repressed horror of the abject hillbilly on which this sub-genre rests. Apparently since the 1950s the enduring legend of 'the mountain man' has been kept alive in the region by a series of disappearances – of hikers, rafters and locals. A macabre *mise-en-scène* of log cabins, horribly disfigured heads, faces, mouths and hands ensues, with knives, blood, female corpses (undressed by malformed fingers) and newspaper headlines outlining the names of the missing. Via stills and written texts moreover all this is linked to 'deformity by inbreeding' and 'inbred related psychosis.' As the microscope shots of boiling and bubbling cells, themselves rather reminiscent of the AIDS anxieties of films such as Frances Ford Coppola's *Dracula* (1992) indicate, something has gone horribly wrong here. At a cellular level there has been a 'genetic mutation' of the pioneering ideal, resulting not only in hunch-backed physical deformity and 'resistance to pain' but in acts of savage and inhuman cruelty perpetrated by these monsters against those 'civilised' American citizens who silently acquiesce to their own oppression.

In its formulaic predictability, and its utterly stereotypical dehumanising of the backwoodsman as inbred and savage mutant, *Wrong Turn* is not only a highly inter-textual work but a knowing illustration as to how the monstrous other may be deployed to serve dominant ideologies of class and nationhood. As such, we have the obligatory gas station scene, complete with slack-jawed local in plaid shirt and undershirt ominously replying to our yuppie hero's clichéd farewell: 'You're the one goin' a need "take care."' We have the obligatory collection of teenage couples sure to meet a sticky end. There is the quickly despatched Evan and Francine whose indulgence in pot-smoking and pre-marital sex and unequivocal assertion that 'nature sucks' spell an early death for both. There is Scott and Carly – he knowingly ironic about their situation and referring to 'a little movie called *Deliverance*,' she a fashionably skinny girl entirely devoid of personality, intelligence or wit. And there is the feisty singleton Jesse whose name alone, in *Easy Rider* style, signals continuity with the Western outlaw tradition, her inventive survival skills underscoring the improvisatory intelligence of her pioneering progenitors.[22] Lastly there is Chris, the identikit heterosexual hero and love interest.

Standard plot devices abound too. The metaphor of the wrong road taken, most potently seen in *Southern Comfort,* gives the film its title. What is more, the film purposefully evokes the historian Frederick Jackson Turner's belief that it was the coming of the road to the wilderness that guaranteed the fulfilment of the United States' manifest destiny to tame the continent first and then redeem the world. But whereas, for Turner, the 1890 closure of the frontier had signified the fulfilment of that destiny, *Wrong Turn* dwells upon the horrors that are still to be found in the United States if one strays too far from the path. For in the extant wilderness of the American imagination, one is still likely to encounter characters like the band of backwoods brothers who slaughter their way through the film. These of course are degenerate and slavering brutes – less a testament to the nobility of the frontier spirit that is now encapsulated in our final boy and girl Chris and Jesse than to the necessity of civilisation's triumph over the largely hidden forces of savagery. As the obnoxious ironist Scott puts it, in a line that clearly references the rhetoric surrounding Operation Enduring Freedom: 'I read in *Newsweek* that economically depressed places are like breeding grounds for all kinds of apocalyptic visionaries: the Order of the Solar Temple, Jim Jones, the Jijong family.' And, of course, Al Qaeda. The ongoing comparison of the backwoods mutants and Al Qaeda reaches its climax as our surviving three are followed to the forester's tower where they have sought a radio to summon help. Aware that the tower is on fire, our hero Chris proclaims 'I'd rather jump than burn to death,' bringing out into the open one of the great unspoken and media-suppressed images of the 9/11 tragedy – the horror of those who chose to jump from the towers rather than be consumed by the flames. The backwoods South in all its gun firing, bow and arrow shooting, torch-carrying and law-defying frenzy thus becomes symbolic analogue for the faceless and savage threat of Islamic anti-Americanism as the media suppressed and psychologically repressed horror of the fallen dead returns once more to haunt us. But unlike *Cabin Fever*, this film has its two survivors: those who reject the spoiled and selfish individualism of their murdered teenage companions and look to cooperative bloodshed to survive. That is not to say that the forces of evil are easily despatched here. We are left in little doubt (and here it is significant that the film is a Canadian production) that urban, 'civilised' America is a degenerate superpower on the cusp of crepuscular collapse. The mutant backwoodsman, the terrorist threat, remains alive and impervious to whatever conventional weapons are used against him. In the final frames of the film, as we will see again in the remade *Texas Chainsaw Massacre,* the South is on the rise once more. New ways of engaging with the forces of savagery must be found.

Like *Cabin Fever* and *Wrong Turn,* Marcus Nispel's remake of *The Texas Chainsaw Massacre* is also stylistically and conceptually engaged with its 1970s progenitors. It nonetheless manages to bring a range of contemporary concerns to the proceedings. Replacing the original Hardesty siblings and their friends with five new victims and framing the film with hand-held monochrome footage of the catastrophic police search of what is now termed the Hewitt house, the action is dated to 18 August 1973, contemporaneous with that of *Southern Comfort* and hence the nation's defeat in the Vietnam War. The 1970s are thus carefully evoked in the material possessions and cultural attitudes of the teenagers: their campervan and clothing, 'pot-smoking' and sexual promiscuity. But the last girl conventions of subsequent slasher films are also visible here. Thus Erin refuses to drink tequila in Mexico, is genuinely outraged that her long-term boyfriend has smuggled two pounds of 'pot' into the country and desires nothing more out of life than an engagement ring. She also displays extraordinary courage, loyalty and inventiveness in protecting her friends throughout. In this, she is not dissimilar to the tightly-knit Hewitts themselves, a genuinely frightening clan of inbred deviants with very bad teeth, adamant 'there's nothin' wrong with us' despite their predilections for normally repressed desires and social practices. And what deviance there is! The facially deformed child Jedidiah who lures unsuspecting travellers into the family's clutches and enjoys playing with the bodies of the dead; the legless grandfather whose toothless unshaven face is always shot in close-up; the clearly unhinged grandmother who condones slaughter but takes exception to the use of profane language; the necrophiliac son and lawman Sheriff Hoyt who enjoys nothing more than to 'grab me a feel' of a freshly dead girl while proclaiming his mission to 'protect and serve;' then there is the large-headed androgynous cousin with childlike voice and a maniac's eyes and her enormously obese and chair-bound trailer-dwelling mother. Finally, of course, there is Leatherface, who is still banging his victims on the head, removing and wearing their faces and collecting their organs in jars. But unlike Hooper's original he is here depicted, at least by his family, as a victim of the 'cruelty and ridicule' heaped upon him because of a skin-complaint that began in childhood. Thus while he retains his penchant for impaling individuals (this time male) on meat hooks[23] and running about in the dark with his chainsaw on full throttle, his predilection for wearing the faces of the dead is presented as a perversely justifiable desire to emulate those who have rejected him in childhood. The stolen face is thus a kind of neurotic mask behind which Leatherface hides, as assuredly as our own unspeakable psycho-sexual desires may be hidden behind a mask of social conformity; as sure as the unseen and faceless terrorist threat is said to invisibly pervade the paranoid nation that is America post-9/11. And as the film's framing device makes clear, and as was the case in *Cabin Fever* and *Wrong Turn*, he remains at large. For he can never be 'brought to justice' by a system he refuses to recognise. You can no more conquer that which is named 'the backwoods' than you can wage war on the abstract noun that is 'terror.'

The impossibility of closure is similarly foregrounded in Alexandre Aja's remake of Wes Craven's *The Hills Have Eyes* which insistently explores the United States' culpability in the perpetration of the crimes that have now led to its currently traumatised status. Here the ill-fated Carter family wander once more into the New Mexico desert, but this time the metaphor of genetic mutation as a product of radioactive fallout is more insistently foregrounded as a means of exploring questions of territorial ambition, essentialised formulations of national identity, the nature and culture of the family and the manipulability of American popular opinion by the nation's political leaders. Produced by a non-American team, though from Wes Craven's original script, the remake adds a significant new location to the original landscape of sun-bleached rocks and barren desert. It is a 1950s nuclear test village, now inhabited by descendants of the desert's original inhabitants who escaped eviction from their land by taking to the mines and later returned, horribly mutated, to inhabit the extant Eisenhower-era village. The juxtaposition of Norman Rockwell-style homes and grotesquely disfigured cannibalistic serial killers is 'bizarre and powerful' here as Wes Craven comments in his DVD commentary to the film. Built in the age when 'everyone was white' and 'the American nuclear family [and] two cars in the garage' exemplified national ambitions, such villages were 'part of a different world [when] everyone thought that America was just a great place.' Before Vietnam, before Watergate and before the failure of Civil Rights called into question the foundational mythology of the nation, this 'was the last moment of innocence in American history' for Craven. But such innocence, the film makes clear, was lost not by the enemy but by the United States government's own actions, specifically the desecration of the land and its people. 'We went into the mines,' says the aptly named grotesque Big Brain from his wheelchair, 'You set off your bombs and turned everything to ashes. You made us what we became.' Thus consistently deploying the wide-angle lenses and extreme distance shots of the Western, its warm ochre pallet and Ennio Morriccone-style score, the film calls into question the very innocence on which essential formulations of freedom, American-style, rest. The nation has been brought to this pass by a fetishisation of military might, a disregard for life and an inability to spot the difference between political rhetoric and existential liberty. 'They'll take away my gun when they pull it from my cold dead fingers' says a bumper sticker on a long-abandoned 1950s car. The current danger, as the country and western theme tune that plays over the opening montage of nuclear explosion and genetic freaks indicates, is that 'More and more [Americans are] forgetting the past.' For in so doing, they condemn themselves to repeat it. It is for the hillbilly axeman, both bad guy and victim, to remind the United States of this uncomfortable truth.

From the very outset, the figure of the backwoodsman has occupied a problematic position at the heart of America's formulation and dissemination of idealised and exeptionalist models of its own national identity. On the one hand, (visible in tales of Kit Carson, Davy Crockett and Daniel Boone) was a wholesale cultural valorisation of the backwoodsman of the republican dream: the 'real

American' of pithy sayings, medicinal, astronomical and meteoro-
logical knowledge whose uncomplicated integrity was guaranteed
by the purifying forces of nature itself, that being a realm entirely
antithetical to the cunning political machinations of the civilised
urban world. On the other hand (clearly visible in the immediate
post-Revolutionary War texts of William Byrd and Hector de
Crèvecoeur and in the post-Civil War writings of local colourists
like Joel Chandler Harris) we can see an innate distrust of those that
occupied the hinterland of fugitives and outlaws that made up the
backwoods of American nightmare. For like the cowboy hero and
his successor the serial killer, the backwoodsman amply illustrates
the limits placed on liberty by an increasingly organised and urbanised
society.[24] But unlike the cowboy or the serial killer who, as we have
seen, are frequently reappropriated by mass culture to serve dominant ideologies of nationhood, the hillbilly is less suited to cultural
assimilation: being tied firmly to a sense of place and an extended
kinship structure, a distinct cultural milieu with its own sense of
history, tradition and class. Being less an individual than a member
of an entire social group that challenges the totalising claims for
national identity embodied in the Declaration of Independence and
other foundational texts, he is a dangerous figure indeed.[25] Thus the
sub-genre that is hillbilly horror comes to encapsulate all the archaic
disorder, medieval darkness, anti-classical savagery and pantheistic
paganism of the American other and the terrorist threat alike while
making amply apparent the simultaneously repressive and oppressive qualities of everyday civilised life.

Notes

1 Hector St John de Crèvecoeur, *Letters From an American Farmer* (1782.
    London: Penguin, 1982).
2 Crèvecoeur, *Letters,* p. 72.
3 Crèvecoeur, *Letters,* p. 77.
4 Quoted in James R. Masterson, 'William Byrd in Lubberland,' *Ameri-
    can Literature.* 9:2 (May 1937), 167.
5 Dominick LaCapra, *Writing History, Writing Trauma,* p. 187.
6 This is not, however, to argue that all depictions of rural life and com-
    munities were necessarily negative, for at times it became necessary to

deploy the image of the hillbilly in service of America's dominant myths. As the Great Depression dispossessed one-third of America's farming families of their land and forced many into the role of internal refugees, for example, John Ford's 1939 film *The Grapes of Wrath* (from John Steinbeck's novel of the same year) not only established the iconicity of the truck piled high with familial effects and elderly relatives that would subsequently appear everywhere from *The Beverley Hillbillies* (1962–71) to *Deliverance* but deployed the star status of the unthreatening good guy Henry Fonda to affirm the validity of the New Deal, rejecting in the process any less American (i.e. communistic) solutions. As the mass migration of some three million Appalachian people to the mid-Atlantic and mid-Western cities of the 1950s threatened to undermine Cold War pretensions to cultural homogeneity and national stability, moreover, television stepped into the breach: with programmes like *The Real McCoys* (1957) Americanising the Appalachian in its tale of West Virginia farmers seeking a new life in California. It was a strategy echoed throughout the 1960s, as the subject of Appalachian poverty or 'the plight of the hill people' became not only a campaign issue for the young John F. Kennedy in the West Virginia primaries but was the subject of a 1962 CBS television special *Christmas in Appalachia* illustrating the failure of Kennedy's New Deal-style Area Development Administration. As if to counter such a deeply subversive impression, American mass culture kicked into action. *The Andy Griffith Show*, based on Griffith's own home town of Mount Airy in North Carolina running from 1960–68 and eclipsed only in popularity by *The Beverley Hillbillies*. This tale of a Jed Clampett, an Ozark farmer whose oil-rich land is bought for $25,000,000 enabling him to subsequently relocate his entire family to Beverley Hills not only underscored pre-existing regional, class and ethnic stereotypes, but re-fashioned them in the context of both Cold War and Vietnam era reaffirmations of a unified national identity. A form of local colour television for the Cold War generation, *The Beverley Hillbillies* was massively commercially successful, going to the top of the ratings within three weeks of its first airing by CBS on 26 September 1962. Here it stayed, the December 1962 episode pulling in a massive 33 million viewers. Only in 1971, in its last season, did it drop from the top twenty, even in 2006 being watched by an estimated 60 million people a week through syndication. For figures see: www.tvparty.com/recbev.html. Accessed 2 November 2006.

7   Its release, moreover, coincided with the beginning of CBS's long-running Depression Era narrative of good country people, *The Waltons*

(1972–81).

8   In the novel, the tune played is the romantic duet 'Wildwood Flower.' Here it is a version of the more recent bluegrass number 'Fighting Banjos.'

9   The image of the pig is, of course, hugely resonant in the culture of the South. Initially brought to the New World by early settlers who, to the disgust of more civilised farmers such as William Byrd, grazed them in the forests or on the open range where many slipped into a wild or feral state akin to that of their despised owners. For the Southern farmer, though, the pig became not only a mainstay in the regional diet but a core component in the rituals of agricultural life, with the hog-killing season being a time in which Southern men enacted their triumph over nature through the public slaughter of hogs. See S. Jonathan Bass, 'How 'Bout a Hand for the Hog: The Enduring Nature of the Swine as a Cultural Symbol in the South,' *Southern Cultures*, 1:3 (Spring 1995), 301.

10 Carol J. Clover, *Men, Women and Chainsaws: Gender in the Modern Horror Film* (London: Bfi, 1992), p. 132.

11 See James T. Patterson, *Restless Giant: The United States from Watergate to Bush vs Gore* (New York: Oxford University Press, 2005).

12 Tom Wolfe, 'The Me Decade and the Third Great Awakening,' in Wolfe, *Mauve Gloves and Madmen, Clutter and Vine* (New York: Farrar, Straus and Giroux, 1976).

13 Shown over eight consecutive nights, *Roots* had received the biggest ever television audience in the history of the medium (outstripping even *The Beverley Hillbillies*) as some eight million people (over half the television sets in the United States) tuned in.

14 In Chapter 4 of *Shocking Representation,* 'Only a Movie: Specters of Vietnam in Wes Craven's *Last House on the Left*' Adam Lowenstein produces an engaging and relevant discussion of the film in the light of contemporary traumatic events.

15 Taking the name of the current president, the first to be elected from the Deep South since the Civil War *and* the legendary folk-singing family.

16 Lew Brighton, 'Saturn in retrograde; or the Texas jump cut,' *The Film Journal,* 7 (1975), 27.

17 The film was banned in France until 1982, in Finland until 1996 and Norway in 1997. In the UK it was shown only in London cinemas, its 1980 video was rapidly withdrawn for almost twenty years. Not until 1998 was the uncut version shown in nationally in UK cinemas. Clips from the film nonetheless found a home in a range of horror tributes,

from comedy horrors like John Waters' *Serial Mom* (1994) to *American Psycho* (2000).

18 Jack Sargeant, 'American Nightmare. The Baying of Pigs: Reflections on the New American Horror Movie,' *Senses Of Cinema* (July 2001), p. 3, www.sensesofcinema.com/contents/festivals/01/15/biff_nightmare.html. Accessed 2 November 2006.

19 George W. Bush, 'Address to a Joint Session of Congress and the American people,' 20 September 2001. www.whitehouse.gov/news/releases/2001/09/20010920–8.html. Accessed 2 November 2006.

20 The same can also be said of films that reached considerably smaller audiences: *The Undertow* (2003) depicts the discovery of a small rural town's guilty secret in the form of 'the boy' – a mutant giant who stalks them through the woods before killing them off in a variety of predictably graphic ways. *The Ruining*, re-edited and released in 2003 (though written and partly shot a decade earlier) sees two couples going to the California backwoods where they discover a remote community poisoned by the government thirty years ago and now dead, insane or degenerated into dog-like mutants. *Shallow Ground* (2005) winner of Edinburgh's Dead By Dawn film festival's Best Feature prize brings a great deal of gallows humour to the proceedings as the staff of a soon-to-close sheriff's station are confronted with a blood-soaked and naked teenager who emerges from the woods. The considerably less inventive *The Attendant* (2004) is also set in the present day but wears its 1970s credentials fairly heavily, the opening titles evoking those of *The Texas Chainsaw Massacre* with its tale of 'six campers who planned to spend a relaxing weekend in those mountains [but] had no idea of the horrible fate that awaited them.' The supernatural infusion of the genre is similarly clear in *The Fanglys* (2004) which amply illustrates just how truly unpleasant camping can be if one is accosted by the soul-gobbling matriarch of a family of cannibalistic hillbillies!

21 Like Eli Roth's *Cabin Fever*, Rob Zombie's *House of 1000 Corpses* and *The Devil's Rejects* self-consciously reference their 1970s progenitors throughout. Set in 1977, each film centres upon the Firefly family, a clan of sadistic, sexually deviant, serial-killing rednecks including Mother Firefly, a grotesque elderly stripper, Baby Firefly her nymphomaniac shorts-and-Stetson wearing daughter, Otis Driftwood her insane Mansonesque son, Rufus Jr., a hideously burned bearskin-wearing monster, the ironically named Tiny and the terrifying Captain Spalding, museum proprietor and mass murderer in full clown make up. Drawing heavily on both *The Hills Have Eyes* and *The Texas Chainsaw Massacre* for character types, *mise-en-scène* and plot these films are

nonetheless visually inventive, interpolating surreal montages and in-
versions of the colour spectrum along the way as a means of disorien-
tating the viewer while intensifying the carnivalesque excesses of the
American tall tale tradition.

22 An analogy made all the more potent in that she is played by Eliza
Dushku, who played Faith the 'bad girl' vampire slayer in Joss Whedon's
Mutant Enemy seven-season production *Buffy the Vampire Slayer*
(1997–2003) and its spin off, the five-season *Angel* (1999–2004).

23 The brutal impalement of a female victim in the original film, a scene
censored in Sweden until 2001, provoked considerable critical comment with regards to the slasher genre's purported misogyny, male
victims being despatched in far cleaner, quicker ways and less linger-
ingly shot. The inverse is true of the remake.

24 The rural population may have doubled between the end of the Civil
War and the beginning of the First World War, but the urban population multiplied sevenfold, so that by 1914 only one-third of the American population was involved in agriculture. See Arthur M. Schlesinger
and Dixon Ryan Fox, *A History of American Life. Volume 10: The Rise
of the City 1878–1898* (New York: Macmillan, 1933), p. 57.

25 And, as such, he was repeatedly the victim of sociological, literary and
pseudo-scientific calumny Thus it was that by 1891, in a climate of
Social Darwinism, that pseudo-evolutionary justification of laissez-
faire capitalism promulgated by Herbert Spencer and others, an in-
vestigator from the Department of Labor could credibly claim that
'the mind of the poor white is feral, fatalistic, bordering on bitterness,
unable to improve, and unwilling to relent.' Sylvia Jenkins Cook, *From
Tobacco Road to Route 66: The Southern Poor White in Fiction* (Chapel
Hill, NC: University of North Carolina Press, 1976), p. 4. Into the
twentieth century, moreover, the Eugenics Records Office would con-
duct some fifteen 'Eugenic Family Studies' between 1880 and 1920,
setting out to expose the genetic defects of the poor white caused, it
was argued, by miscegenation, incest and alcoholism. In literature such
a perspective would be echoed in William Faulkner's picture of the
rural South and in Ellen Glasgow's Southern Gothic School of writing. It was a form of cultural validation of class-based regional stereotypes which would not only enable popular writers like H.L. Mencken
to foreground for a mass audience a misogynistic, ignorant and brutal
vision of much poor white southern society in his coverage of the
Scopes Monkey Trial in Dayton, Tennessee, but would loan credibil-
ity to influential academic works like W.J. Cash's *The Mind of the
South* (1941). Clearly by the mid-twentieth century, binaristic

conceptions of the distinction between urban progress and rural regression, good country people and the savagery of poor white communities traceable to the eighteenth century had solidified into a lexicon of essentialising prejudice most commonly applied by whites to blacks. And if, during the eighteenth century, the binarism had functioned as a vindication of the continued existence of social hegemonies, class distinctions and slavery within this ostensibly egalitarian nation, then it continued to operate in the interests of dominant interest groups here.

PART IV

New Labour new horrors:
the post-Thatcherite crisis of
British masculinity

Introduction

In the United Kingdom the 1980s were characterised by the avaricious individualism of the Thatcherite agenda, which dismantled the industrial economy on which the nation's class-based and regionally-distinctive culture had historically rested, promoted narcissistic consumerism as acme of human aspiration through wholesale valorisation of the cultural products of American capitalism and turned to military action in the Falklands and the Gulf as a means of ensuring electoral victory and cementing the much-vaunted 'special relationship' with the United States. As Jeffrey Richards has put it, the zeitgeist of the Thatcher years was that of 'aggressive and uncompromising individualism which glories in combat and which rejects consensus and concern as wet and wimpish,' this being of course a world view that created not national cohesion but promoted a vision of British society as 'a mass of struggling individuals each out for what they could get.'[1] With the fall of the Berlin Wall in 1989 and the collapse of the Soviet Union two years later the victory of Conservative ideology seemed assured and a sense of right-wing triumphalism saturated British social life: from the Porsche-driving yuppies of the deregulated City of London Stock Exchange to an increasingly rootless working class aspiring to participation in Britain's new property-owning, share-owning democracy even as nationalised industry and the welfare state were dismantled around their ears. Film culture was not slow to respond to such a perilous state of affairs – numerous films, (many of which were made with the financial support of Channel 4's Film Four label) despairing at the depths of social injustice, intolerance and hatred to which the nation had unashamedly descended.[2]

But even as the liberal left railed against the horrors of the present age in ways broadly in keeping with Britain's history of cinematic realism, new developments in video technology were introducing a mass audience to a range of innovative cultural products that would come to alter the ways in which filmic narratives were conceived of, structured and shot. Launched in 1981, the music channel MTV bombarded viewers with a plethora of highly disposable and commercially driven mini-narratives in the form of music videos. From Duran Duran's *Rio* (1982) to Wham's *Club Tropicana* (1983) to Spandau Ballet's politically unequivocal capitalist anthem *Gold* (1983) these gloried in the libertarian avarice of the present. Breaking down traditional generic distinctions between music, television and film, they conflated their own glamorous fictionality and the greedy, self-seeking intolerance of the real world into a single simulacral realm of fun and sunshine, glamour and glittering economic rewards. Thus setting out to 'plunder the image bank and the word-hoard for the material of parody, pastiche and in extreme cases, plagiarism,'[3] the 1980s music video encapsulated that ideologically saturated flattening of history visible across contemporary visual and political culture. Highly popular in the UK, for example, was that genre of US comedy-romance that deployed the pre-Vietnam, pre-Civil Rights 1950s or early 1960s as a decidedly Edenic backdrop while conveniently omitting the terrors of its Cold War, McCarthyite actuality.[4] Thus, even as British directors struggled to deploy the past as a means of social critique of the present, mass audiences thrilled to imported television dramas, such as the soap *Dynasty* (1981–89) the cop drama *Miami Vice* (1984–89) and the gumshoe romance *Moonlighting* (1985–89).[5] Each self-consciously foregrounded the surface, the look and the style of consumer fetish objects while blurring the boundaries between film, television and music video. Enthusiastically consuming such imports while displaying a decidedly equivocal response to the politics of contemporary British cinematic realism, the public appeared to concur with Thatcher's outlandish assertion that it was no longer possible to speak of 'society' at all: only of 'individuals and their families.'[6] As real-life and its representations collapsed into a single simulacral realm, it became possible to claim that despite the deaths of some 40,000 soldiers and 113,000 civilians,[7] 'the Gulf War did not take place.'[8]

By the 1990s though, it had become apparent that the legacy of the Thatcher years had been to make the rich richer and the poor poorer by destroying the nation's industrial base and promoting a culture of self-seeking social irresponsibility that valued hyper-masculine characteristics such as aggressively individualistic ambition over all others.[9] It was equally apparent that any political party that sought to overturn eighteen years of Conservative rule must engage not only with mass popular culture's polyphonic and multi-genred celebration of the signifier, but with the crisis in masculine identity that was all too visible within that culture; caused in part by the economically-driven dispersion of patriarchal authority across social and commercial institutions, in part by the dissipation of male status engendered by the wholesale dismantling of British industry and in part by the cultural consolidation of earlier equal rights legislation such as the 1970s Equal Pay Act and the Sex Discrimination Act of 1975.

On 1 May 1997, a party purporting to address such issues swept to power, Tony Blair's New Labour winning a record number of seats, a record majority and a record swing in votes and so ending a run of four successive electoral defeats for Labour.[10] Or so it seemed. From the outset New Labour was itself a hybrid entity; its 'third way' professing to synthesise economic growth with a concern for social justice while repudiating any Old Labour-style attempts to actually redistribute wealth.

Similarly hybridised was New Labour's conception of gender identity, Blair being keen to embody in his public persona those 'dominant constructions of masculinity' that under Thatcher had 'dictated that assertiveness, toughness, decisiveness and, when necessary, the capacity for violence' lay 'at the core of what it is to be a man.'[11] He was nonetheless keen to temper such qualities by presenting himself as a nurturing family man, working in tandem with his professionally successful wife to raise their children in keeping with Labour's own history of social justice for all.[12] Responding to the challenges that feminism and gay liberation had made to both the hyper-masculine ethos of the warrior ideal of Britain's imperial past *and* the ways that 'patriarchal structures of authority, domination and control' were currently 'diffused throughout social,

economic, political and ideological activities,'[13] Blair set out to promote a political culture that was simultaneously tough *and* caring,
proactive *and* stable, decisive *and* nurturing. While heading a government that boasted record numbers of female MPs (deemed 'Blair's
babes' by the tabloid press), the new Prime Minister thus sought to
retain a 'traditional left concern for equity and social cohesion' while
insisting on the proactive virility of the neo-liberal emphasis he placed
'on economic efficiency and dynamism.'[14] In a world in which the
British man's traditional role as familial provider has been dispersed
both by the destruction of the nation's industrial base and by increasing numbers of working wives and mothers, themselves demanding equal rights in civil society and the workplace, New Labour set
out to appeal to a post-patriarchal demographic. And the complex-
ity of its mission can be seen in the British horror film of the period;
specifically as its will to generic hybridity evokes a pronounced sense
of a crisis in available models of British masculinity – themselves
called into question by the traumatic social changes wrought to
Britain's industrial base and cultural practices by the Thatcher years.

   Chapter 6 of this study addresses itself to these concerns with
specific reference to an extraordinary proliferation of what Noël
Carroll would term 'fusion monsters': which our questing heroes
must invariably overcome in order to forge for themselves a mode of
masculinity fitted to their time and place. Such monsters include
the zombies of *Shaun of the Dead* the werewolves of *Dog Soldiers*, the
vampiric serial killer of *Cradle of Fear* (2000), the Arab fire spirit of
Long Time Dead (2001), the dragons of *Reign of Fire*, the murderously infected citizenry of *28 Days Later* and the invisible malevo-
lence of *Deathwatch* and *The Bunker*. In each of these highly
self-reflexive films a new kind of 'fusion hero' can also be seen to
emerge: one who undertakes a hybidisation of earlier models of British masculinity in his mission to conquer the monster and become a
man. Thus, in new millennial British horror we can see not only a
tendency to parody and pastiche earlier horror texts but a will to
explore earlier models of British masculinity – specifically those
drawn from Britain's imperial past.

   There are, in short, a lot of warrior figures in British horror of
the new millennium, their struggle with their own particular demons

bespeaking the trauma wrought to long-established modes of masculine selfhood by the socio-economic and cultural changes that over the past thirty years have challenged traditional gender hegemonies to the clear advantage of women. As such, attitudes to women are highly significant in each of these films. Some, such as *Deathwatch* and *The Bunker*, entirely exclude women from the narrative, centring the action on traditional spheres of masculine endeavour such as war. Others, such as *Creep* (2005) and *Cradle of Fear*, are overweeningly misogynistic, women being subject to brutal and graphically depicted sexual punishment for their perceived transgression of patriarchal norms. Others, such as *The Descent*, go so far as to dwell at length on the utterly monstrous destructive potential of the feminine abject. But this is not to argue that new millennial British horror is entirely dominated by a traumatised will to punish women. In films such as *28 Days Later* and *Reign of Fire* and to a lesser extent *Shaun of the Dead* we can in fact see a new form of adult masculinity emerging – one that rejects gender essentialism in favour of a hybridised New Labour-style selfhood. Thus a new form of masculine identity can be seen to emerge from the ruins: one that is simultaneously hard-hitting and gentle, innovative and steady, decisive and compassionate. Thus, as Chapter 6 will argue, British horror of the new millennium not only points to the traumatised nature of contemporary British male self-image but to the ways in which it is possible to work through the horror and, in so doing, become a new kind of man.

Notes

1 Jeffrey Richards, *Films and British National Identity From Dickens to Dad's Army* (Manchester: Manchester University Press, 1997), pp. 23–4.
2 Including Lindsay Anderson's *Britannia Hospital* (1982), Stephen Frears' *My Beautiful Laundrette* (1985) and *Sammy and Rosie Get Laid* (1987) and Derek Jarman's *The Last of England* (1987).
3 Peter Wollen, 'Ways of Thinking about Music Video (and Postmodernism),' *Critical Quarterly*, 28:1–2, (Spring–Summer 1986), 169.
4 Such films would include John Sayles's *Baby It's You* (1983), Laurence Kasdan's *The Big Chill* (1983), Gerry Marshall's *The Flamingo Kid*

(1984), Robert Zemekis's *Back to the Future* (1985) and Francis Ford Coppola's *Peggy Sue Got Married* (1986), Emile Ardolino's *Dirty Dancing* (1987) and Richard Benjamin's *Mermaids* (1990).

5   Such a return to the past was also visible in British films of the period, but here a more political agenda appeared to be at work: James Ivory's *Maurice* (1987) and David Lean's *A Passage to India* (1984) indicting the homophobia and racism of the British imperial past while a range of realist dramas resurrected real-life characters from that past to illustrate how their cultural construction as villains was an ideologically expedient justification for contemporary racist, sexist and classist attitudes. These included an exploration of failure of the criminal justice system in the execution of David Bently in 1952 in Peter Medak's *Let Him Have It* (1991) and Ruth Ellis in Mike Newell's *Dance With a Stranger* (1984) and a plea for the humanity of the demonised gangster in Tom Clegg's *McVicar* (1980) and Peter Medak's *The Krays* (1990).

6   Thatcher, Margaret, *Woman's Own* (31 October 1987), pp. 8–10. See The Margaret Thatcher Foundation. www.margareththatcher.org/speeches/displaydocument.asp?docid=106689. Accessed 28 April 2006.

7   Edmund L. Andrews, 'Census Bureau to Dismiss Analyst who Estimated Iraqi Casualties,' *New York Times* (7 March 1992), p. 7.

8   Jean Baudrillard, *The Gulf War Did Not Take Place,* trans. Paul Patton (Bloomington and Indianapolis, IN: Indiana University Press, 1995).

9   Yvette Walcsak, *He and She: Men in the Eighties* (London and New York: Routledge, 1988).

10 Steve Ludlum, 'The Making of New Labour,' in Steve Ludlum and Martin J. Smith (eds), *New Labour in Government* (Basingstoke and New York: Palgrave, 2001), pp. 1–31.

11 Suzanne E. Hatty, *Masculinities, Violence and Culture.* Sage Series on Violence against Women (Thousand Oaks, CA: Sage, 2000), p. 173.

12 It was the Labour Party that had been responsible for the introduction of the Welfare State, including the foundation of the National Health Service (1945–51), the introduction of Comprehensive education (1964–70), the State Earnings Related Pension and universal Child Benefit (1974–79) and the decriminalisation of abortion and homosexuality (1967).

13 Michael Kaufman, 'The Construction of Masculinity and the Triad of Men's Violence,' in Michael S. Kimmel and Michael A. Messner (eds), *Men's Lives* (Boston: Allyn and Bacon, 1995), p. 15.

14 S. White, 'Interpreting the Third Way: Not One Road, but Many,' *Renewal,* 6:2, (1998) 17.

6

Zombies, dog men and dragons: generic hybridity and gender crisis in British horror of the new millennium

> Horror thrives best when emotions are bottled up and nobody bottles them up quite like us.[1]

For over twenty years British horror cinema has been characterised by a will to generic hybridity, as earlier film texts and genres are endlessly worked and re-worked as a means of exploring the traumatic legacy that Thatcherite machismo bequeathed to those who grew either to hyper-masculine empowerment or economic and political emasculation in its shadow. Standing at the junction between cultural policy and mass-cultural articulation of the traumas wrought to models of manhood by the Thatcher years, the horror film was recognised from the early 1980s onwards as proffering a dangerous challenge to establishment ideology; leading initially to the Video Nasty controversy that raged across the British media in the early 1980s and thence to the infamous Video Recordings Act of 1985. Seeking to 'protect' British video audiences from a swathe of predominantly American and Italian horror imports that were said to threaten the moral fabric of the nation, this piece of legislation effectively ended Britain's 250-year history of government non-interference in censorship issues. It led to between sixty and seventy-five horror videos including *The Texas Chainsaw Massacre* and *The Evil Dead* being banned and provided retrospective justification for those thousands of videos that had already been confiscated by police raids authorised by the Director of Public Prosecutions.[2] That some 96 per cent of films banned were foreign-made merely confirmed the fact that since 1983's repeal of the British Cinematograph Act (1927) fewer films had been made in the United Kingdom than at any time since the 1920s. Most significantly, those that did reach production tended to be derivative pastiches of earlier American successes. Hence, *Dust Devil* (1992) was described by its director Richard Stanley as '*A Dry White Season* meets *El Topo* and *The Texas Chainsaw Massacre*;'[3] *Split Second* (1991), said Laura Gregory of Challenge Films, was 'a British *Terminator 2* at a tenth of its budget;'[4] while producer Paul Brooks of Metronome Films characterised *Beyond Bedlam* (1994) as 'falling somewhere between *The Silence of the Lambs* and *Flatliners*;'[5] *Proteus* (1995) as '*Alien* meets *The Thing*'[6] and *Darklands* (1996) as 'a cross between *Rosemary's Baby* and *The Wicker Man*.'[7] By the 1990s, it seems, the British horror film was little more than a self-reflexive exercise in pastiche; most often of earlier American texts and their attendant ideologies.

Having been legislatively recognised as potentially offering a potent challenge to the prescriptively normative and intrinsically hegemonic formulation of British social and cultural life propounded first by the Conservative policies and then consolidated by those of New Labour, horror cinema of the new millennium was thus ideally positioned to articulate the trauma wrought to individuals, families, communities and the nation as a whole by the socio-cultural and economic changes of the previous thirty years. Unsurprisingly, the site of trauma on which these New Labour horrors consistently focused, the particular wound they exposed and explored, was masculine subjectivity: specifically the ramifications of the erosion of the British man's traditional role as head of the family that had been engendered by the destruction of the nation's industrial base and the ongoing realisation of women's longstanding calls for economic, political and cultural equality. Echoing such seismic alterations to the nature and texture of British life, horror cinema would come to display an overweening preoccupation with the theme of hybridised mutation, as across a range of film texts otherwise ordinary Britons were repeatedly transformed into what Noël Carroll would term 'fusion monsters.'[8] In Neil Marshall's *Dog Soldiers*, for example, 'good people' are seen to mutate into bloodthirsty werewolves while *Shaun of the Dead* sees very ordinary Londoners turn into flesh-eating zombies. Virulent infection changes men, women and children into rage-driven maniacs in *28 Days Later*, while *The Descent* illustrates how closely related we all are to blind, cannibalistic and evolutionarily regressive troglodytes. What is equally notable is the fact that a whole new generation of what may be termed 'fusion heroes' have arisen in the new millennium to do battle with said monsters and with themselves. Operating within a culture which, in Andrew Spicer's words, is itself:

> decentred and heterogeneous, no longer recognising clear national, ethical or sexual boundaries, where forms of masculinity are becoming increasingly hybrid and audiences delight in the knowingness and self-reflexivity of popular culture[9]

such heroes are self-reflexively comprised of a range of archetypally British cinematic variations on the masculinity theme (from stoical everyman to Byronic romantic lead to stiff-lipped action hero). And as such, they allow for an exploration of the ways in which gender-specific models of national identity may be traumatically shaped and reshaped by the historically specific needs and imperatives of the national culture. Thus the self-reflexive, hybridised and composite heroes of *Cradle of Fear*, *Long Time Dead*, *The Bunker*, *Reign of Fire* and *Deathwatch* can be seen to do battle with malevolent spirits, demons, dragons and themselves in their exploration of gendered national identity.[10]

In *The Hero with a Thousand Faces*, Joseph Campbell traced the ways in which mythological narratives have allegorised the young man's quest for freedom from the bonds of home and family through his survival of initiation rituals that enable him to win a place for himself in the world. In traditional folk tales, such a quest would take the form of leaving home, facing a series of tests that culminate in a supreme ordeal such as a fight with a dragon or sea monster; this leading to the reward of the treasure hard to attain, such as marriage to an eligible princess and in time the throne.[11] Intriguingly, this selfsame narrative of masculinisation is admirably evoked, in decidedly mythographic terms, in the Anglo-Irish co-production *Reign of Fire*. This is an apocalyptic tale that quite literally pits two competing models of masculinity against each other and jointly against the dragon – as mythic species that has traditionally challenged mankind's ambitions to master the planet.[12] An extraordinarily potent trans-cultural and trans-historical symbol, the fire-breathing dragon with its scaly hide, leathery wings and taloned feet stretches back to human pre-history, specifically at the point at which human societies were coming into being.[13] Emerging at exactly the point at which patriarchal rule consolidated its grip on early societies through the emergence of a 'centralised structure of chiefdoms or kingdoms,' themselves coincident with the acceptance of 'a monotheistic form of religious belief,'[14] the dragon of Western mythology is a 'bloodthirsty, antisocial and violent' beast, its challenge to patriarchal rule depicted as 'the quintessential image of evil.'[15] Offering a contemporary twist on such fantasies, then, the present film is an exercise in near-future apocalypticism; intimately concerned with the nature of what it means, in a devastated present moment to be human, British and male.

In a manner highly reminiscent of the classic British horror film *Quatermass and the Pit* (1967), *Reign of Fire* opens in 2008 when a female engineer supervising the construction of a new London Underground station at Trafalgar Square awakes a dragon; the name of the station stop significantly evoking the British imperial past, specifically its longstanding enmity with its nearest neighbour, France. The engineer and her crew perish in the subsequent conflagration but her young son survives, taking up the story in voice-over as a montage of semi-animated newspaper clips and documentary footage illustrate how humanity wiped itself out by launching nuclear strikes on the entirely impervious dragons. By 2020 the remnants of British society huddle together in a monastic outpost in Northumberland, as Christian monks of the Dark Ages had done over a thousand years before. Here the adults teach the children how to live, not through biblical scholarship but through acted-out versions of half-remembered films, specifically the fight scene between two competing models of filmic masculinity, Darth Vader and Luke Skywalker in *The Empire Strikes Back* (1980); an archetypal narrative our hero Quinn nonetheless claims to be of his own making.

Quinn's attempts to create a nurturing and sustainable agrarian community nonetheless seem doomed to failure in the face of the dragon's traditional predilection for the slaughter of livestock and destruction of crops. Clearly what is needed to return the nation to statehood is not a peaceable farmer but a dragon slayer, one who can 'ensure the future of the population as it moves towards a state-like governmental form.'[16] He comes in the shape of the heavily tattooed, excessively muscled and aggressively American Denton Van Zan and his bellicosely macho helicopter-flying band of Kentucky Irregulars. Opining on their arrival that there's only one thing worse than a dragon, and that's Americans, Quinn gives voice to a generation of Britons disgruntled by the subservient role their nation has invariably taken in its 'special relationship' with the United States. And from here onwards, the conflict between Van Zan and Quinn's schools of masculinity drives the narrative. In a manner that is reminiscent of the ways in which Americans 'taught' the British how to defeat fascism in the Second World War and are currently 'teaching' them how to root out terrorist insurgency in Iraq and Afghanistan, Van Zan demonstrates how the American capacity to think the unthinkable, the rebel's capacity to yell in the face of overwhelming odds, might lead humanity to freedom.

But for all Van Zan's impressively muscled physique, for all his breathtakingly anachronistic display of twenty-first-century technology to an audience of quasi-medieval peasants, his is precisely the model of masculinity that launched the nuclear strikes that wiped out humankind. Having arrogantly refused to listen to Quinn's counsel, and in the process having ensured the theft of his equipment and the death of his men, Van Zan is forced to acknowledge Quinn's superior knowledge of the land of his birth and hence his capacity to lead the attack against the dragon king, sole patriarch of his entire species. Together they leave the ostensible safety of the castle and travel to London, where Quinn will quite literally defeat his own dragon in a devastated capital, complete with ruined Big Ben and burned-out London cabs. His is, moreover, a highly significant victory for consensual and democratic modes of masculinity that turn their backs on old tribal enmities in order to secure a peaceful future. It was a mode of masculinity, of course, which in his first term of office Tony Blair was keen to call his own, specifically in the negotiation of the Good Friday Agreement of 1998 which brought peace to the highly sectarian communities of Northern Ireland. It is thus significant that some three months after the last attack Quinn's adopted son Jared picks up a radio broadcast from France. The old

enmities between the nations evoked in the earlier Trafalgar reference appear to be at an end. Quinn, moreover, is now capable of
absorbing both masculine and feminine subject positions into a very
New Labour style of masculinity. 'If they come they'll burn, we'll
build,' he says, 'or maybe I'll just kill them.' Both are viable and
valid solutions; and neither is dogmatically advocated. Quinn may
have found Jared 'in a village near Bray,' but his story moves far
beyond the hegemonic gender roles of the period-piece horrors of
the Bray-based Hammer Studios.

Steering a path between Van Zan's martial proclivities and his
own tendency to feminised nurture, Quinn can thus be seen to have
forged his own 'third way' to self-knowledge – as a Briton and a
man. His is moreover a mode of self-discovery that echoes mythopoetic explorations of masculinity undertaken since the early 1990s
in the United States by the poet Robert Bly, the Jungian psycholo-
gist James Hillman, the storyteller Michael Meade and thousands of
predominantly white, middle-class participants in workshops and
retreats across the United States (and to a far lesser extent the United
Kingdom). Responding to feminism's perceived denigration of the
immorality of men, such groups self-consciously sought a form of
masculine community wherein the roles, status and power of individuals was suspended and the collective identity of men explored
through talking, ritual and drumming. Theirs was a kind of 'resistance to domination' through which men might reply to the 'alienation and isolation that stem from living in a capitalist society that
encourages people to be greedy, selfish and predatory;'[17] a society
that calls on men to promote these qualities as culturally necessary
norms regardless of their own needs and desires. Theirs was a means
of breaking free of the conceptual constraints of late twentieth-century society in all its stultifying actuality to imagine a world in which
being a man was not to be an agent of oppression. And it is intriguing that it is precisely this aspiration that is foregrounded by the two
most successful British horror films to emerge to date under Blair's
premiership: the grimly hilarious *Shaun of the Dead* and the apocalyptic sci-fi–horror crossover that is *28 Days Later*.

Edgar Wright's *Shaun of the Dead* is self-consciously steeped in
the iconography of both contemporary British life and American

horror cinema. From its opening in The Winchester, a pub named for the totemic American rifle, we are slowly steeped in the cultural stasis of the contemporary UK, this being a smoke-filled, traditionally-styled venue complete with fruit machines, pool table, nicotine-stained walls, red velvet curtains, a heavy wooden bar, juke box, brown-painted cast iron radiator, decorative plates on the walls and numerous pints of lager. 'Things will change,' opines our hero Shaun to his discontented girlfriend Liz, but he says it to the strains of The Specials' *Ghost Town* (1981) as 'time' is called on his unconvincing optimism. Unsurprisingly, Liz's main complaint is that Shaun and his best friend Ed refuse to grow up and embrace the responsibilities of manhood. In their late twenties they are still living in student-style shared house, itself trapped in time – with its saggy 1970s-style brown sofa, its coffee table groaning with unidentifiable detritus and its overgrown garden. Theirs is a mode of masculinity endlessly trapped in its own fast-receding adolescence, where a great deal of time is spent avoiding meaningful contact with one's biological family and no effort is made to establish an adult home and family of one's own; the preferred alternative being a life of computer games and corner-shop lager, fart gags, dead-end jobs and small-scale dope deals.

This is a way of life admirably encapsulated in the two scenes in which Shaun makes his morning visit to the corner shop – once before and once after the events that will come to be known as 'Z Day'. In the first, Shaun leaves his house, passes a boy playing football, a beggar with a dog, a man washing a car, the row of mopeds on display at a bike shop and a National Lottery advertisement outside the corner shop where the Asian proprietor greets him with 'Hello my friend, no beer today?'[18] The second occurs after a heavy night's drinking when Shaun, who has failed to notice the escalating military presence, the sirens in the street and the running, terrified people, braves the morning to buy himself and Ed a Cornetto and a Coke to assuage their terrible hangovers. The street this time is oddly empty, though the beggar from earlier is now a zombie who shuffles on a clearly broken ankle down the road, holding a lead but walking no dog. Burglar and car alarms are going off, bollards are knocked over, the windscreen of the now-clean car is smashed, a terrified man runs down the street past the knocked-over National Lottery sign and pile of tumbled mopeds. In the shop, Hindi pop still plays but the floor is sticky, there is a bloody handprint on the refrigerator and no newspapers have been delivered. Shaun notices none of this. As assorted zombies shuffle about, Shaun returns safely home. Entirely blind to all that surrounds him he is one of the atomised and isolated living, cut off from each other by their Ipod-wearing lack of interest in anything beyond their own immediate gratification. In this, of course, he is remarkably like the dead.

Like Thoreau's nineteenth-century Americans, the vast majority of contemporary Britons lead lives of quiet desperation; men in particular being trapped within a stultifying present that prevents them from developing beyond their teenage years. One might as well be a zombie. And certainly the quality of television programming offered to the British public is seen as appropriate for such an audience. The national culture is a pastiche of simulacral representations, a triumph of style over content where anaesthetising platitudes and clichés stand in for genuine thought, engagement or interaction. It is truly horrific and yet grimly funny. Shaun's refusal to engage with current events thus leads him to ignore tabloid headlines that warn of a 'New Super Flu,' 'Mutilated Remains' and the 'GM Crops Blamed' for recent unfortunate events. Even at work in an electrical goods store, as army trucks roll down the street outside, Shaun ignores the news on the banked television screens, preferring a diet of the chat show *Tricia* or toddler-tv programmes like *Teletubbies*. Following his lucky avoidance of zombies at the corner shop, Shaun still insists on channel-hopping to avoid anything as serious as news. This results in a wonderful montage of TV genres, ranging from football to a wildlife documentary to a music show; the juxtaposition of which admirably evokes the climate of anodyne disposability that distracts us all from the horrors of actuality. Much of Britain may be in a state of panic, but if one wishes it, one can immerse oneself in the vapid exclamations of the DJ and television presenter Vernon Kay, a man as reality-free as Sean himself, who loudly pronounces himself 'dead excited' by another unspecified media non-event. Even funnier, even more shocking, is the montage of programmes screened after the annihilation of the zombie hoard, when it seems that life has largely returned to normal. Now Vernon Kay proclaims the launch of the philanthropic 'Zombaid' by Coldplay members Chris Martin and Jerry Beckland 'dead exciting!' Meanwhile a news programme illustrates how the 'mobile deceased' have proved useful in tedious and badly paid unskilled jobs formerly taken by teenagers and the elderly, having a hitherto untapped potential to entertain in *It's a Knockout*-style physical challenges by running for meat while attached to an elastic ropes and being pelted with pudding!

In tandem with the communal drummers of the mythopoetic movement, *Shaun of the Dead* thus seems to explore how late-capitalist society infantilises its males, bombarding them with mass cultural simulacra of their own desires so insistently that they exist in tranquillised isolation from each other; unable to think, act or live for themselves. Described in its own publicity as 'a romantic comedy with zombies,' the film is thus happy to juxtapose in its opening sequence a bleached-out supermarket checkout (drawn from 1974's *The Stepford Wives*) and shopping-centre car park (from *Dawn of the Dead*) with hooded youths whose rhythmic shuffling is reminiscent of *West Side Story* (1961). And throughout, playful references to films within and without the horror genre abound. The swinging bathroom cabinet door, revealing the zombified flatmate Pete is a delightful tribute to *An American Werewolf in London* (1981). The shot through the hole in the zombie-girl's stomach echoes a very similar piece of cinematography in the remade *Texas Chainsaw Massacre*. Shaun's headband, donned when under siege in The Winchester evokes that of the Russian roulette-playing Christopher Walken in *The Deer Hunter* (1978). David is pulled out of the window to his doom just like Barbara in Romero's *Night of the Living Dead* and eviscerated like Captain Rose in *Day of the Dead* – the opening of which is repeatedly referenced in Shaun's foot-shuffling early morning walk, the end of which is neatly inverted at this film's denouement as the elevator in the pub cellar lifts Shaun and Liz to safety. But references to British comedy culture are equally frequent, most notably when our band of survivors encounters Shaun's friend Yvonne, whose own accompanying group exactly mirrors them in terms of age, physical type and dress. What is more, each is a significant figure in British radio and television comedy culture.[19] There is no such thing as authentic and autonomous human subjectivity in Britain of the present, it seems; only media-constructs aware of their own stereotypical status. In the light of this, 'Z Day' becomes the best thing that ever happened to Shaun. Admittedly he loses his mother and stepfather, but this is necessary if he is ever to move on to attain an autonomous adult subjectivity free of the past. From a man unable to book a restaurant table or buy a gift for his mother's birthday, Shaun evolves into a capable decision maker. That these decisions result in the death of his friends and family is of course testament to the potentially destructive potential of such incisive and purposeful masculinity. And it is for this reason, within the insistently hererosexist logic of the film, that Shaun's potential for hyper-masculinity must be tempered by Liz, who moves into his flat and takes over his domestic arrangements in classic gender-defined ways. By the end of the film Shaun's house has been transformed by new lighting, cushions and throws. His friend Ed, now a zombie, has been exiled to the garden shed where his video-gaming, meat-eating, fart-unleashing life continues much as before. Only by re-pressing his adolescent yearning for homosocial camaraderie and redirecting his desire towards heterosexual romance, domesticity and putative paternity, the film seems to say, can Shaun come fully to life and face his destiny and his responsibilities as a heterosexual and a man.

But as Danny Boyle's *28 Days Later* is keen to explore, such a journey is not without risk: specifically from the overweening machismo that underpins decisive and authoritative masculinity but is normally tempered in society by those qualities of cooperative endeavour and altruistic nurturance that, as we have seen in *Shaun of the Dead*, is normatively associated with the traditionally feminine spheres of child-rearing, education, healthcare and welfare provision. Thus exploring the ways in which patriarchy is embodied in and perpetuated by hegemonic institutions such as the military, *28 Days Later* is a fascinating exercise in generic hybridity, being a highly effective amalgam of science fiction's 'end of the world' preoccupations, body horror's interrogation of the nature and culture of humanity and the quest narrative's recounting of the hero's voyage to adult masculinity in the face of overwhelming odds. As such, it echoes and references British films such as *The Day the Earth Caught Fire* (1961) and *The Day of the Triffids* (1962) while providing a very British take on eschatological fantasies like *The Omega Man* (1971). But unlike the cult offering *Cradle of Fear*, this film is far more than a collection of references to other cinematic works, being an engaged and engaging exploration of the ways in which the modern world is shaped both by the material manifestations of the state (such as the government, the police or the army) and the state's ideological apparatuses (such as television, radio or film.) The horrors of twenty-first-century life are on display, in fact, from the opening sequence's visually arresting documentary-realist montage of acts of human violence. These range from small-scale private-enterprise lynchings to public execution as state-sponsored homicide. Ironically the footage is being watched by our closest primate relative: a chimpanzee trapped in a laboratory. For all the chimp is the ostensible experimental subject, then, it is clearly humanity itself that is under scrutiny here; for only humanity experiences the rage depicted on screen and only human beings would be both brilliant enough and stupid enough to synthesise a viral agent capable of destroying the species.[20]

Some four weeks after the release of the virus, then, a naked young man awakes in an intensive care unit. Staggering from the hospital into the silence of a deserted London's dawn he moves like *Reign of Fire*'s Quinn through a city made strange by its total lack of inhabitants.[21] By reading a series of dispassionate newspaper headlines that knowingly echo Romero's *Day of the Dead* our hero discovers what has happened. By reading the desperate hand-written notes pinned around the statue of Eros in Piccadilly by those in search of loved ones, he discovers how those events felt to those who lived through them, however briefly. Functioning as testament to humanity's capacity for love in the face of horror, such notes clearly echo those posted by relatives in the devastated cities of Germany and Japan and more recently in Manhattan's business district. But the scale of the catastrophe outstrips even these, the messages being interspersed with children's pictures of intra-familial slaughter and Biblical quotations from the Book of Nahum that tells of the destruction of Nineveh. Graffiti on a nearby church may read 'Repent

– for the end is extremely fucking nigh,' but for the majority of Britons the end has come and gone, the corpse-strewn church being tended by a priest every bit as infected as his remaining flock. In a world in which love, tenderness and cooperation has passed away, the infected lie in wait for potential victims. Even the domestic sphere offers our hero no refuge, his parents lying dead in their beds, having committed suicide in the belief that their son would never wake from his coma.

Jim, accordingly, is forced to move on – in time forging a surrogate family with the pharmacist Celina, the taxi driver and alpha male Frank and Frank's teenage daughter Hannah. It is Frank who persuades the group to travel north in response to a military broadcast urging survivors to make their way to the forty-seventh blockade on the M602 outside Manchester, a city now burned to the ground. But Jim's role as Frank's surrogate son is soon to end as Frank is infected and shot dead by soldiers and Jim is forced to become a man by doing battle with the evocatively named Major Henry West who asserts 'women mean a future' while sanctioning Celina and Hannah's rape by his troops. From being a boyish bicycle courier living with his parents in an affluent London suburb, Jim must now become a new kind of hero for a post-apocalyptic age. To do so he must reject the soldiers' hyper-masculine equation of manly power and sexual violence; redirecting his energies to preservation of the family unit. As such, his actions echo those of the classical figure Laocoön, whose statue stands in the hall of the soldiers' billet, being a priest of the healing-god Apollo who lost his life defending his two children from giant serpents sent to destroy them. Clearly, the aggressively phallic 'serpents' in this tale are the forces of military might unchecked by any authority higher than their commanding officer, a professional soldier who proudly asserts that normality for him is 'people killing people.' That Jim destroys West's platoon by adopting the guerrilla tactics of an insurgent functions as something of a tribute to the powers of the freelance freedom fighter who acts in service of those he loves and thus, through that love, triumphs over the might of the military machine. It is a lesson that Tony Blair and George Bush might have profitably heeded prior to embarking on their invasions of Afghanistan and Iraq.[22] As the

Apollonian references make clear then, Jim's assault upon the military might of West's platoon are not essentially destructive but redemptive; leading to the infected over-running the artificial sanctuary the soldiers have constructed for themselves and illustrating in their murderous rage the logical consequence of militaristic hyper-masculinism. Only with the eradication of the equation of military strength and essential masculinity can the future be contemplated. Celina's conjecture that the virus had wiped out the entire world was clearly wrong, as was that of the ill-fated Sergeant Farrell who believed that the planet was purging itself of humanity's harmful presence. By the time our survivors are rescued, the last of the infected are now dying in the streets, making the 'civilised' world that engendered the disaster ripe for re-colonisation. It appears unlikely though that the traumatised survivors of the horrific events of recent months will return to the 'real world' unscathed. For not only have Jim, Celina and Hannah been forced to kill everyone who stood in the way of their survival, but they have attained a profound personal knowledge of the horrors of unchecked machismo and the necessity of social cooperation and personal self-sacrifice if one is to survive as a civilised human being, and in Jim's case, a man.

The unequivocally anti-militaristic sentiments of *28 Days Later* (however tempered by the merciful energies of the Finnish Air Force who rescue our survivors from their Lake District hideaway) find their way into a number of British horror films of this period. This displays a pronounced discomfort with Britain's imperial past and with the ways in which 'warfare and the militaristic masculinity integral to combat' have been historically used 'as a means by which young men are socialised into the essential ingredients of contemporary manliness.'[23] Thus set in the trenches of the First World War, the British–German co-production *Deathwatch* locates its horror in the no-man's-land between enemy lines and between biological, socio-cultural and supernatural explanations of the hyper-masculine will to destruction; a locale entirely appropriate to an exploration of the gulf between the manly rhetoric of jingoistic war and the entirely emasculating horrors of protracted and bloody fighting that leads to a terrifying and agonising death. Thus opening with a fabulously realistic depiction of British soldiers going 'over the top' by night in a doomed attempt to capture more corpse-strewn Flanders mud, the film admirably explores a young conscript's horror at the model of murderous yet self-sacrificing masculinity arbitrarily demanded by the abstract entity that is the nation-state. Following a gas attack the troops find themselves walking by daylight in an eerie, misty and depopulated wood. Taking and then securing a German trench that is running with blood and capturing its two terrified inhabitants, the group are gradually differentiated by their actions and beliefs, but they remain unified by an insistent filmic awareness of the complicity of masculinity discourses with oppression. For in gender theorist Bob Connell's words, it is impossible to escape the fact that:

> the vast majority of the world's soldiers are men. So are most of the police, most of the prison warders, and almost all of the generals, admirals, bureaucrats and politicians who control the apparatus of coercion and collective violence.[24]

Thus we have McNess, the bright and slightly rebellious Scot, Quinn the chirpy cockney sadist, Shakespeare the frightened boy soldier, Storinski the masturbating everyman, Fairweather the medic, Tate the capable Sergeant whose initiative and bravery would have ensured officer status in any culture less divided by class, Bradford the cowardly chaplain and Bramwell, the aristocratic commander who lacks all the qualities of decisive leadership and empathic camaraderie possessed by his sergeant. Each provides a snapshot of the differing class positions and personal aspirations available to young men of this time and place, illustrating in the process that even within the ostensibly monolithic totality of the army, men exist in complex patterns of shifting relations in which 'dominant, subordinated and marginalised masculinities are in constant interaction.'[25] Having said this, it is unsurprising that this seemingly cohesive fighting unit, itself a microcosm of the class hegemonies of early twentieth-century British society, effectively implodes under the enormous pressures of warfare exacerbated by the ostensible presence of a malevolent supernatural force.[26] As unearthly howls resound through the still air and the German prisoner cranks up the hysteria with his prophesies of doom the soldiers turn upon each other, all but the adolescent Shakespeare meeting their end. Those not killed by their comrades are sucked down by mud or strangled by possessed barbed wire that entwines them in a manner entirely evocative of the ideology of imperialistic machismo that already binds them. And it is neither the cowardly officer nor the nurturing sergeant who prevail in such circumstances. It is Quinn: a man perfectly adapted to this horrific environment, a man who indulges his will to sadistic violence by knifing his commanding officer, crucifying the German prisoner and leaving his sergeant for dead in no man's land. Quinn *is* war in all its horror; a totemic figure far closer to Robert Duvall's Colonel Kilgore of *Apocalypse Now* (1979) than Laurence Olivier's epony-mous *Henry V* (1944). In such a world, it is only at the hands of supernatural justice that men like Quinn will be destroyed. And in the absence of that justice a sense of the utter futility of battle abounds, with the once-glorious cause that was the Great War exposed as a murderous travesty that not only failed to elevate men into heroes but transformed them into crying children and bloodthirsty beasts. Through such an ordeal the boy soldier Shakespeare may find his courage and learn to trust his own judgement – becoming a man despite the class hegemonies that position him as child – but he is certainly destined to be damaged by the experience, for only a traumatised form of masculinity can emerge from this.

That little has changed in British military culture is made ap-parent in Neil Marshall's *Dog Soldiers*, a darkly comic film that re-counts the horrors visited on a group of soldiers who discover that they have been sent to the Scottish Highlands as an expendable means of testing the military potential of a family of werewolves who have inhabited an isolated valley for generations and who for most of the month are 'good and kind people.' In adopting the metaphor of the werewolf, of course, the film evokes the slaughtered campers of *An American Werewolf in London* (1981), replaying that film's frequent shots of a cloud-scudded full moon and soundtrack of terrifying howls by night. In ostensible tribute to that film's special effects, it refuses to use CGI in the creation of its 9ft-high bipedal lycanthropes, whose monochrome points-of-view we intermittently share. *Dog Soldiers* thus vacillates between *Southern Comfort*'s narrative of sol-diers lost in hostile territory to *Night of the Living Dead*'s siege para-digm, via *Assault on Precinct 13* (1976) and *Zulu* (1963), the classic of British imperial pluck. The first soldier to die is even called Bruce

Campbell, self-evidently named for the star of Sam Raimi's *Evil Dead*. Such intertextuality of course ensnares us in a web of textual referents as effectively as the soldiers themselves are trapped in the Highlands and in the macho culture of the military. And it is in our shared entrapment within ideological systems that this film sets out to highlight, producing in the process a pointed critique of the British class system and the militaristic underpinning of British notions of national identity, in both the imperial past and the neo-imperialist present.

Clearly, the overweening preoccupation with the military world of men without women visible in contemporary British horror indicates a certain discomfort with Britain's imperial past and a reluctance on behalf of contemporary men to identify unquestioningly with the hyper-masculine ethos that underpins nationalistic war. It also bespeaks an awareness that over the course of the last thirty years or so the social world of men's experience has so altered that traditional models of masculinity are in need of substantial reconceptualisation. For not only has there been a radical increase in the number of British households headed by women and a corresponding decrease in the number of traditional families headed by a sole male breadwinners in recent years, but as the comprehensive failure of the Child Support Agency has illustrated, men appear increasingly reluctant to accept even financial responsibility for the children they have fathered. With the mechanisation of domestic labour taking the drudgery out of homemaking, and with consumer capitalism enabling men to become their own status objects, the desirability of maintaining a non-productive trophy wife could also be said to have decreased. Accordingly, it is now uncommon for men to advocate a return to the responsibilities of patriarchal authority, preferring as Susan Faludi has indicated to complain about the oppression they are now suffering at the hands of women and to wish for a kind of 'hegemonic-masculinity-lite' – with all the privileges of hierarchical superiority over women and children but few of the responsibilities such paternalism entails.[27] For those women who seek to challenge the hierarchical proclivities of hegemonic masculinity, of course, little has changed: punishment of the transgressive female being as swift now as it was for the *film noir* heroines of the

1940s. In films such as the British–German co-production *Creep*, reactionary retribution for the end of patriarchal privilege is thus visited not on those institutions and economic practices that are de facto responsible, but on women; specifically those women who are seen to be complicit with or advantaged by society's evolution away from the gender norms of the past.

Creep follows the nocturnal misadventures of a German student Kate in the subterranean tunnels and empty stations of the London Underground as she is chased by the eponymous monster, abandoned as a child in an underground medical facility where scientists conducted secret and unspecified experiments upon him. Haunting the sewers, the stations and an extant operating theatre while hunting people as food and medical subjects, the hairless, wall-eyed and sinuously malformed Creep bears a marked similarity to the inbred mutants of Neil Marshall's *The Descent*, themselves related to earlier Appalachian inbreeds of *Deliverance* or incest-spawned desert cannibals of *The Hills Have Eyes*. But for all the film attempts to distance the monstrous actions of the Creep from those of above-ground and post-patriarchal masculinity, what emerges is an intense feeling of violently retributive male powerlessness. Given that the normative male society depicted here consists of coke-sodden rapists, the smack-addled homeless, drug-dealing absent fathers and child-abusing mad scientists, it is hardly surprising that this film attempts to exert a sadistic control over its female protagonists that is worthy of the Italian *giallo* and entirely symptomatic of a state of emasculated helplessness engendered by the very existence of non-submissive women.

As is customary with British horror of this period, inter-textual references abound. At the opening of the film, for example, a victim lurches into the torch beam of two ill-fated sewer workers in a manner directly reminiscent of the blood-caked, demonically-possessed zombies of *The Evil Dead*. Kate's early wanderings in the abandoned station echo Charlton Heston's peregrinations around a depopulated Los Angeles in *The Omega Man* and Cillian Murphy's in *28 Days Later*, while the location itself and certain high-angle shots used to depict it directly evoke *An American Werewolf in London*. Most significant though is the film's close similarity to the classic

British horror *Death Line* (1972). Inspired like *The Texas Chainsaw Massacre* and *The Hills Have Eyes* by the legend of Sawney Bean and itself inspiring Guillermo del Toro's *Cronos* (1993), *Death Line* is also set on the London Underground beneath Soho, being a film that itself explores the legacy of Britain's imperialistic and capitalistic past. Depicted in highly sympathetic ways through an insistent use of point-of-view shots, *Death Line*'s monsters are the last descendants of a group of eight men and four women who were trapped by a tunnel collapse when working on the construction of the Underground and abandoned to their fate by their bankrupt employers. Thus, while the pornography-saturated world of Soho above offers loveless liberation from the sexual repressions of the past through the objectification and commodification of women's bodies, the world below has formed a mutally supporting dynasty, respectful of their ancestors and tenderly supportive of each other. Having now reached an evolutionary dead-end though, the remaining male now tends for the remaining female in her final days in the only way he knows – by killing her a fresh commuter and kidnapping her a female student for food.

For all its setting and eponymous anti-hero then, *Creep* is no new *Death Line*. It is hampered from the outset by its extraordinarily unsympathetic heroine: Franka Potente playing a coke-snorting, dope-smoking rich kid directly descended from the 'yuppie' Thatcherites of the 1980s, a hypocrite who sneers disgustedly at drug-addicted homeless people while aspiring to do nothing more meaningful with her own life than sleep with George Clooney. In fact, if this were not a German co-production one would be tempted to read Kate as a typically racist British depiction of Germans as arrogant, cold and humourless. For while Kate attempts to escape the murderous medico-romantic attentions of the killer, she still fails comprehensively to attain the kind of emotional investment that is typical of Clover's 'last girl.' If Patricia Wilson, the kidnapped student of *Death Line* had displayed great kindness to a fallen commuter and empathy for the mutants as economically exploited waste products of the capitalist system, there is no such kindness in Kate whom we are encouraged to dislike so strongly that we become inescapably complicit with the film's will to punish her. She may come to resemble the homeless at the film's close when she sits filthy and tattered on the station platform, a little dog on her knee. Nonetheless, her encapsulation of that 1980s ethos of individualistic self-seeking self-consciously positions her as prick-teasing bitch who, in fighting off the sexual attentions of the attempted rapist Guy, has brought her troubles upon herself.

So, whereas *Death Line* invents a plausible back story to the horror and roots this firmly in the economic exploitation to which the Victorian underclass were subject in an age of imperial ambition abroad and material acquisition through technological innovation at home, *Creep* does no such thing. It is, in fact, so disengaged from historical materiality that its events occur in a kind of durational present notable only for its overweening misogyny. Its monster, moreover, attains neither the iconic nastiness of a Leatherface nor the empathy of *Death Line's* subterranean mutant repeatedly howling 'mind the doors.' Thus, in a decidedly mawkish sepia-toned scene, we are shown 'Surgery Site 12' from which Creep came, complete with extraordinarily hackneyed *mise-en-scène*: cribs bearing the names of the facility's young experimental subjects, a clockwork doll playing a xylophone, rows of deformed foetuses in bottles and a fully equipped operating theatre. What is worse, in a breathtaking hateful scene the homeless woman Mandy, flat on her back and with her legs strapped in stirrups, is 'operated upon' by the Creep who goes through the motions of hand-washing beneath a broken tap, putting on a gown and administering fictive anaesthesia from a disconnected mask. He then takes an 18-inch curved serrated knife and thrusts it, repeatedly and with great force, into her vagina. Beyond even the wider shores of Dario Argento's imagination, it is difficult to imagine such a horrific violation being committed to celluloid for mainstream consumption. It serves no narrative or thematic purpose and even appears to shy away from assuming responsibility for its own woman-hating by concealing the actual penetration of the blade in off-screen space beneath the Creep's chest and then slowly panning, to the sound of a multi-tracked crying baby, across serried ranks of bottled mutants to settle on the picture of a bespectacled and balding middle-aged white man in lab coat and stethoscope. And this is the closest we ever get to an explanation of or justification for what has gone before – being entirely typically of this under-conceived and flashily executed pastiche of earlier films better done. What are we to surmise? That the monster here is the product of exploitative and abusive experimentation? That he is simply exercising the will of the father in his ongoing abuse of victims less powerful than himself? That this is somehow a comment on the exploitative nature of patriarchal relations? That the Creep bespeaks the invidious position of all males inducted into patriarchy? That he is in fact the real victim in all of this? Perhaps that was the intention. But given the director's exclusion of the Creep's back story, it is hard to know precisely what the film thinks it is doing, if indeed it thinks at all. What is certain is that *Creep* embodies an entirely problematic set of attitudes towards women that themselves bespeak an attempt by disempowered men 'to affirm their personal power in the language of our sex gender system' serving in the process to underline 'the fragility, the artificiality, the precariousness of masculinity' at the present time.[28]

This will to punish iconic agents of the demise of patriarchy is equally visible in Neil Marshall's *The Descent* which, in the manner of his earlier film *Dog Soldiers*, illustrates the strength of the survival instinct while exploring precisely what it means to call oneself a human being. Instead of a party of soldiers though, we have a group of professional women with a taste for nature-defying sports such as white water rafting and mountaineering who meet on an annual basis to test their courage, skill and friendship in a way that owes far more to male bonding rituals championed by the mythopoetic movement than stereotypically empathic (and considerably more commonplace) modes of female interaction. A year prior to their present adventure, moreover, the group's only mother loses her husband and daughter in a horrific car accident that leaves her emotionally devastated and subject to visions of the dead child advancing towards her and carrying a cake complete with birthday candles. Sarah's loss is made even more poignant by clear evidence that her husband was planning to leave her for Juno, the Asian-American amazon and self-appointed leader of the group who has organised its current adventure into an unexplored cave network beneath the iconic Appalachians.

Thus providing us with an emotionally charged insight into the interior life of our key protagonist (who remains a strong and decisively heroic type) the film sets out to deconstruct the male–active/female–passive binarism beloved of patriarchal models of human agency. In having our protagonists descend into a cave network whose wet, dark tunnels and expansive caverns evoke the female reproductive organs in a pronouncedly *Alien*-esque manner, Marshall thus delineates patriarchy's 'impossible and disastrous drive to conquer the natural world'[29] while evoking the paradoxical position of modern women who have been the historical objects of that conquest but now seek to become its subject. Such impertinence is clearly asking for trouble, and sure enough the women are quickly disoriented and desperate. Attempting to navigate their way out of the labyrinthine network of passages with the help of a prehistoric wall painting that points to an ancient history of human settlement within the cave system, they are forced to confront their own humanity and that of the monsters they find there. For there is something particularly nasty lurking in this decidedly id-like underground space: something that either evolved along a different trajectory from humanity in the period following the cave painting or is the product of rapid evolutionary degeneration, having devolved from miners trapped there in the Great Depression. In either case, with their sightless eyes, superb sense of smell and vampiric ability to crawl up the walls and hang on the ceiling, these creatures are not human beings as we tend to understand the term: most closely resembling the bastard child of H.G. Wells's Morlocks, Max Schreck's Nosferatu and Andy Serkis's Gollum with a little crawling *onryou* thrown into the genetic mix for maximum visual impact![30]

As each of the women are picked off by the Crawlers (some undergoing gut-chomping deaths referencing Romero's *Day of the Dead* via Marshall's own *Dog Soldiers*) Sarah and Juno find themselves the sole survivors of the group; their inevitable and violent conflict owing much to the duelling traditions of the post-Peckinpah Western. That Sarah effectively kills Juno as much for the theft of her husband's affections as for her accidental attack on and deliberate abandonment of Sarah's best friend Beth bespeaks Marshall's own engagement with gender binarisms here. In the conceptual vocabulary of the Western, Juno has become the lone frontier hero destined to die alone, being alienated from her erstwhile friends by her self-seeking agenda and her lack of attachment to any family group. Sarah meanwhile turns her back on her earlier role as agent of civilisation. In an astonishingly bold deployment of the mythic imagery that has pervaded the text throughout, Sarah becomes the archetypal female, crouching far below ground and giving birth to visions of her own dead child. Significantly, we do not see Sarah being killed by the mutants – the final frame fading as she stares into the darkness of her own vision, surrounded by crouching monsters that show no signs of pouncing. For Sarah has become the monstrous mother of the patriarchal imagination, at one with the mutants and embodying in her blood-smeared oneness with them 'all those aspects of the self that society and civilisation, in the service of social inequalities, have required both men and women to lose, to repress, stigmatise and disown.'[31]

If the werewolves of Marshall's *Dog Soldiers* had illustrated the belief that 'human beings are of one nature: that of a savage, brutal, voracious, vicious being which needs only to rise to the surface'[32] then a coda to that view of humanity is offered here. Becoming all that is identified with our animal nature, Sarah has been rendered truly monstrous by Marshall, her expedition into the cave system being a voyage to true knowledge of her mother-self in all its terrifying potentiality. For a few moments she may believe that she has been reborn into the world of men above, ascending a Jacob's Ladder of bones towards the well-lit world of horn-blaring logging trucks and gas-guzzling automobiles. But her fantasy is cut short by a vision of the dead Juno staring impassively at her from the passenger seat of the SUV. It is only in the world of subterranean darkness that Sarah can attain the wisdom and peace entailed by acceptance of her own position as totemic mother – bringer of life and of death – surrounded by the cave-dwellers as cannibalistic fetish-objects that both embody and defer to her monstrous potentiality.

From a patriarchal and post-patriarchal perspective, of course, Sarah's position is both horrific and frightening; the fear of the totemic mother being a consistent feature of recent British horror. Certainly, in the films considered here, the mother is either absent (as in *Creep* and *Dog Soldiers*) or already dead (as in *28 Days Later* and *Long Time Dead*). She may die within the course of the film (as in *Reign of Fire* and *Shaun of the Dead*) or be excluded by definition from the militaristic world of men (as in *Deathwatch* and *The Bunker*). However she is absented though, such narrative punishment of the maternal figure clearly bespeaks an ongoing set of problematic attitudes towards women that remain in contemporary British society, for all Blair's attempts to promote a political culture that synthesises traditional gender positions. For in an age in which traditional masculine lifestyles, modes of work and patterns of leisure have been transformed by socio-economic and cultural changes that have challenged traditional gender hegemonies to the clear advantage of women, Blair's own attempts to head a government that appeaed simultaneously tough and caring, proactive and stable, decisive and nurturing foundered. As the economy slowed down and the Blair administration was forced to face increasing military fatalities in the never-popular occupation of Iraq and Afghanistan, the difficulties inherent in the Prime Minister's will to social, economic and cultural hybridity became increasingly apparent. For as the inveterate misogyny of films such as *Creep* have shown us, a dark set of patriarchal drives continued to bubble away beneath the entrenchedly simulacral culture of Blair's New Labour administration. In order to transcend such drives, as *28 Days Later* and *Reign of Fire* illustrated, it had become necessary to move beyond the gender essentialism of the past towards a more hybridised future. Only then, it seemed, might the United Kingdom put the horrors of the past behind it and heal.

Notes

1 Annie Bilson, 'Horror in the Home Counties,' *Sunday Telegraph* (4 August 1996), quoted in Jonathan Rigby, *English Gothic: A Century of Horror Cinema* (London: Reynolds and Hearne, 2002), p. 250.

2 See James Kendrick, 'A Nasty Situation: Social Panics, Transnationalism, and the Video Nasty,' in Steffen Handke (ed.), *Horror Film: Creating and Marketing Fear* (Jackson, MI: University Press of Mississippi, 2004), pp. 153–72.

3 Richard Stanley, *Shivers*, 1 (June 1992), quoted in Rigby, *Century*,

p. 246.

4   Laura Gregory, interviewed in *The Dark Side*, 15 (December 1991), quoted in Rigby, *English Gothic*, p. 246.

5   Paul Brooks, interviewed in *Shivers*, 10 (January 1994), quoted in Rigby, *English Gothic*, p. 246.

6   Paul Brooks, interviewed in *Shivers*, 20 (August 1995), quoted in Rigby, *English Gothic*, p. 247.

7   Paul Brooks, interviewed in *Shivers*, 20 (August 1995), quoted in Rigby, *Century*, p. 247.

8   Carroll, *The Philosophy of Horror*.

9   Andrew Spicer, *Typical Men: The Representation of Masculinity in Popular British Cinema* (London: I.B. Tauris, 2003), p. 204.

10 A similar will to hybridity can be seen in Alex Chandon's *Cradle of Fear*, a portmanteau horror referencing both 1945's *Dead of Night* and 1972's *Asylum*. The villain here is a Dark Metal vampire semiologically derived from Brandon Lee's eponymous role in *The Crow* (1994) who hunts his prey in fetish clubs that purposefully echo those of *The Hunger* (1983) and impregnates a young clubber in the manner of *Rosemary's Baby* (1968) leaving her open to visions of distorted faces and people akin to those of *Jacob's Ladder* (1990) and fated to deliver his child in a scene that is a *mélange* of some of the nastier moments from Jörg Buttgereit's *Nekromantik*, Ridley Scott's *Alien* and John Carpenter's *The Thing* (1982). Similarly self-referential is *Long Time Dead*, the storyline of which echoes the Jamil Dehlavi's *Born of Fire* (1988) and earlier possession narratives such as *The Exorcist* and teen slashers from *Friday the 13th* on. It repeatedly uses *The Evil Dead*'s signature high-speed low-level tracking shot, makes reference to *Halloween*'s 'hiding in the closet' sequence and believes itself witty when having its Moroccan demon paraphrase *Casablanca*'s (1942) great romantic line 'We'll always have Paris.'

11 Joseph Campbell, *The Hero With a Thousand Faces* (Princeton, NJ: Princeton University Press, 1990).

12 As David E. Jones outlines, names for the dragon appear across a wide range of languages including Chinese, Hawaiian, Croatian, Finnish, Cherokee, Polish, Turkish, Maori, Hungarian, Japanese, Welsh, German, Dutch, Lakota Sioux, Astek, Arabic, Danish, Estonian, Greek, Hebrew, Icelandic, Momanian, Russian, Turkish and, of course, English. David E. Jones, *An Instinct for Dragons* (New York and London: Routledge, 2000), p. 1.

13 For the ancient Egyptians the dragon Orboros, depicted eating its own tail, was a symbol of eternity. For the Greeks he was Typhon, the

flame-breathing winged serpent Zeus must defeat to consolidate his victory over his own father and gain mastery of the gods. For the Vikings he was Jormungander, a carving of which appeared on ships' prows as they wreaked havoc on settled agrarian Europe.

14   Jones, *Dragons,* p. 100.

15   Jones, *Dragons,* p. 111.

16   Jones, *Dragons,* p. 111.

17   Michael Schwalbe, 'Mythopoetic Men's Work,' in Michael S. Kimmel and Michael A. Messner (eds), *Men's Lives* (Boston: Allyn and Bacon, 1995), p. 518.

18   *Shaun of the Dead,* like *28 Days Later,* was funded in part with grants from the National Lottery and in return both carry several advertisements for it.

19   Yvonne herself is played by Jessica Stephenson, co-star and co-writer with Shaun's Simon Pegg of the surreal sitcom *Spaced.* Her best friends are played by Tamsin Greig (who appeared in the comedy *Black Books* with Dylan Moran who plays David and Lucy Davis who plays Dianne), Martin Freeman (who was in *The Office* with Lucy Davis) and Reece Shearsmith of *The League of Gentlemen.* Her mother is played by Julia Deakin, also of *Spaced,* while Matt Lucas of *Little Britain* brings up the rear.

20   The parallels between this film and Terry Gilliam's time-travelling dystopian horror *12 Monkeys* (1995) are pronounced. For not only does *12 Monkeys* see twelve billion people wiped out by a similarly man-made virus, but Bruce Willis turns in an introspective and bewildered central performance that foreshadows that of Cillian Murphy as Jim in *28 Days Later.*

21   He crosses Westminster Bridge, trampling Big Ben souvenirs underfoot. Passing an overturned Routemaster bus on the Mall he moves along Horse Guard's Parade to pause by the bronze statues of fallen British soldiers at the Cenotaph. He stops to collect bundles of cash littering the stairs next to the ICA, central London's premier arts venue, before heading to Trafalgar Square, past the National Gallery and up Charing Cross Road to Centrepoint. All are recognisable signifiers of London and many evoke resonances of the military and imperial past that Jim, by virtue of his Irishness, is a priori absolved of.

22   Interestingly, a very similar impulse can be seen to be at work in Roland Emmerich's *The Patriot* (2000) that pits Mel Gibson's Revolutionary War freedom fighter against the massed force of the British Empire for like Gibson's Benjamin Martin, Jim also has to learn to control and direct his rage in service of his new-found family.

23 Hatty, *Masculinities*, p. 172.

24 Bob Connell, 'Masculinity, Violence and War,' in Kimmel and Messner (eds), *Men's Lives*, p. 125.

25 R.W. Connell, 'The History of Masculinity,' in Rachel Adams and David Sauran (eds), *The Masculinity Studies Reader* (Oxford: Blackwell, 2002), p. 254

26 This sense of the trans-historical and trans-cultural inexcusability of war is also evoked in *The Bunker* (2001), a film set in the closing days of the Second World War when a group of German soldiers take refuge from advancing American troops in a forest bunker on the German–Belgian border. That the bunker was built on the site of a mass grave containing the bodies of local townspeople driven into the forest by a stranger or 'Priest of the Unholy' in the Middle Ages and slaughtered by their own neighbours, all adds to the tension. Given that prior to their descent into the bunker the soldiers were engaged in executing deserters and throwing their bodies into a pit of their own making, the parallels between the medieval priest and Hitler's genocidal Final Solution are inescapable. As each soldier descends into his own mental bunker, re-living the horrors he has participated in, these terrors take shape. Ghostly figures haunt the tunnels as assuredly as *die Unbewaltigte Vergangenheit* or the un-addressed past, was seen to haunt the cinematic imagination of Jörg Buttgereit while the heroes of German myth offer no models as to how to survive the terrifying isolation of one's own memories, one's own conscience.

27 Susan Faludi, *Backlash: The Undeclared War Against American Women* (New York: Anchor Books, 1992).

28 Kaufman, 'The Construction of Masculinity,' in Kimmel and Messner (eds), *Men's Lives*, p. 18.

29 Kaufman, 'Construction,' in Kimmel and Messner (eds), *Men's Lives*, p. 15.

30 Of H.G. Wells's *The Time Machine* (1895), F.W. Murnau's *Nosferatu: Eine Symphonie des Grauens* (1922), Peter Jackson's *The Lord of the Rings* trilogy (2001, 2002, 2003) and Nakata Hideo's *Ringu* respectively.

31 Jane Caputi, *Goddesses and Monsters: Women, Myth, Power and Popular Culture* (Madison, WI: University of Wisconsin Press, 2004), p. 317.

32 Denis Duclos, *The Werewolf Complex: America's Fascination with Violence* (Oxford and New York: Berg, 1998), p. 141.

Conclusion: horror cinema and traumatic events

In exploring the response of genre films from Japan and Germany, the United States and the United Kingdom to the traumatic social, cultural and personal legacies of the Second World War, Vietnam and 9/11 and to the broader cultural changes engendered by transformations to traditional gender roles since the 1970s, this study has engaged with a number of debates drawn from horror film scholarship, trauma theory, post-colonial studies and cultural studies. Specifically though, it has been concerned with the ways in which the generic strategies of horror cinema allow for an exploration of those traumatic events and processes that in the post-war period have come to define 'the nation' as site of cultural production and identity formation. Thus horror cinema's specific sub-genres, such as the *onryou*, the necrophiliac romance, the hillbilly horror adventure and others have been shown not only to allow for a mediated engagement with acts so disgusting or violent that their real-life realisation would be socially and psychologically unacceptable, but for a re-creation, re-visitation or re-conceptualisation of traumatic memories that lie buried deep within the national psyche; memories themselves so outrageous that their very actuality as past events appears a logical impossibility. In this, the power of horror may be to effect a certain productive re-engagement with the traumas of national history, their cultural legacy and the possibility of being (and narrativising) otherwise. Self-evidently then, it has not been the purpose of this study to provide either a rigid set of criteria to which historic events must conform in order to be 'traumatic,' or to comparatively quantify the magnitude of specific national traumas. For although it may be tempting to argue that the damage inflicted on the national psyche by Margaret Thatcher or Ronald Reagan was of a similar magnitude to that of Vietnam or Hiroshima, such qualitative evaluations are not only empirically contentious but rather beside the point.

What this study has been concerned with though is the way in which an already-traumatised socio-cultural and historical context may have shaped the generic representational strategies of horror cinema and thus the ways in which an exploration of those strategies allows access to the nature and significance of that trauma, specifically within the context of debates concerning nationhood, national culture and popular cultural forms. For as the horror directors contributing to the enlightening documentary *American Nightmare* all speculated, it does appear to be the case that the shocking viscerality of post-war horror cinema allows for the creation of generically specific characters, narratives, images and conceptual spaces in which traumatic events that lie often buried in the nation's past or continue to reverberate in its present may be reanimated or reconceptualised for the visual pleasure and putative psycho-cultural benefit of audiences. Thus the narrative of the decomposing corpse as object of erotic attachment can be seen to take on a particular significance once located within the broader context of a wounded post-war Germany, its exposure of those prematurely bound wounds fulfilling a specific socio-cultural function. Similarly, the narrative of the banjo-plucking rural deviant that forms the mainstay of hillbilly horror can also be seen to allow for a timely reconsideration of the limits placed on individual freedoms by the ostensibly democratic state, specifically when the imperatives of that state are called into question in times of national crisis such as war.

But this is not to argue that distinctive generic forms can only operate within a single historically determined national context, for once mobilised certain horror sub-genres do seem to be capable of offering a trans-historical and trans-cultural critique of dominant ideologies of race, class and gender. Hence, in both its American and Japanese manifestations, the *onryou* retains a powerful ability to warn against the dominant ideology's coercive normalisation of state-sponsored or culturally sanctioned acts of violence. Similarly the zombie apocalypse, mobilised initially by Romero as a terrifying means of exploring the legacy of the Nixon years still retains a potent socially critical function when satirically remobilised as a means of illustrating the Thatcherite emasculation and infantilisation of British men.

That said, it does seem to be the case that a culturalist location of horror film texts within specific socio-cultural and historical contexts enables us to undertake a politically engaged exploration of the ways in which in which horror cinema dramatically encapsulates and articulates the impact of historical events on conceptions of individual, national and cultural identity. It was for this reason that this study began with consideration of the traumatic legacy that the Second World War bequeathed to Germany and Japan – two defeated nations subject at all levels of social and cultural organisation to an enforced repudiation of the models of national identity that had brought them to war in the first place. Such a repudiation, as has been argued, led to a pronounced reluctance on behalf of mainstream 'national' cinema to address the question of individual and collective responsibility for those acts of wartime atrocity that had been perpetrated in the name of 'the nation' by 'the people.' In the case of the horror films considered here though, such silence is purposefully broken as the unquiet dead return as victims and as perpetrators to witness past events, to apportion blame, to extract retribution and to atone. Thus horror cinema can be seen to fulfil a function that sets it apart from other more 'respectable' branches of the culture industry: providing a visceral and frequently non-linguistic lexicon in which the experience of cultural dislocation may be phrased; in which the dominant will to repudiate post-traumatic self-examination through culturally sanctioned silence may be audibly challenged.

Within a traumatised culture in which hegemonic conceptions of national identity *are* loudly contested by dissenting groups whose challenges are nonetheless marginalised or suppressed by their economic and political masters, horror cinema can be seen to fulfil an additional function. To explore this we turned to the dislocations wrought to American self image by the Vietnam War, the civil rights struggle, economic collapse and the neo-conservative ascendancy of the Reagan years. For in the face of a pronouncedly bifurcated national culture in which entirely antithetical conceptions of the individual, the state and the people fought it out over the 'meaning' and 'destiny' of the United States, horror cinema allowed for a highly affective and effective enactment of what was at stake in the current struggle for national self-definition. Thus resorting to allegorical depictions of culturally embedded narratives of their nation's coming into being, film makers such as George A. Romero and Jonathan Demme not only facilitated a vibrant revivification of complex historical debates regarding the historical meaning and trans-historical mission of the United States, but threw down a challenge to all monumentalising or totalising narratives of national identity.

In the light of this it is unsurprising that in the post-9/11 climate of paranoia, economic self-interest and cultural essentialism, horror can be seen to undertake another form of cultural work. For as this study has argued, recent hillbilly horror's resurrection of the popular 1970s genre allows us to trace continuities between that period and our own, specifically the ways in which ideas of nationhood are re-narrativised, re-visioned and re-remembered in the service of nationally-specific military-industrial ends, whether this is in the aftermath of traumatic events such as military atrocity, terrorist outrage or the impending threat of total thermonuclear war. In this, once again, horror may offer an insight into our current predicament that is every bit as immediate and considerably more affective that conventional polemical forms such as the documentary.

But if all of this appears to emphasise an unnecessarily grim picture of what it is to be the member of a nation-state, subject to its laws and engaged with its cultural products, then the concluding chapter does offer a rather more hopeful perspective. For the final characteristic of horror cinema explored in this study has been its ability to offer traumatised subjects a means of initially recognising, subsequently conceptualising and finally overcoming the traumatic dislocations of the past. In the exploration of British horror of the new millennium, this study has thus attempted to indicate how horror cinema might point the way to a new, desirable and indeed necessary model of masculinity for a post-patriarchal age. This is not of course to deny or marginalise the sense of violently retributive misogyny that is very much alive in several of these films and in aspects of the culture that created them. But it is to illustrate how horror cinema's socially engaged deployment of humorous pastiche and affectionate parody (both of earlier horror films and previously available ways of being a British man) might bring forth a new form of subjectivity from the trauma of the past, unbinding the wounds of the nation and in so doing offering them the opportunity to heal.

Filmography

Films

12 Monkeys. Terry Gilliam, 1995.
28 Days Later. Danny Boyle, 2002.
AI: Artificial Intelligence. Stephen Spielberg, 2001.
Akira. Otomoto Katsuhiio, 1988.
Alien. Ridley Scott, 1979.
American Nightmare. Arlam Simon, 2000.
American Psycho. Mary Harron, 2000.
American Werewolf in London, An. John Landis, 1981.
Amoklauf. Uve Boll, 1994.
Anatomy. Stefan Ruzowitzky, 2000.
Anatomy 2. Stefan Ruzowitzky, 2002.
Apocalypse Now. Francis Ford Coppola, 1979.
Arlington Road. Mark Pennington, 1998.
Assault on Precinct 13. John Carpenter, 1976.
Asylum. Roy Ward Baker, 1972.
Attendant, The. Corbin Timbrook, 2004.
Audition. Miike Takeshi, 2001.
Baby It's You. John Sayles, 1983.
Babylon. Ralph Heuttner, 1992.
Back to the Future. Robert Zemekis, 1985.
Badlands. Terrence Malick, 1974.
Battle Royale. Fukasaku Kinji, 2001.
Battle Royale II. Fukasaku Kinji, 2003.
Bell of Nagasaki, The. Ohna Hideo, 1950.

Beyond Bedlam. Vadim Jean, 1994.

Big Chill, The. Laurence Kasdan, 1983.

Birds, The. Alfred Hitchcock, 1963.

Black Forest Girl. Hans Deppe, 1950.

Black Past. Olaf Ittenbach, 1989.

Black Rain. Imamura Shohei, 1989.

Black Rain. Ridley Scott, 1989.

Black River. Kobayashi Masaki, 1956.

Bloody Excesses in the Leader's Bunker. Jörg Buttgereit, 1982.

Blue Velvet. David Lynch, 1986.

Boiling Point. Kitano Takeshi, 1990.

Bone Daddy. Mario Azzopardi, 1998.

Bonnie and Clyde. Arthur Penn, 1970.

Born of Fire. Jamil Dehlavi, 1988.

Boston Strangler, The. Richard Fleischer, 1968.

Britannia Hospital. Lindsay Anderson, 1982.

Brother. Kitano Takeshi, 1997.

Bunker, The. Rob Green, 2001.

Burning, The. Tony Maylam, 1980.

Burning Moon. Olaf Ittenbach, 1992.

Butch Cassidy and the Sundance Kid. George Roy Hill, 1969.

Cabin Fever. Eli Roth, 2002.

Cabinet of Dr Caligari, The. Robert Wiene, 1919.

Casablanca. Michael Curtiz, 1942.

Cat Ballou. Elliot Silverstein, 1965.

Children of Hiroshima. Shindo Kaneto, 1952.

Cradle of Fear. Alex Chandon, 2000.

Crazies, The. George A. Romero, 1973.

Creep. Christopher Smith, 2005.

Cronos. Guillermo del Toro, 1993.

Crow, The. Alex Proyas, 1994.

Cujo. Lewis Teague, 1983.

Dance With a Stranger. Mike Newell, 1984

Dark Water. Nakata Hideo, 2003.

Dark Water. Walter Salles, 2005.

Darklands. Julian Richards, 1996.

Dawn of the Dead. George A. Romero, 1978.

Day of the Dead. George A. Romero, 1985.

Day the Earth Caught Fire, The. Val Guest, 1961.

Day of the Triffids, The. Steve Sekely, 1962.

Dead or Alive. Miike Takeshi, 1999.

Dead of Night. Alberto Cavalcanti, Charles Chrichton, Basil Dearden, Robert Hamer, 1945.

Death Line. Gary Sherman, 1972.

Deathmaker, The. Romuald Karmakar, 1995.

Deathwatch. Michael J. Bassett, 2002.

Deer Hunter, The. Michael Cimino, 1978.

Deliverance. John Boorman, 1972.

Demonium. Andreas Schnaas, 2001.

Descent, The. Neil Marshall, 2005.

Devil's Rejects, The. Rob Zombie, 2005.

Dirty Dancing. Emile Ardolino, 1987.

Dog Soldiers. Neil Marshall, 2001.

Donnie Darko. Richard Kelly, 2002.

Dracula (aka *Bram Stoker's Dracula*). Francis Ford Coppola, 1992.

Driller Killer. Abel Ferrara, 1978.

Dry White Season, A. Euzhan Palcy, 1989.

Dust Devil. Richard Stanley, 1992.

Easy Rider. Dennis Hopper, 1969.

Empire Strikes Back, The. George Lucas, 1980.

Empire of the Sun. Stephen Spielberg, 1987.

Evil Dead, The. Sam Raimi, 1982.

Evil Dead II. Sam Raimi, 1987.

Exorcist, The. William Friedkin, 1973.

Extreme Pestilence. Andreas Schnaas, 1991.

Fahrenheit 9/11. Michael Moore, 2004.

Fallen. Gregory Hoblit, 1998.

Fanglys, The. Barry Meyer, 2004.

Fisher Girl of Lake Constance. Haral Reinl, 1956.

Flamingo Kid, The. Gerry Marshall, 1984.

Flatliners. Joel Schumacher, 1990.

Flight 93. Peter Markle, 2006.

Freeze Me. Ishii Takeshi, 2002.

Friday 13th. Sean S. Cunningham, 1980.

German Chainsaw Massacre, The. Christoph Schlingensief, 1990.
German Sisters, The. Margarethe von Trotta, 1981.
Ghost in the Shell. Oshii Mamoru, 1995.
Golem, The. Paul Wegener, 1920.
Gone With the Wind. Victor Fleming, 1939.
Grapes of Wrath, The. John Ford, 1939.
Grudge, The. Shimizu Takashi, 2004.
Grudge 2, The. Shimizu Takashi, 2006.
Gummo. Harmony Korine, 1997.
Halloween: H20. John Carpenter, 1998.
Halls of Montezuma. Lewis Milestone, 1951.
Hannibal. Ridley Scott, 2001.
Happy Birthday to Me. Andre Link, 1981.
Heimat. Edgar Reitz, 1984.
Hell in the Pacific. John Boorman, 1968.
Henry V. Laurence Olivier, 1944.
Henry: Portrait of a Serial Killer. John McNaughton, 1986
Hidden Fortress, The. Kurosawa Akira, 1958.
Hills Have Eyes, The. Wes Craven, 1977.
Hills Have Eyes, The. Alexandre Aja, 2006.
Hiroshima. Sekigawa Hideo, 1953.
Hitler – A Film From Germany. Hans-Jürgen Syberberg, 1977.
Homunculus. Otto Ripert, 1916.
Hot Love. Jörg Buttgereit, 1985.
House of 1000 Corpses. Rob Zombie, 2004.
Hunger, The. Tony Scott, 1983.
Ichi the Killer. Miike Takeshi, 2001.
I Know What you Did Last Summer. Jim Gillespie, 1997.
In Dreams. Neil Jordan, 1998.
Intentions of Murder. Imamura Shohei, 1964.
I Spit on your Grave (Day of the Woman). Meir Zarchi, 1978.
I Walked with a Zombie. Jacques Touneur, 1943.
Jacob's Ladder. Adrian Lyne, 1990.
Jesus: The Film. Michael Brynntup, 1985–86.
Jud Süßß. Veit Harlan, 1940.
Ju-On: The Grudge. Shimuzu Takashi, 2000.
Kids. Larry Clark, 1995.

Kill Bill Part One. Quentin Tarantino, 2004.

Krays, The. Peter Medak, 1990.

Kuragejima: Tales from a Southern Island. Imamura Shohei, 1968.

Kuruneko. Shindo Kaneto, 1968

Kwaidan. Kobayashi Masaki, 1964.

Land of the Dead. George A. Romero, 2005.

Last of England, The. Derek Jarman, 1987.

Last House on the Left. Wes Craven, 1972.

Last Samurai, The. Edward Zwick, 2003.

Let Him Have It. Peter Medak, 1991.

Little Big Man. Arthur Penn, 1970.

Locals, The. Greg Page, 2003.

Long Time Dead. Marcus Adams, 2001.

Lord of the Rings, The: The Fellowship of the Ring. Peter Jackson, 2001.

Lord of the Rings, The: The Two Towers. Peter Jackson, 2003.

Lord of the Rings, The: The Return of the King. Peter Jackson, 2004.

M. Fritz Lang, 1931.

McCabe and Mrs Miller. Robert Altman, 1971.

McVicar. Tom Clegg, 1980.

Magnificent Seven, The. John Sturgis, 1960.

Man Bites Dog. Rémy Belvaux, André Bonzel, Benoît Poelvoorde, 1992.

Manhunter. Michel Mann, 1986.

Marriage of Maria Braun, The. Rainer Werner Fassbinder, 1978.

Martin. George A. Romero, 1976.

Maurice. James Ivory, 1987.

Mein Papi. Jörg Buttgereit, 1981.

Mermaids. Richard Benjamin, 1990.

My Beautiful Laundrette. Stephen Frears, 1985.

My Bloody Valentine. Andre Link, 1981.

My Dinner With André. Louis Malle, 1981.

Natural Born Killers, Oliver Stone, 1994.

Nekromantik. Jörg Buttgereit, 1987.

Nekromantik 2. Jörg Buttgereit, 1991.

Night and Fog. Alain Resnais, 1955.

Night of the Living Dead. George A. Romero, 1968.

Nightmare on Elm Street, A. Wes Craven, 1984.
Night Time. Peter Fratzcher, 1997.
Nosferatu – Eine Symphonie des Grauens. F.W. Murnau, 1922.
Nosferatu. Werner Herzog, 1979.
Omega Man, The. Boris Sagal, 1971.
Onibaba. Shindo Kaneto, 1964.
Over My Dead Body. Rainer Matsutani, 1995.
Passage to India, A. David Lean, 1984.
Patriot, The. Alexander Kluge, 1979.
Patriot, The. Roland Emmerich, 2000.
Pearl Harbor. Michael Bay, 2001.
Peeping Tom. Michael Powell, 1960.
Peggy Sue Got Married. Francis Ford Coppola, 1986.
Premutos: Lord of the Living Dead. Olaf Ittenback, 2002.
Prom Night. Paul Lynch, 1980.
Proteus. Bob Keen, 1995.
Psycho. Alfred Hitchcock, 1960.
Psycho. Gus Van Sant, 1998.
Quatermass and the Pit. Roy Ward Baker, 1967.
Rambo: First Blood Part II. George Pan Cosmatos, 1985.
Rear Window. Alfred Hitchcock, 1954.
Red Dragon. Brett Ratner, 2002.
Reign of Fire. Rob Bowman, 2002.
Ring, The. Gore Verbinski, 2002.
Ring 2, The. Nakata Hideo, 2005.
Ring Virus, The. Kim Dong-bin, 1999.
Ringu. Nakata Hideo, 1998.
Ringu 0. Tsuruta Norio, 2000.
Ringu 2. Nakata Hideo,1999.
Rosemary's Baby. Roman Polanski, 1968.
Ruining, The. Chris Burgard, 2004.
Sammy and Rosie Get Laid. Stephen Frears, 1987.
Sands of Iwo Jima. Allan Dwan, 1949.
Sayonara. Joshua Logan, 1957.
Scary Movie. Keenan Ivory Wayans, 2000.
Schramm. Jörg Buttgereit, 1993.
Scream. Wes Craven, 1996.

Scream 2. Wes Craven, 1997.

Scream 3. Wes Craven, 2000.

Se7en. David Fincher, 1995.

Serial Mom. John Waters, 1994.

Seven Samurai, The. Kurosawa Akira, 1951.

Shallow Ground . Sheldon Wilson, 2004.

Shaun of the Dead. Edgar Wright, 2004.

Shinzuku Triad Society. Miike Takeshi, 1995.

Shoah. Claude Lanzmann, 1985.

Silence of the Lambs, The. Jonathan Demme, 1990.

Soldier Blue. Ralph Nelson, 1970.

Sonatine. Kitano Takeshi, 1993.

Southern Comfort. Walter Hill, 1981.

Spirited Away. Miyazaki Hayao, 2001.

Split Second. Tony Maylam, 1991.

Star Wars. George Lucas, 1977.

Stepford Wives, The. Brian Forbes, 1974.

Taxi Driver. Martin Scorsese, 1976.

Terminator 2: Judgement Day. James Cameron, 1991.

Terror 2000. Christoph Schlingensief, 1992.

Terror Train. Roger Spottiswoode, 1979.

Tetsuo: The Iron Man. Tsukamoto Shinya, 1991.

Tetsuo 2: Bodyhammer. Tsukamoto Shinya, 1991.

Texas Chainsaw Massacre, The. Tobe Hooper, 1974.

Texas Chainsaw Massacre, The. Marcus Nispel, 2003.

That Was S.O.36. Jörg Buttgereit, 1984–85.

Thing, The. John Carpenter, 1982.

Tin Drum, The. Volker Schlöndorff, 1979.

Tödesking, Der. Jörg Buttgereit, 1990.

Topo, El. Alejandro Jodorowsky, 1971.

Trend – Punk Rockers Speak About Their Lives, The. Jörg Buttgereit, 1981–82.

Triumph of the Will, The. Leni Riefenstahl, 1935.

Two Thousand Maniacs. Hershell Gordon Lewis, 1964.

Undertow, The. Jeremy Wallace, 2003.

Versus. Kitamura Ryuhei, 2000.

Violent Cop. Kitano Takeshi, 1989.

Violent Shit. Andreas Schnaas, 1987.
West Side Story. Robert Wise, 1961.
Wicker Man, The. Robin Hardy, 1973.
Windtalkers. John Woo, 2002.
Woman in the Dunes, The. Teshigahara Hiroshi, 1964.
World Trade Center. Oliver Stone, 2006.
Wrong Turn. Rob Schmidt, 2003.
Yesterday Girl. Alexander Kluge, 1966.
Zulu. Cy Endfield, 1963.

Television series and programmes

Andy Griffith Show, The. CBS, 1960–68.
Angel. WB Television Network, 1999–2004.
Beverley Hillbillies, The. CBS, 1962–71.
Black Books. Channel 4, 1999–2001.
Buffy the Vampire Slayer. Twentieth Century Fox Television, 1997–
    2003.
Christmas in Appalachia. CBS, 1962.
Davy Crockett. Disney/Warner Bros, 1954–55.
Dynasty. ABC, 1981–89.
League of Gentleman, The. BBC, 1999–2002.
Little Britain. BBC, 2003–05.
Miami Vice. NBC, 1984–89.
Moonlighting. ABC, 1984–89.
Office, The. BBC, 2001–03.
Real McCoys, The. CBS, 1957.
Roots. ABC/Warner, 1977.
Spaced. Channel 4, 1999–2001.
Teletubbies. BBC, 1997–2001.
Waltons, The. CBS, 1972–81.

Music

Club Tropicana. Wham. Columbia, 1983.
Ghost Town. The Specials. 2 Tone/Chrysalis, 1981.
Gold. Spandau Ballet. Chrysalis, 1983.
Psycho Killer. Talking Heads. Sire Records, 1977.
Rio. Duran Duran. Capitol/EMI, 1982.
White Album, The. The Beatles. Apple/Parlaphone/EMI, 1968.

Bibliography

Achenbach, Joel. 'Serial Killers: Shattering the Myth.' *Washington Post* (14 April 1991), 17.

Adorno, Theodor and Max Horkheimer. *Dialectic of Englightenment*. London: New Left Books, 1979, pp. 120–68.

Agee, James and Walker Evans. *Let Us Now Praise Famous Men*. 1941. New York: Lexington Books, 1988.

Althusser, Louis. *For Marx*. London: Allen Lane, 1969.

Althusser, Louis. 'Ideology and Ideological State Apparatuses.' *Lenin and Philosophy and Other Essays*. 1971. New York: Monthly Review Press (2001), pp. 127–86.

Altman, Rick. *Film/Genre*. London: Bfi Publishing, 1999.

Anderson, Benedict. *Imagined Communities: Reflections on the Origins and Spread of Nationalism*. London: Verso, 1983.

Andrews, Edmund L. 'Census Bureau to Dismiss Analyst who Estimated Iraqi Casualties.' *New York Times* (7 March 1992), 7.

Arnheim, Rudolph. 'A Note on Monsters.' *Towards a Psychology of Art*. Ed. Rudolph Arnheim. Berkeley, CA: University of California Press, 1972, pp. 248–59.

Badley, Linda. *Film, Horror and the Body Fantastic*. Westport, CT: Greenwood Press, 1995.

Barker, Martin. *The Video Nasties: Freedom and Censorship in the Media*. London: Pluto, 1984.

Barthes, R. *Camera Lucida: Reflections on Photography*. Trans. Richard Howard. London: Vintage, 1993.

Bartholomew, David. 'The Horror Film.' *The Political Companion to American Film*. Ed. Gary Crowdus. New York: Lake View Press,

1994.

Bass, Jonathan. 'How 'Bout a Hand for the Hog: The Enduring Nature of the Swine as a Cultural Symbol in the South.' *Southern Cultures.* 1.3 (Spring 1995), 301–4.

Batailles, Georges. 'History and Memory after Auschwitz.' 1947. *Trauma: Explorations in Memory.* Ed. Cathy Caruth. Baltimore, MD: Johns Hopkins University Press, 1996.

Bates, Milton J. *The Wars We Took to Vietnam: Cultural Conflict and Storytelling.* Berkeley, CA: University of California Press, 1996.

Baudrillard, Jean. *Symbolic Exchange and Death.* 1976. Trans. Iain Hamilton Grant. Intro. Mike Gane. London: Sage, 1993.

Baudrillard, Jean. *The Gulf War Did Not Take Place.* Trans. Paul Patton. Bloomington and Indianapolis, IN: Indiana University Press, 1995.

Baudrillard, Jean. *The Transparency of Evil: Essays on Extreme Phenomena.* 1990. Trans. James Benedict. London and New York: Verso, 2002.

Beasley-Murray, J. and Moreiras, Alberto (eds). *Subaltern Affect. Special issue of Angelaki: Journal of the Theoretical Humanities.* 6.1 (2001).

Belau, Linda and Petar Mamadanovic (eds). *Topologies of Trauma: Essays on the Limit of Knowledge and Memory.* New York: Other Press, 2002.

Benjamin, Walter. 'The Work of Art in the Age of Mechanical Reproduction.' 1936. *Illuminations.* Ed. Hannah Arendt. Trans. Harry Zohn. New York: Schocken Books, 1969, pp. 217–52.

Benjamin, Walter. 'Theses on the Philosophy of History.' 1940. *Illuminations.* Ed. Hannah Arendt. Trans. Harry Zohn. New York: Schocken Books, 1969, pp. 253–64.

Benjamin, Walter. *The Origin of German Tragic Drama.* 1928. Trans. John Osborne. London: Verso, 1996.

Benshoff, H.H. *Monsters in the Closet: Homosexuality and the Horror Film.* Manchester: Manchester University Press, 1997.

Berger, James. *After the End: Representations of Post-Apocalypse.* Minneapolis, MN: Minnesota University Press, 1999.

Berger, John. *Another Way of Telling.* New York: Pantheon, 1982.

Bergfelder, Tim, Erica Carter and Deniz Göktürk (eds). *The German*

Cinema Book. London: Bfi, 2002.

Bhabha, Homi K. *The Nation and Narration.* Ed. Homi K. Bhabha. London: Routledge, 1990.

Billington, Ray. *The Far Western Frontier 1830–1860.* New York: Bloat, 1996.

Bilson, Annie. 'Horror in the Home Counties.' 1966. Quoted in Jonathan Rigby. *English Gothic: A Century of Horror Cinema.* Foreword Barbara Shelley. London: Reynolds and Hearne, 2002, p. 250.

Bly, Robert. 'The Collapse of James Dickey.' *The Sixties.* 9 (Spring 1967), 70–9.

Boot, Andy. *Fragments of Fear: An Illustrated History of British Horror Films.* London: Creation Books, 1996.

Bordwell, David and Kristin Thompson. *Film Art: An Introduction.* Fifth Edition. New York: McGraw-Hill, 1996.

Bordwell, David. *On the History of Film Style.* Cambridge, MA: Harvard University Press, 1997.

Boswell, Charles and Lewis Thompson. *The Girls in Nightmare House.* New York: Fawcett, 1995.

Bradbury, Osgood. *The Mysteries of Boston.* New York: n.p., 1844.

Brighton, Lew. 'Saturn in Retrograde; or the Texas Jump Cut.' *The Film Journal.* 7 (1975), 24–7.

Broderick, Mick (ed.) *Hibakusha Cinema: Hiroshima, Nagasaki, and the Nuclear Image in Japanese Film.* London: Kegan Paul, 1996.

Brottman, Mikita. *Offensive Films: Towards an Anthropology of Cinema Vomitif.* Westport, CT: Greenwood Press, 1997.

Brown, Charles Brockden. *Wieland.* 1798. London: Penguin, 1991.

Browne, Nick (ed.) *Refiguring American Film Genres.* Berkeley, CA: University of California Press, 1997.

Bugliosi, Vincent and Gentry, Kurt. *Helter Skelter.* New York: W.W. Norton, 1976.

Burch, Nöel. *To the Distant Observer: Form and Meaning in the Japanese Cinema.* Berkeley, CA: University of California Press, 1979.

Buruma, Ian. *A Japanese Mirror: Heroes and Villains of Japanese Culture.* London: Penguin, 1985.

Buruma, Ian. *The Wages of Guilt: Memories of War in Germany and Japan.* London: Vintage, 1994.

Bush, George W. 'Address to a Joint Session of Congress and the American People.' 20 September 2001. www.whitehouse.gov/news/releases/2001/09/20010920–8.html.

Bush, George W. 'State of the Union Address.' 29 January 2002. www.whitehouse.gov/news/releases/2002/01/print/200020129-11.html.

Butler, Ivan. *Horror in the Cinema.* New York: Paperback Library, 1967.

Butow, R.J.C. *Japan's Decision to Surrender.* Bloomington, IN: Stanford University Press, 1954.

Byrd, William Byrd. *A History of the Dividing Line Betwixt Virginia and North Carolina.* 1728. Ed. W.K. Boyd. Raleigh, NC: n.p., 1929.

Campbell, Joseph. *The Hero with a Thousand Faces.* 1949. Princeton, NJ: Princeton University Press, 1990.

Caputi, Jane. *Goddesses and Monsters: Women, Myth, Power and Popular Culture.* Madison, WI: University of Wisconsin Press, 2004.

Carroll, Nöel. *The Philosophy of Horror, or, Paradoxes of the Heart.* London and New York: Routledge, 1990.

Caruth, Cathy (ed.) *Trauma: Explorations in Memory.* Baltimore, MD: Johns Hopkins University Press, 1995.

Caruth, Cathy. *Unclaimed Experience: Trauma, Narrative and History.* Baltimore, MD: Johns Hopkins University Press, 1996.

Caruth, Cathy. 'Trauma and Experience.' *The Holocaust: Theoretical Readings.* Ed. Neil Levi and Michael Rothberg. Edinburgh: Edinburgh University Press, 2003, pp. 192–8.

Cash, W.J. *The Mind of the South.* New York: Knopf, 1941.

Chomsky, Noam. *9/11.* New York: Seven Stories, 2002.

Chow, Rey. 'Film and Cultural Identity.' *Film Studies: Critical Approaches.* Eds John Hill and Pamela Church Gibson. Oxford: Oxford University Press, 2000, pp. 169–75.

Clover, Carol J. *Men, Women and Chainsaws: Gender in the Modern Horror Film.* London: Bfi, 1992.

Coates, Paul. *The Gorgon's Gaze: German Cinema, Expressionism and the Image of Horror.* Cambridge: Cambridge University Press, 1991.

Collins, Jim (ed.) *Film Theory Goes to the Movies.* London and New

York: Routledge, 1993.

Comar, P. *The Human Body: Image and Emotion*. London: Thames & Hudson, 1999.

Connell, Bob. 'Masculinity, Violence and War.' *Men's Lives*. Eds Michael S. Kimmel and Michael A. Messner. 1989. 1992. Boston: Allyn and Bacon, 1995, pp. 125–30.

Connell, R.W. 'The History of Masculinity.' *The Masculinity Studies Reader*. Ed. Rachel Adams and David Sauran. Oxford: Blackwell, 2002, pp. 245–61.

Conrich, Ian. 'Traditions of the British Horror Film.' *The British Cinema Book*. Ed. Robert Murphy. London: Bfi, 1997, pp. 226–43.

Cook, Sylvia Jenkins. *From Tobacco Road to Route 66: The Southern Poor White in Fiction*. Chapel Hill, NC: University of North Carolina Press, 1976.

Cooper, James Fenimore. *The Last of the Mohecans*. 1826. London: Penguin, 1986.

Cooper, James Fenimore. *The Prairie*. 1840. New York: Penguin, 1987.

Cooper, James Fenimore. *The Pioneers*. 1823. New York: Penguin, 1988.

Cooper, James Fenimore. *The Pathfinder*. 1840. Oxford: Oxford World Classics, 1999.

Cooper, James Fenimore. *The Deerslayer*. 1841. Oxford: Oxford World Classics, 1999.

Crane, Jonathan Lake. *Terror and Everyday Life: Singular Moments in the History of the Horror Film*. Thousand Oaks, CA, London and New Delhi: Sage, 1994.

Crang, M. *Cultural Geography*. London: Routledge, 1998.

Creed, Barbara. *The Monstrous Feminine: Film, Feminism, Psychoanalysis*. London and New York: Routledge, 1993.

Crèvecoeur's, Hector St John de. *Letters from an American Farmer*. 1782. Harmondsworth: Penguin, 1982.

Cubbitt, G. 'Introduction.' *Imagining Nations*. Ed. G. Cubbitt. Manchester: Manchester University Press, 1998, pp. 1–21.

cummings, ee. 'Buffalo Bill.' *ee cummings: Selected Poems 1923–1958*. Ed. ee cummings, 1958. Harmondsworth: Penguin, 1960.

Davidson, John E. *Deterritorializing the New German Cinema*. Minneapolis, MN and London: University of Minnesota Press, 1999.

Desser, David. *Eros Plus Massacre: An Introduction to the Japanese New Wave Cinema*. Bloomington, IN: Indiana University Press, 1988.

Dica, Barbara. *Games of Terror: Halloween, Friday the 13th, and the Films of the Stalker Cycle*. Rutherford, NJ: Fairleigh Dickinson University Press, 1990.

Dissanayake, Wimal (ed.) *Cinema and Cultural Identity: Reflections on Films from Japan, India and China*. Lanham, New York and London: University of America Press, 1988.

Douglas, John and Mark Olshaker. *Journey into Darkness*. New York: Pocket Star, 1997.

Duclos, Denis. *The Werewolf Complex: America's Fascination with Violence*. Oxford and New York: Berg, 1998.

Dyer, Richard. *Heavenly Bodies: Film Stars and Society*. New York: St Martin's, 1986.

Edensor, Tim. *National Identity, Popular Culture and Everyday Life*. Oxford: Berg, 2002.

Ehrenreich, Barbara. 'The Decline of Patriarchy.' *Constructing Masculinities*. Ed. Maurice Berger, Brian Wallis and Simon Watson. New York: Routledge, 1995, pp. 284–90.

Elsaesser, Thomas. *New German Cinema: A History*. London: Bfi/Macmillan, 1989.

Faludi, Susan. *Backlash: The Undeclared War Against American Women*. New York: Anchor Books, 1992.

Fassbinder, Rainer Werner. 'Six Films by Douglas Sirk.' *Douglas Sirk*. Ed. L. Mulvey and J. Halliday. Edinburgh: Edinburgh Film Festival, 1972, pp. 95–107.

Featherstone, Mike (ed.) *Global Culture*. London: Sage, 1990.

Foucault, Michel. *Madness and Civilization: A History of Insanity in the Age of Reason*. 1961. Trans. Richard Howard. London: Tavistock, 1965.

Freeland, Cynthia. *The Naked and the Undead: Evil and the Appeal of Horror*. Boulder, CO: Westview Press, 1999.

Friedlander, Saul. *Probing the Limits of Represetation: Nazism and the 'Final Solution.'* Cambridge: Harvard University Press, 1992.

Friedlander, Saul. *Reflections of Nazism: An Essay on Kitsch and Death.* Trans. Thomas Weyr. Bloomington, IN: Indiana University Press, 1993.

Friedman, Lester (ed.) *British Cinema and Thatcherism.* Minneapolis, MN: University of Minnesota Press, 1993.

Gagne, Paul R. *The Zombies that Ate Pittsburgh: The Films of George A. Romero.* New York: Dodd, Mead, 1987.

Gay, Paul du, Jesica Evans and Peter Redman *et al.* (eds). *Identity: A Reader.* London: Sage, 2000.

Gelder, Ken (ed.) *The Horror Reader.* London and New York: Routledge, 2000.

Gellner, Ernest. *Nations and Nationalism.* Blackwell: Oxford, 1983.

Gerraghty, Christine. *British Cinema in the Fifties: Gender, Genre and the 'New Look.'* London: Routledge, 2000.

Giddens, Antony. *The Nation State and Violence: A Contemporary Critique of Historical Materialism Volume 2.* Cambridge: Polity Press, 1985.

Giddens, Antony. *Modernity and Self Identity.* Cambridge: Polity, 1991.

Goddu, Teresa A. *Gothic America: Narrative, History and Nation.* New York: Columbia University Press, 1997.

Goodwin, Andrew. *Dancing in the Distraction Factory.* London: Routledge, 1993.

Guibernau, M. *Nationalisms: The Nation State and Nationalism in the Twentieth Century.* Cambridge: Polity Press, 1996.

Gurwell, John K. *Mass Murder in Houston.* Houston, TX: Cordovan, 1974.

Hake, Sabine. *German National Cinema.* London: Routledge, 2002.

Halberstam, Judith. *Skin Shows: Gothic Horror and the Technology of Monsters.* Durham, NC: Duke University Press, 1995.

Hall, Stuart and Peter Gay (eds). *Questions of Cultural Identity.* London: Sage, 1996.

Hall, Stuart. 'The Question of Cultural Identity.' *Modernity and Its Futures.* Eds S. Hall, D. Held and A. McGrew. Cambridge: Polity Press, 1992, 165–75.

Halle, Raymond and Margaret McCarthy (eds). *Light Motives: German Popular Film in Perspective.* Detroit: Wayne State University

Press, 2003.

Harkins, Antony. *Hillbilly: A Cultural History of an American Icon.* New York: Oxford University Press, 2004.

Harper, Graham and Xavier Mendik (eds). *Unruly Pleasures: The Cult Film and its Critics.* Guildford: FAB Press, 2000.

Harris, Thomas. *Red Dragon.* 1981. London: Corgi, 1992.

Harris, Thomas. *The Silence of the Lambs.* 1988. London: Mandarin, 1992.

Harris, Thomas. *Hannibal.* 1999. New York: Delacourt, 1999.

Hatty, Suzanne E. *Masculinities, Violence and Culture.* Sage Series on Violence Against Women. Thousand Oaks, CA: Sage, 2000.

Hawkins, Joan. *Art Horror and the Horrific Avant-Garde.* Minneapolis, MN: University of Minnesota Press, 2000.

Heimer, Mel. *The Cannibal.* New York: Lyle Stewart, 1971.

Hellman, John. *American Myth and the Legacy of Vietnam.* New York: Columbia University Press, 1986.

Hendry, Joy. *Understanding Japanese Society.* Nissan Institute/ Routledge Japanese Studies Series. London: Routledge, 1996.

Higashi, Sumiko. 'Night of the Living Dead: A Horror Film about the Horrors of the Vietnam Era.' *Hanoi to Hollywood: The Vietnam War in American Film.* Eds Linda Dittmar and Gene Michaud. New Brunswick: Rutgers University Press, 1990, pp. 175–88.

Hills, Matt. *The Pleasures of Horror.* London and New York: Continuum, 2005.

Hirano, Kyoko. *Mr Smith Goes to Tokyo: Japanese Cinema Under the American Occupation 1945–1952.* Washington and London: Smithsonian Institution Press, 1992.

Hjort, Mette and Scott MacKenzie (eds). *Cinema and Nation.* London: Routledge, 2000.

Hobsbawm, Eric. *The Age of Capital 1848–75.* London: Weidenfeld & Nicolson, 1975.

Hobsbawm, Eric. *The Age of Empire 1875–1914.* London: Weidenfeld & Nicolson, 1987.

Hogan, Michael J. *Hiroshima in History and Memory.* Cambridge: Cambridge University Press, 1996.

Hunt, Leon. *British Low Culture: From Safari Suits to Sexploitation.*

London: Routledge, 1998.

Hunter, Jack. *Eros in Hell: Blood and Madness in Japanese Cinema.* London and New York: Creation Publishing Group, 1999.

Hunter, Jack (ed.) *The Bad Mirror.* New York and London: Creation Books, 2002.

Hutchings, Peter. *Hammer and Beyond: The British Horror Film.* Manchester: Manchester University Press, 1993.

Hutchings, Peter. *The Horror Film.* Harlow: Pearson, 2004.

Hutchinson, John and Anthony D. Smith (eds). *Nationalism.* Oxford and New York: Oxford University Press, 1994.

Huyssen, Andreas. *After the Great Divide: Modernism and Mass Culture.* New York: Columbia University Press, 1987.

Huyssen, Andreas. 'Trauma and Memory: A New Imaginary Temporality.' *World Memory: Personal Trajectories in Global Time.* Eds Jill Bennett and Rosanne Kennedy. Basingstoke: Palgrave Macmillan, 2003.

Ingram, Joseph Holt. *The Mysteries of New York.* New York: n.p., 1842.

Jackson, Rosemary. *Fantasy: The Literature of Subversion.* 1981. London and New York: Routledge, 1995.

Jancovich, Mark (ed.) *Horror: The Film Reader.* London and New York: Routledge, 1992.

Jancovich, Mark, Antonio Lázaro Peboli and Julian Stringer *et al.* (eds). *Defining Cult Movies: The Cultural Politics of Oppositional Taste.* Manchester: Manchester University Press, 2003.

Jenkins, Philip. *Using Murder: The Social Construction of Serial Homicide.* New York: de Gruyter, 1994.

Johnson, Paul. *A History of the Modern World From 1917 to the 1990s.* London: Weidenfeld & Nicolson, 1991.

Jones, David E. *An Instinct for Dragons.* New York and London: Routledge, 2000.

Kaes, Anton. *From Hitler to Heimat: The Return of History as Film.* Cambridge, MA and London: Harvard University Press, 1989.

Kaplan, Cora. *Rocking Around the Clock: Music, Television, Postmodernism and Consumer Culture.* London: Methuen, 1987.

Kaufman, Michael. 'The Construction of Masculinity and the Triad of Men's Violence,' *Men's Lives.* 1989. 1992. Eds Michael S.

Kimmel and Michael A. Messner. Boston: Allyn and Bacon, 1995, pp. 13–25.

Keith Grant, Barry (ed.) *The Dread of Difference: Gender and the Horror Film*. Austin, TX: University of Texas Press, 1996.

Keith Grant, Barry (ed.) *Planks of Reason: Essays on the Horror Film*. Oxford: Scarecrow, 2004.

Kendrick, James. 'A Nasty Situation: Social Panics, Transnationalism, and the Video Nasty.' *Horror Film: Creating and Marketing Fear*. Ed. Steffen Handke. Jackson, MS: University Press of Mississippi, 2004, pp. 153–72.

Kerekes, David. *Sex, Murder, Art: The Films of Jörg Buttgereit*. 1994. Manchester: Headpress, 1998.

Kerekes, David and David Slater. *See No Evil: Banned Films and Video Controversy*. Manchester: Critical Vision, 2000.

Kerouak, Jack. *On the Road*. 1957. London: Penguin, 1985.

Kesey, Ken. *One Flew Over the Cuckoo's Nest*. 1962. London: Picador, 1988.

King, Brian (ed.) *Lustmord: The Writings and Artefacts of Murderers*. Burbank, CA: Bloat, 1997.

Kluge, Alexander, Edgar Reitz and Haro Senft *et al. The Oberhausen Manifesto*. University of Victoria, Department of Germanic and Russian Studies. http://web.uvic.ca/geru/439/oberhausen.htlm. Accessed 1 May 2006.

Krackauer, Siegfried. *From Caligari to Hitler: a Psychological History of the German Film*. Princeton, NJ: Princeton University Press, 1947.

Kristeva, Julia. *Powers of Horror: An Essay in Abjection*. Trans. Leon S. Roudiez. New York: Columbia University Press, 1982.

Kristeva, Julia. *Nations Without Nationalism*. Trans. Leon S. Roudiez. New York: Columbia University Press, 1993.

LaCapra, Dominick. *Representing the Holocaust: History, Theory, Trauma*. Ithaca, NY: Cornell Univeristy Press, 1994.

LaCapra, Dominick. *History and Memory After Auschwitz*. Ithaca, NY: Cornell University Press, 1998.

LaCapra, Dominick. *Writing History, Writing Trauma*. Baltimore: Johns Hopkins University Press, 2001.

LaCapra, Dominick. 'Trauma, Absence, Loss.' 1998. *The Holocaust:*

Theoretical Readings. Eds Neil Levi and Michael Rothberg. Edinburgh: Edinburgh University Press, 2003, pp. 199–205.

Lake Crane, Jonathan. *Terror and Everyday Life: Singular Moments in the History of the Horrror Film*. Thousand Oaks, CA and London: Sage, 1994.

Levi, Primo. 'The Drowned and the Saved.' *The Holocaust: Theoretical Readings*. Eds Neil Levi and Michael Rothberg. Edinburgh: Edinburgh University Press, 2003), pp. 25–35.

Lincoln, Abraham. 'Second Inaugural Address.' (4 March 1864). University of Oklahoma, College of Law. Historical Documents. http://www.law.ou.edu/ushistory/lincoln2.shtml. Accessed 2 November 2006.

Lippard, George. *The Quaker City*. New York: 1844.

Lowenstein, Adam. *Shocking Representations: Historical Trauma, National Cinema and the Modern Horror Film*. New York: Columbia University Press, 2005.

Lu, David J. *Japan: A Documentary History. Volume II. The Late Tokugawa Period to the Present*. Armonk and London: East Gate Press, 1999.

Ludlum, Steve.'The Making of New Labour,' *New Labour in Government*. Eds Steve Ludlam and Martin J. Smith. Basingstoke and New York: Palgrave, 2001, pp. 1–31.

McRoy, Jay. 'Introduction.' *Japanese Horror Cinema*. Ed. Jay McRoy. Edinburgh: Edinburgh University Press, 2005, pp. 15–17.

Marcuse, Herbert. *One Dimensional Man*. 1964. London: Abacus, 1972.

Masterson, James R. 'William Byrd in Lubberland,' *American Literature*. 9:2 (May 1937), 153–70.

Maugham, W. Somerset. *Sheppey*. London: William Heinemann, 1933.

Melville, Herman. *Moby Dick*. 1851. London: Penguin, 1981.

Mitscherlich, Alexander and Margaret Mitscherlich. *The Inability to Mourn: Principles of Collective Behaviour*. Trans. Beverley R. Placzek. New York: Grove Press, 1967.

Mulvey, Laura and John Halliday (eds). *Douglas Sirk*. Edinburgh: Edinburgh Film Festival, 1972.

Neale, Stephen. *Genre*. London: Bfi, 1980.

Neale, Stephen. *Genre and Hollywood*. London: Routledge, 1999.

Newman, Kim. *Nightmare Movies: A Critical History of the Horror Movie from 1968*. London: Bloomsbury, 1988.

Newton, Michael. *Hunting Humans: The Encyclopedia of Serial Killers*. New York: Avon, 1990.

Newton, Michael. *Serial Slaughter: What's Behind America's Murder Epidemic?* Port Townsend, WA: Loompanics Unlimited, 1992.

Norris, Joel. *Serial Killers*. New York: Anchor, 1988.

O'Brien, Daniel. *The Hannibal Files*. London: Reynold and Hearn, 2001.

Patterson, James T. *Restless Giant: The United States from Watergate to Bush vs Gore*. New York: Oxford University Press, 2005.

Paul, William. *Laughing Screaming: Modern Horror and Comedy*. New York: Columbia University Press, 1994.

Perks, Marcelle. 'A Descent into the Underworld: Death Line.' *British Horror Cinema*, Eds Steve Chibnall and Julian Petley. London: Routledge, 2002, pp. 145–55.

Phillips, Kendall R. *Projected Fears: Horror Films and American Culture*. Westport, CT: Praegar, 2005.

Pinedo, I.C. *Recreational Terror: Women and the Pleasures of Horror Film Viewing*. New York: State University of New York Press, 1997.

Poe, Edgar Allan. 'The Murders in the Rue Morgue.' *Graham's Magazine* (April 1841).

Prawer, S.S. *Caligari's Children: The Film as Tale of Terror*. New York: Da Capo, 1980.

Punter, David. *The Literature of Terror*. London: Longmans, 1980.

Ressler, Robert. *Whoever Fights Monsters*. London: Simon and Schuster, 1992.

Ressler, Robert. *I Have Lived in the Monster*. London: Pocket Books, 1997.

Ressler, Robert, Ann W. Burgess and John E. Douglas. *Sexual Homicide: Patterns and Motives*. New York and London: Lexington Books/Free Press, 1988.

Richards, Jeffrey. *Films and British National Identity from Dickens to Dad's Army*. Manchester: Manchester University Press, 1997.

'*Ring, The.*' *The Numbers: Box Office Data, Movie Stars, Idle*

Speculation. www.the-numbers.com/movies/2002/TRING/html. Accessed 4 November 2005.

Ring World, The. www.theringworld.com. Accessed 9 September 2005.

Robins, Joyce and Peter Arnold. *Serial Killers.* London: Chancellor, 1993.

Rockoff, Adam. *Going to Pieces: The Rise and Fall of the Slasher Film, 1978–1986.* Jefferson, NC and London: McFarland, 2002.

Roebuck, Julian B. and Mark Hickson III. *The Southern Redneck.* New York: Praeger Publications, 1982.

Romero, George A. and Susanna Sparrow. *Dawn of the Dead.* 1978. London: Sphere, 1979.

Russo, Mary J. *The Female Grotesque: Risk, Excess and Modernity.* New York and London: Routledge, 1995.

Russo, Mary J. 'Female Grotesques: Carnival and Theory.' *Writing on the Body: Female Embodiment and Feminist Theory.* Eds Katie Conboy, Nadia Mdiena and Sarah Stanbury. New York: Columbia University Press, 1997, pp. 318–36.

Said, Edward. *Orientalism: Western Conceptions of the Orient.* 1978. London: Penguin, 1991.

Salinger, J.D. *The Catcher in the Rye.* 1951. London: Penguin, 1994.

Salmon, Wesley C. *Causality and Explanation.* New York: Oxford University Press, 1998.

Sanders, Ed. *The Family.* London: Panther, 1974.

Santer, Eric. *Stranded Objects: Mourning, Memory and Film in Postwar Germany.* Ithaca, NY and London: Cornell University Press, 1993.

Sargeant, Jack. 'American Nightmare. The Baying of Pigs: Reflections on the New American Horror Movie, *Senses of Cinema.* www.sensesofcinema.com/contents/festivals/01/15/biff_nightmare.html. Accessed 2 July 2002.

Sarup, M. *Identity, Culture and the Postmodern World.* Edinburgh: Edinburgh University Press, 1996.

Schilling, Mark. *Contemporary Japanese Film.* New York and Tokyo: Weatherhill, 1999.

Schlesinger, Arthur and Dixon Ryan Fox. *A History of American Life. Volume 10: The Rise of the City 1878–1898.* New York: Macmillan,

1933.

Schneider, Steven Jay. *New Hollywood Violence*. Manchester and New York: Manchester University Press, 2004.

Schwalbe, Michael. 'Mythopoetic Men's Work.' *Men's Lives*. Eds Michael S. Kimmel and Michael A. Messner. Boston: Allyn and Bacon, 1995, pp. 507–19.

Sharrett, Christopher. 'The Horror Film in Neoconservative Culture.' *Journal of Popular Film and Television*. 21:3 (1993), 100–11.

Shaw, Daniel, 'The Master of Hannibal Lecter.' *Dark Thoughts: Philosophic Reflections on Cinematic Horror*. Eds Stephen Jay Schneider and Daniel Shaw. Lanham, MD and Oxford: Scarecrow Press, 2003, pp. 10–24.

Skal, David J. *The Monster Show: A Cultural History of Horror*. New York: W.W. Norton, 1993.

Smith, Antony. *Nationalism and Modernism*. London: Routledge, 1998.

Smith, Bonnie G. *Global Feminisms Since 1945*. London and New York: Routledge, 2000.

Sontag, Susan. *On Photography*. New York: Dell, 1977.

Spicer, Andrew. *Typical Men: The Representation of Masculinity in Popular British Cinema*. 2001. London: I.B. Tauris, 2003.

Spivak, Gayatri Chakravorty. 'Can the Subaltern Speak? Speculations on Widow Sacrifice.' 1988. *The Post Colonial Studies Reader*. Eds Bill Ashcroft, Gareth Griffiths and Helen Tiffin. London and New York: Routledge, 1995, pp. 24–9.

Spofford, Harry. *The Mysteries of Worcester*. New York, 1846.

Stalin, Joseph. 'The Nation.' *The Essential Stalin: Major Theoretical Writings 1905–1952*. Ed. Bruce Franklin. London: Croom Helm, 1973, pp. 57–61.

Standish, Isolde. *A New History of Japanese Cinema: A Century of Japanese Film*. New York and London: Continuum, 2005.

Steinbeck, John. *The Grapes of Wrath*. New York: Viking/Penguin, 1939.

Stevens, Shane. *By Reason of Insanity*. New York: Caroll and Graf, 1979.

Suzuki, Koji. *Spiral*. London: Harper Collins, 1995.

Thatcher, Margaret. *Woman's Own* (31 October 1987): 8–10. The Margaret Thatcher Foundation. www.margareththatcher.org/speeches/displaydocument.asp?docid=106689. Accessed 28 April 2006.

Thompson, John. *The Media and Modernity.* Cambridge: Polity Press, 1995.

Toffler, Alvin. *Future Shock.* 1970. London: Pan, 1981.

Tuan, Yi-Fu. *Landscapes of Fear.* Oxford: Basil Blackwell, 1979.

Tudor, Andrew. *Monsters and Mad Scientists: A Cultural History of the Horror Movie.* Oxford: Blackwell, 1989.

Tudor, Andrew. 'Why Horror?: The Peculiar Pleasures of a Popular Genre.' *Cultural Studies.* 11:3 (October 1997): 443–63.

Turner, Frederick Jackson. 'The Significance of the Frontier in American History.' 1893. *The Early Writings of Frederick Jackson Turner.* Madison, WI: Wisconsin University Press, 1938.

Twain, Mark. *The Adventures of Huckleberry Finn.* 1884. London: Minster, 1967.

Twitchell, James B. *Dreadful Pleasures: An Anatomy of Modern Horror.* New York: Oxford University Press, 1985.

Van Doren Stern, Philip (ed.) *The Portable Poe.* New York: Viking Penguin, 1979, pp. 332–76.

Walcsak, Yvette. *He and She: Men in the Eighties.* London and New York: Routledge, 1988.

Walker, Janet. *Documenting Incest and the Holocaust.* Berkeley, CA and London: University of California Press, 2005.

Waller, Gregory A. *The Living and the Undead: From Bram Stoker's Dracula to Romero's Dawn of the Dead.* Urbana and Chicago, IL: University of Illinois Press, 1986.

Waller, Gregory A. (ed.) *American Horrors: Essays on the Modern American Horror Film.* Urbana and Chicago, IL: University of Illinois Press, 1987.

Ward, M. Review of *Necromantic* [*sic*]. www.aboutcultfilm.com/reviews/nekromantic.html. Accessed 13 September 2005.

Warner, Marina. *Managing Monsters: Six Myths of Our Time.* New York: Vintage, 1994.

Webb, Walter Prescott. *The Great Plains.* New York: Grosset and Dunlap, 1931.

Wells, H.G. *The Time Machine*. 1895. London: Penguin, 2005.

Wheeler, Edward L. *Deadwood Dick's Dream; or, The Rivals of the Road. A Mining Tale of Tombstone*. Beadle's Half Dime Library, 572 (1888).

Wheen, Francis. *How Mumbo-Jumbo Conquered the World*. London: Harper Perennial, 2004.

White, Hayden. 'Historical Emplotment and the Problem of Truth.' *Probing the Limits of Representation: Nazism and the Final Solution*. Ed. Saul Friedlander. Cambridge, MA: Harvard University Press, 1992, pp. 37-53.

White, Hayden. 'The Modernist Event.' *The Persistence of History: Cinema, Television and the Modern Event*. Ed. Vivienne Sobchack. New York and London: Routledge, 1996, pp. 17-38

White, S. 'Interpreting the Third Way: Not One Road, But Many.' *Renewal*. 6:2 (1998), 17–30.

Wikpedia, the Free Encyclopedia. http://en.wikipedia.org/wiki/Onryou. Accessed 9 September 2005.

Williams, Alan. 'Introduction.' *Film and Nationalism*. Ed. Alan Williams. New Brunswick: Rutgers University Press, 2002, pp. 1–22.

Williams, Linda. *Hardcore: Power, Pleasure and the 'Frenzy of the Visible.'* Berkeley, CA: University of California Press, 1989.

Williams, Linda. 'Learning to Scream,' *Sight and Sound* (December 1994), 14–17.

Williams, Tony. 'Wes Craven: An Interview.' *Journal of Popular Film and Television* 8:3 (October 1980), 10–4.

Williams, Tony. *Hearths of Darkness: The Family in the American Horror Film*. London: Associated Universities Press, 1996.

Williams, Tony. *The Cinema of George A. Romero: Knight of the Living Dead*. London and New York: Wallflower, 2003.

Williamson, J.W. *Hillbillyland: What the Movies did to the Mountains and what the Mountains Did to the Movies*. Chapel Hill, NC: University of North Carolina Press, 1994.

Winthrop, John. 'A Model of Christian Charity.' 1630. *The Norton Anthology of American Literature*. Ed. Ronald S. Gottesman, Laurence B. Holland and David Kalstone *et al*. New York: W.W. Norton, 1979, pp. 11–25.

Wolfe, Tom. 'The Me Decade and the Third Great Awakening.'
  Mauve Gloves and Madmen, Clutter and Vine. New York: Farrar,
  Strauss and Giroux, 1976, http//us.hist.wisc.edu/hist102/pdocs/
  wolfe_me.pdf. Accessed 8 January 2008.
Wollen, Peter. 'Ways of Thinking about Music Video (and
  Postmodernism),' *Critical Quarterly,* 28:1–2 (Spring–Summer
  1986): 167–70.
Wood, Robin. *Hitchcock's Films.* 1965. New York: A.S. Barnes, 1969.
Wood, Robin. *Hollywood from Vietnam to Reagan.* New York: Co-
  lumbia University Press, 1986.
Wood, Robin and Richard Lippe (eds). *The American Nightmare:
  Essays on the Horror Film.* Toronto: Festival of Festivals, 1979.
Woods, Stuart. *Chiefs.* New York: Avon, 1981.
Wray, Matt and Annale Newitz (eds). *White Trash: Race and Class in
  America.* New York: Routledge, 1997.
Žižek, Slavoj. 'Introduction: The Spectre of Ideology.' *Mapping
  Ideology.* Ed. Slavoj Žižek. London: Verso, 1994, pp. 1–33.
Žižek, Slavoj. *Everything You Wanted to Know about Lacan (But Were
  Afraid to Ask Hitchcock).* London: Verso, 1995.
Žižek, Slavoj. 'Are We in a War? Do We Have an Enemy?' *London
  Review of Books* (23 May 2002), 24.

Index

Note: 'n.' after a page number indicates the number of a note on that page.